ALSO BY ERIC BURNETT

Children's Books

Trapped in Tenochtitlan

Skateboarder Steve Stops Falling Down

Gymnastics Jenny Stands on Her Own

For the Classroom

Aztec Plays for the Classroom

Middle Ages for the Classroom

History Through Film

History Through Film

Volume I

Edited by Eric Burnett

Table of Contents

To John Bonds, Paul Breakman, Paul Moore and Jon Sorensen
For helping me avoid places where rivers run.

Introduction

Most people today gain their first exposure to historical events through movies – not the Ken Burns-type, painfully researched documentaries found on the History Channel, but the frivolous pulp spewed out on a regular basis by the Hollywood dream factory. In the year 2007 alone, audiences could learn about the Battle of Thermopylae (*300*), an escape from a Vietnam prisoner of war camp (*Rescue Dawn*), the end of the Roman Empire (*The Last Legion*), the building of the Transcontinental Railroad (*3:10 to Yuma*), the Iraq War (*In the Valley of Elah*), the *The Assassination of Jesse James by the Coward Robert Ford*, the Civil Rights Movement (*Hairspray*), the history of Saudi Arabia (*The Kingdom*), Queen Elizabeth (*Elizabeth: The Golden Age*), the war in Afghanistan (*Lions for Lambs*), the Battle of Dunkirk (*Atonement*), Robber Barons in the Gilded Age (*There Will be Blood*), and the end of the Cold War (*Charlie Wilson's War*).

And that was just one year.

At a pace of ten to fifteen historical films a year, the movie industry has done an admirable job trying to recreate the past. Unfortunately for some, directors and scriptwriters oftentimes are conflicted. On one hand they want to breathe life into people and events from long ago, but on the other hand they must fill seats. Oftentimes, these two realities mean that studio heads, directors, producers and screenwriters alter history to fit their needs.

Does this mean that all Hollywood films should merely be discarded? Ignored? Written off as unsubstantiated trash? Not at all. Just as the *Harry Potter* series awakened a previously apathetic generation to the joy of reading, Hollywood has the power to do what countless history teachers have failed to accomplish over the years – entice the everyman to wonder about the past.

However, even if an exiting filmgoer never looks further into the history topic introduced, he should be able to readily recognize why and how history has been altered. Before launching into detailed analyses of key films from Hollywood's catalogue, it helps to be familiar with the principal motivations and standard alterations made by filmmakers.

Even though oftentimes the actual history is more engaging than the modified version, filmmakers take creative liberties for a variety of reasons – some necessary and some personal. Directors assume each audience member enters the theater with minimal to no knowledge of the subject matter, and with an equally limited ability to keep track of multiple plotlines and complex characters. Subsequently, the version put on screen almost always simplifies the reality of the situation.

Therefore, directors take the history which is often complex, involving countless personalities and events, and fit it into the predictable plot structure that has come to represent almost all of Western fiction. Each film must have 1) an exposition – introduction of the setting and characters, 2) a conflict – the problem the protagonist must solve, 3) rising action – mini-conflicts that prevent the good guy from solving the problem, 4) a climax – the critical scene where the protagonist and antagonist square off, 5) a resolution - where the problem is eventually solved, and 6) a conclusion - where the protagonist either inspires a change in society or journeys on to a better life for himself.

Here's the problem – life doesn't fit into such nice, linear categories. Life rarely follows a plot arc that builds into a climactic event that can then be solved in 15-20 minutes. Instead, events evolve with the help of numerous characters, all with varying motivations, all dealing with a world where dramatic events rarely occur, but are instead overshadowed by the drudgery of day to day existence. But this reality doesn't work on screen. Subsequently, the director's alterations, additions, and deletions all enable the audience to follow a predictable plot arc, maintaining their interest for 2+ hours.

One of the most obvious alterations is the depiction of critical characters. Again, characters are chosen not so much for their actual contributions to history, but the extent to which they can match the characteristics of fictional archetypes the audience has come to expect. To be commercially successful, films must have a non-conformist, considerate protagonist, a hedonistic, cruel antagonist, and a series of complimentary characters who appear to exist solely to amplify the characteristics of the two vital figures.

When crafting a protagonist, filmmakers usually create the super male. He will have long hair, love his family, speak his mind, never cheat on his lady love, hate to fight, have a sense of humor, be at home in nature, build with his hands, be respected by his peers, and if ever anyone hurts someone he loves, he will be able to turn into a homicidal maniac able to massacre entire armies with his expert usage of a cornucopia of weapons. As for the antagonist, he is usually the guy in power, the one who has deviant sexual interests, the one who has access to all the wealth, weaponry, and training to be superior to all challengers, and the one who finds joy in hurting women and children. He is everything the protagonist is not. Because in reality humans aren't all good or all evil, filmmakers selectively omit information that takes away from their super-protagonist or that might make audiences side with the antagonist. In addition to selective omission, composite characters are also created where traits of numerous individuals (sometimes even across eras) are combined into one person.

Films also must have other characters to advance the plot and illustrate the influence, moral fiber of the protagonist or the vile temperament of the antagonist. There must be a love interest. This woman will dress plainly, wear little make-up, and her sole purpose will be to love the protagonist unconditionally (until of course she is threatened, raped or killed). There must be a foil, a character from the same social standing as the protagonist, but a man who chooses a different route in life. He exists to show the resolve of the protagonist. There might be a naughty girl who tempts the protagonist, but he will not partake in her affection, because he only has one true love. There are the protagonist's friends – the IQ challenged buddy who is his faithful sidekick; the token minority (a man whose only purpose is to be Black, Hispanic, or French); the aging sage (a follicly-challenged character that gives advice and is the voice of reason); and the crazed lunatic who likes to fight, but, unlike the protagonist, doesn't have the ability to also use calm reason.

As for the events, history can take years, even decades, before coming to a resolution, whereas movies have two to three hours. Therefore, directors will usually choose 2-3 supplementary events and one big climax. In each of these "mini-events" of the rising action, the protagonist appears to be the underdog, but only through his inner strength does he vanquish his enemies. Usually, by the third event, the protagonist's weakness has been revealed, and he might even contemplate not confronting the antagonist. However, either through his inner resolve or after hearing the advice of the aging sage, he will persevere and enter into one final climatic battle with the antagonist.

This climax usually showcases all the traits of both key characters. The protagonist will employ wit, honor, and courage. The antagonist will resort to his material advantages or even cheat. After a few minutes of showcasing their verbal and physical skills, the protagonist will be on the verge of defeat. However, right when it appears the antagonist will win, right when the protagonist appears near death, unable to continue, right when it appears all hope for humanity is lost, the protagonist will reach deep inside and summon the intestinal fortitude needed to rise up and defeat evil, allowing everyone in the theater to leave with a happy joy-joy feeling.

Of course, history doesn't usually have these scenes, and unfortunately, when faced with death, individuals rarely embody the fictional ideal. Consequently, like with character creation, both the supplementary events and the climax are merely rewritten – omitting any inconvenient details that might distract from the formula or inventing elements that could add to the suspense. What the audience is left with are entertaining scenes that exist in the filmmakers' minds, but bare little resemblance to the truth.

And lastly, there are anachronisms – events, people, objects, beliefs, or words that are placed in the incorrect time period. Oftentimes, directors make these alterations because it's what they think the audience has come to expect. Subsequently, what is included in a film oftentimes represents more the world of the director and the audience than the history he is recreating. Here are some of the more common inclusions: values of today (possibly alter the main character's sexual preference or racist ideology), language (have everyone Shakespearean English), casting (make your good guys all Northern European...bad guys should be whoever Americans hate that decade), vernacular (throw in some contemporary slang), director's political views (make the king/emperor embody the president you don't like), costume/make-up (choose what matches today's styles), or setting (create sets that match the audience's preconceived notions).

Obviously, this list is not an exhaustive rule book and few films exactly follow this formula (unless of course Mel Gibson plays a starring role), but it provides a blueprint for what directors usually alter when bringing history to the screen.

However, knowing that something is altered doesn't actually help with knowing the truth. You might be able to guess that *Braveheart's* William Wallace wasn't the super man Mel created, but did you know he was instead a morally-questionable noble who murdered sometimes for pleasure? You can probably figure out that Pocahontas and John Smith didn't have a romantic liaison, but were you aware that she actually married another Virginian colonist John Rolfe and later lived in London as an ambassador for her people? And yes, you probably realize that *300's* King Xerxes wasn't a sexually deviant "oversized drag queen," but did you know he actually ruled over an empire more open to civil liberties than any Europe would construct for centuries?

This is why I created *History through Film*. I wanted to find out where history ended and where fiction began. Over the past couple years, I became the man in the back of the theater, notebook in hand, waiting for the daylight scene in the film to provide me with the light needed to scribble details I could research later. I then combined my research with the essays of others to create an anthology that will give you insight into the movies that for many define their historical experience. It is through these movies, and countless others, that I hope you too will be able to appreciate and learn from history through film.

10,000 B.C.

2008

Director: Roland Emmerich

Starring: Steven Strait, Camilla Belle, Cliff Curtis

109 minutes – Rated PG-13

By Eric Burnett

Synopsis:

The film *10,000 B.C.* explores the early phases of human civilization as a band of hunter-gatherers fights for survival in the midst of an expanding society bent on enslaving the surrounding population to build their temples to the gods. The story traces the journey of mammoth hunter D'Leh as he attempts to rescue his childhood love, Evolet, from slavery, while finding a way to ensure the continued existence of his diminishing tribe. After climbing frozen mountains, surviving deadly tropical jungles, and crossing barren deserts, D'Leh eventually unites all the tribes of the region for one final battle against the civilized god-kings living in the "mountain of the gods." However, before the final battle can be fought, D'Leh will have to choose between saving the woman he loves and saving his people.

Historically Relevant Scenes	
00:09:23-00:17:08	- Hunting Mammoth
00:43:28-00:48:07	- Early Agricultural Village and Saber-Toothed Cat
01:17:54-01:26:04	- Early Walled City and Pyramid Construction

Ratings:

Entertainment - ★ ★ ☆ ☆

Historical Accuracy - ★ ☆ ☆ ☆

Historical Analysis:

Probably the greatest error made by the creators of this feeble attempt at a prehistoric epic was their film's title – *10,000 B.C.* Once they pinned a date to the film, uncovering its inaccuracies becomes almost too easy: Psychotic ostrich-chicken predators – 1.2 million years B.C.

Egyptian sailboats – 3200 B.C. Egyptian pyramids – 2300 B.C. Metal spears – 2400 BC. The list goes on and on.

If there was ever a movie created to introduce the topic of anachronisms, this would have to be the one. In films, anachronisms are any objects, events, ideologies, or customs that are placed in the wrong time period. Obviously, nobody drove cars in Ancient Greece; a World War II G.I. can't have a dinosaur for a pet; and cavemen probably don't know the lyrics to Elvis Presley tunes. However ludicrous the above examples might appear, the film *10,000 B.C.* equally misses the mark on several occasions, so, although they might have a few historically accurate details, for the most part, this movie merely pulls together details from a hodgepodge of eras in hopes that the audience will suspend all logic for a couple hours. Director Roland Emmerich promised to bring to the audience a world "like nothing they have ever seen." He could have added, "…or like nothing they could have ever seen even if they were able to travel back in time."

First, let's start with D'Leh and his small band of mammoth hunters. Many people left the theater thinking they are cavemen. They are definitely not cavemen. In fact, by 10,000 B.C. the men roaming Earth had all the cognitive functions of modern day humans, but without all the fancy gadgets later generations would invent. They were a far cry from the world's first hominids – Australopithecus - a group of upward walking primates that roamed Africa close to 4 million years ago. The most famous collection of bones from this era belongs to the archaeological find nicknamed "Lucy" (named after the Beatles' song "Lucy in the Sky with Diamonds" which was playing on the radio when Donald Johanson and Tom Gray made the pivotal discovery in 1974). Over the next four million years, the stature of these early hominids grew more upright and their cognitive function improved, until about 250,000 years ago when Homo Neanderthalensis (Neanderthals) emerged, later to be joined by Cro-Magnon man who many archaeologists argue were responsible for wiping out the Neanderthals. These Cro-Magnons roamed Europe and are the ones you think of when you hear the word "Caveman." However, by 10,000 B.C. they all had essentially died off, paving the way for Homo Sapiens to emerge as the sole hominid group on Earth.

A better way to refer to the mammoth hunters depicted in the film would be nomadic hunter gatherers. They hunted, they gathered, they roamed. In the film, D'Leh's Yagahl tribe lives in mammoth skeleton-framed shelters and waits for a herd of woolly mammoths (called "manick" by these prehistoric wanderers) to pass their hilltop village. Finding out how prehistoric man actually lived is fairly difficult due to the fact that early man rarely buried the deceased underground, instead choosing to bury them in trees where the corpse could be shredded by scavengers. However, from archaeological digs of preserved village sites, from the shattered remains of prehistoric prey of early man, and from studying the behavior of contemporary hunter gatherer societies, scientists believe these early humans survived on root vegetables and berries and divided the world of animals into two categories "edible and inedible." Unlike in the movie where the tribe remains stationary, in reality they would have had to move frequently to avoid exhausting the region's food supply and also to avoid the constant threat of human and animal predators.

Because of this constant movement, by 10,000 B.C. man inhabited all current continents of the globe, and their domiciles varied to fit the environmental demands of the region. The skeleton-framed homes depicted in the film did exist 10,000 years ago, as numerous sites have been found across Siberia and Northern Europe where animal hides covered mammoth bones. In addition to this type of dwelling, Stone Age man would have also lived in huts built from stick/tree lean-tos supported by stones at the base. However, many nomads chose stretched animal hide shelters that provided increased mobility.

Although conditions varied from region to region due to varying climate conditions and topographical realities, some historical validations of the film's depictions can be made. For one, did the tribes remain in relatively small groups? Yes. Unable to feed larger groups, each tribe usually held between 10-30 people and had fluid leadership that regularly changed from generation to generation. Did they wear dreadlocks? Probably. The first historical reference to dreadlocks was made in the Ancient Indian Vedas about how a god stored the power of a river in his hair, but all continents have evidence mentioning their existence. Also, because dreadlocks form naturally when washed but not combed or brushed, they most almost certainly did exist in prehistoric times. Did the men have goatees? Sorry. This fashion statement more reflects today's male grooming techniques. Considering early man only had access to stone tools during this time, it would have been impossible for a group of men to maintain a well-manicured goatee while on a walkabout. Today, even with the five-bladed Gilette Fusion, men still knick their faces, so those prehistoric boys with their obsidian rock blades didn't have a chance.

How about the romance between the two lead characters? Did prehistoric boys and girls gaze adoringly into each other's eyes and profess their undying love? Again, probably not. Throughout human history, romantic love has been the anomaly, not the norm, and truly cheesy love where men claim, "You will always be in my heart" did not occur until the mid 1990s when Celine Dion started belting out some easy listening classics.

As for jewelry, characters in the film have bracelets, earrings, necklaces and one gentleman even has a tusk through his chin. Although jewelry has been worn by humans for over 80,000 years, the types of jewelry seen in the film could not have been crafted using tools available to humans in 10,000 B.C. Remember, this was the Stone Age, which meant the only shaping tool would have been a sharp piece of stone.

How about the character "Old Mother"? If you're wondering if a human could feel the pain and the temperature of clansmen hundreds of miles away, or transfer her own spirit to the dead body of a young girl in a far off land, ummm...no...103% of all scientists agree that prehistoric man had not perfected these skills. However, did comparable spiritual leaders exist? Maybe. Because they lacked surplus food storages, specialization of labor was not possible and all men and women needed to develop and focus on only those skills necessary for survival. There was no place in the prehistoric world for such superfluous careers as doctors, lawyers, teachers or even priests. However, some early man societies had shamans, spiritual leaders who were in touch with the "invisible world" and through self-mutilation, hypnosis or herbal concoctions could cure or cause illnesses or "predict" the future. Like with "Old Mother," these shamans were respected by the villagers and their "non-traditional" behavior was seen as needed to satisfy the spiritual world. So yes, a character like "Old Mother" could have existed, but her superhuman telepathic powers did not.

What did exist was the need to hunt. Although humans more often than not hunted the more abundant deer, caribou, rabbits, and turtles, megafauna like the wooly mammoth were always desired, though they did pose considerable risk. Because of their vast size (nearly fifteen feet tall and weighing close to 20,000 pounds) and ornery disposition, the wooly mammoth could only be taken down through a coordinated effort that combined the best projectile technology of the time with a synchronized attack. Like their distant cousin the elephant who "don't behave like animals [but] like enemies," the mammoth could readily dispatch a singular hunter, so the scene in which D'Leh downs a bull with a lone spear was impossible. However, prehistoric men were "not primitive cave people. Strategy, cunning, and guile [were] all part of their arsenal." After days of tracking their movement, the hunters would wait until the landscape was favorable – either near a canyon, a swamp or some other water source. Then, using a device known as an atalatl that could launch a stone tipped spear over a hundred yards at a speed of 60 miles per hour, the hunters simultaneously launched their projectiles at the beast. They then followed the wounded beast as it staggered away, gradually losing strength, and only when it was near death would they "administer the coup de grâce." Here, at the kill site, the tribe would then set up camp, taking advantage of every organ available. Like the meat packing plants of the 20th century, they would use everything from "the squeak to the tail." So, unlike in the movie where the brief, violent solitary kill of the mammoth allowed the hunters to return to the camp with food, in reality, the kill would have taken an extended amount of time and the tribe would have moved their "village" to the fallen beast.

As for being able to tame the mammoths and use them as beasts of burden to help construct pyramids - also not possible. The first domesticated animal was the dog, about 14 thousand years ago, but they served primarily for hunting, protection and companionship. As for the first draught animals used to drag objects, civilizations in the Middle East used the ox around 4,000 B.C. In the Indus Valley, man first domesticated elephants around 2000 B.C., using them for both agriculture and military purposes. So, in 10,000 B.C., no animal was used for moving objects, let alone a 20,000 pound hairy beast with tusks taller than a man.

In the film, aside from his run-in with the mammoth, D'Leh must also survive three other beasts – the saber-toothed tiger, an unidentified dinosaur-chicken beast that seemingly travels at the speed of light (unless of course it is chasing the lead character), and the "four-legged demon" horses. Although nearly extinct by the year 10,000 B.C., numerous species of saber-toothed cats did roam the Americas, Eurasia and Africa from as far back as 40 million years ago. Unlike in the movie where the saber-toothed cat looks to be about the size of a bus and has the ability to remain indebted to those that help him, in reality saber-toothed cats were about the size of humans, and there is no scientific proof that it befriended humans and thanked them for their hospitality. As for the dinosaur-chicken beast, the closest animal to the film's creation would be the Phorusrhacids, or "terror birds" that died out over 1.2 million years ago and only existed in North and South America.

Then there are the horses. The entrance of the slave trading warlords who sweep through the village firmly strapped into the stirrups of horses is yet another event that never could have happened. Man didn't ride the horse until 4,000 B.C., and even then he would have ridden merely on a blanket-like saddle. Stirrups didn't appear until around 400 A.D. in China. So…final score on the depiction of prehistoric animals: wooly mammoth – maybe; saber-toothed cat – probably not; terror bird – impossible; and horses – no.

HISTORY THROUGH FILM

Although the battles between men and beasts were probably the more engaging scenes from the film, the protagonist must also survive a changing environment and a nearby civilization dedicated to enslaving the entire region. The beginning of the film mentions how a shift in their world forced prehistoric man to adapt or perish. It is difficult to ascertain the setting because the lead characters are able to walk from a mountainous region to a tropical rainforest to a desert to a river valley. Making it even more difficult is that the characters are racially ambiguous. The movie starts in what appears to be a European mountain, but the chosen actors appear Asian, Native American, African and European. In the desert region, the villagers are primarily African, and in the river valley and tropical region they appear Middle Eastern (This final casting fits quite conveniently with Hollywood's post-9/11 depiction of most protagonists as Middle Eastern).

But could such a climate disparity have existed in 10,000 B.C.? No. By 10,000 B.C., the world was coming out of its last Ice Age, and the glacier ice pack was gradually rescinding, but at no point could the three distinct climates depicted been within walking distance of each other.

However, some archaeologists do believe that climate played a role in the birth of civilization, although not in the manner normally accepted. The accepted early civilization theory states that free of climatic turmoil, man was able to establish his roots near a river valley where he gradually developed agriculture, leading to surplus food and specialization of labor – the hallmarks of a first civilization. Dr. Nick Brooks believes the opposite. "On the contrary, what we tend to think of today as 'civilisation' was in large part an accidental by-product of unplanned adaptation to catastrophic climate change. Civilisation was a last resort - a means of organising society and food production and distribution, in the face of deteriorating environmental conditions." Brooks believes that an adjustment of the earth's orbit led to a massive shift in the earth's climate, creating arid regions where the only source of water were the great rivers in regions like Egypt, Mesopotamia, the Indus Valley and China. He believes humans reluctantly settled in these civilizations, giving up their freedom and consigning themselves to a life of toil, all as a last effort to ensure their survival. So, although the film was correct in depicting a correlation between climate and the rise of civilizations, current historians would argue that the film's traditional cause/effect depiction could be erroneous.

Regardless of whether Brooks' view or the traditional view proves correct, the fact is that the first river civilizations did not appear until around 6000 B.C. near the Tigris and Euphrates Rivers of Mesopotamia (modern day Iraq), the Indus River (modern India), and the

Yellow River (modern China). However, the "mountain of the gods" civilization depicted in *10,000 B.C.* most closely resembles that of Egypt, but the familiar Egypt pyramid building civilization didn't start until about 2700 B.C.

As for some of the conditions illustrated in the film, Egypt also created a hierarchical society near a river (the Nile River); subjugated its people by rulers seen as deities and through administrators serving as priests; and organized an expansive system of slavery to construct its mammoth (pardon the pun) pyramids. But they never housed four story high sailboats in a pyramid-like boathouse, and they didn't have scale maps of Europe and Africa that the world would not see until the time of Christopher Columbus. However, numerous hunter gatherers still existed in surrounding regions, considering in the year 1000 B.C., probably 70% of the world's population continued to lead a nomadic existence. And a nomadic people known as the Hebrews were even enslaved by the pharaohs of Egypt until a man named Moses came along in the 13th century B.C. and guided them across the Red Sea to the Holy Land. So, maybe director Roland Emmerich should have renamed the film *1300 B.C.* and then he could have kept true to his tale of a long-haired man, orphaned as a boy, who later unites a people and saves them all from slavery, all while convincing the slave-holding civilization that they believed in false deities (if you're not getting the Biblical allusion, please head down to your local video store and check out *The Ten Commandments* or *Prince of Egypt*).

Overall, *10,000 B.C.* introduces numerous events, inventions, individuals, and settings that have actually existed over the course of human history, just not all at the same time, and definitely not all in 10,000 B.C. Nonetheless, although the plot's climax is predictable (the evil king is actually slain this time around – not like *300*'s Xerxes) and the dialogue stands out as minimalistic cheese, a fair amount of action sequences were created and the CGI civilization and animal recreations give the viewer a sense of life a long, long time ago. But as for the penultimate prehistoric tale, we'll all still have to wait for Hollywood to spin a true Stone Age masterpiece.

Key Quotes

D'Leh: (pointing to the North Star) That light is like you in my heart; it will never go out.

D'Leh: (talking to the Saber-tooth cat before freeing him) Do not eat me when I save your life!

Troy

2004
Director: Wolfgang Peterson
Starring: Brad Pitt, Orlando Bloom, Diane Kruger and Eric Bana
163 minutes – Rated R

By Sophie Greene

Synopsis:

Based on Homer's legendary epic poem *The Iliad*, the movie *Troy* tells the story of the Trojan War and the famous Greek heroes involved. The war begins after Paris, the Prince of Troy, falls in love with and then abducts Helen, the wife of Menelaus, King of Sparta. Enraged with jealousy, Menelaus calls on his warrior brother Agamemnon, and together they journey off to recapture Helen, the "face that launched a thousand ships." Greek hero Achilles joins this Trojan War, not for the glory of his king, but to secure his own immortality. After a series of battles and individual clashes, the Greeks finally enter the walls of Troy for one final encounter that will secure the combatants' legacy for all eternity.

Historically Relevant Scenes

0:09:23>0:14:31	- Paris and Helen's secret relationship
0:14:40>0:16:20	- Helen leaves with Paris
0:18:13>0:21:14	- Menelaus and Agamemnon decide to go to war
0:35:40>0:49:10	- Achilles' assault on the Trojan beach
1:52:00>2:02:36	- Hector and Achilles battle outside Troy
2:15:34>2:19:56	- Trojan Horse and siege of Troy

Ratings:

Entertainment - ★ ★ ★ ★

Historical Accuracy - ★ ☆ ☆ ☆

Historical Analysis:

What causes war? For the American Civil War, it was the attack on Fort Sumter. For World War I, it was the assassination of Franz Ferdinand. For World War II, it was Hitler's invasion of Poland.

For the Trojan War, it was a woman. It was "the face that launched a thousand ships" - the stunningly beautiful Helen of Troy. According to the film *Troy*, while surviving a loveless marriage to her repulsive husband King Menelaus, Helen falls in love with the Trojan ambassador, Prince Paris, and then she foolishly returns to Troy with Paris, provoking her jealous husband. King Menelaus, humiliated and seeking revenge, and backed by his more-powerful brother Agamemnon, wages war on Troy. In the movie, after weeks of back and forth skirmishes, the Greek forces plan a surprise attack by faking surrender and giving the Trojans a giant wooden horse as a gift. After a night of revelry, while the Trojans slumber, the Spartan soldiers, hidden inside the horse, emerge to massacre the city. During this night, Paris kills super-warrior Achilles by shooting him in the one place he was defenseless – his heel. Paris and Helen eventually escape, but the impregnable fortress that was Troy lay forever in ruins.

Versions of this story have passed down though the ages – with the phrases "Trojan Horse" and "Achilles Heel" becoming regulars in the Western lexicon. But here's the problem with this epic battle.

It probably never happened.

The only "source" for the Trojan War is Homer's epic poem, the *Iliad*, which dates back to the 8th century BC. The problem with this account is that it comes almost five hundred years after the alleged incident. Believing the accuracy of a poem written five centuries after the historical event would be like accepting as fact a Britney Spears' song about Christopher Columbus' voyage of discovery. Now, granted, Homer has a bit more credibility than the princess of the tabloids, but his *Iliad* not only recounts the so-called war, but also speaks of moody gods giving humans immortality by dipping them in rivers or sending plagues to opposing armies. Not exactly rock solid proof.

At the time of the early Greeks, many believed the Trojan War was an actual event, but also realized Homer was probably drawn to hyperbole or metaphor at times to suit the needs of his poem. Others thought maybe he merely combined numerous events and characters into one engaging, climactic narrative. Today most historians have settled on the fact that there probably were a series of engagements from the Mycenaean cities of Greece against the region of Troy.

However, one man made it his life's mission to discover the truth. For nearly two decades, Manfred Korfmann, a German archaeologist from the University of Tubingen, Germany, supervised the excavation of ruins in the northwest region of Turkey. At this site lies archaeological proof that there was in fact a walled city that survived numerous sieges and was destroyed for the last time in approximately 1180 BC (which puts it fairly close to Homer's version of the Trojan War). Aside from skeletons, walled remains, and sling bullets, there is an elevated platform that might be the sanctuary discussed in the *Iliad*. However, some archaeologists believe the discovered city was too small to be the legendary Troy, and that it wasn't destroyed by war, but by fire. In response to historical critics, Korfmann noted:

> "However, everything currently suggests that Homer should be taken seriously, that his story of a military conflict between Greeks and the inhabitants of Troy is based on a memory of historical events--whatever these may have been. If someone came up to me at the excavation one day and expressed his or her belief that the Trojan War did indeed happen here, my response as an archaeologist working at Troy would be: Why not?"

In spite of its historical questionability, the story never gets old and has survived in Western Civilization for over three thousand years. And the movie *Troy* provides yet another chapter in this legendary love story, providing entertainment value for every demographic. There's a gorgeous woman, Helen, the dashingly romantic Paris, and the hero that everyone loves to hate, Achilles. Wolfgang Peterson's *Troy* got it right. Diane Kruger, with her blue eyes and golden hair, plays Helen; teenage heartthrob Orlando Bloom plays Paris, and last but most certainly not least, Brad Pitt, a favorite in everyone's books, buffed up to play the role of the fearless Achilles. Along with a stellar cast, *Troy* is packed with battle scenes of epic proportions, one even depicting the ever-so-famous "thousand ships" that Helen's face "launched." Granted the ships depicted were themselves from 800 BC – 400 years after the alleged battle.

Speaking of anachronisms, after one of these amazing battle scenes, Achilles is seen burying his cousin/close friend Patroclus with coins over his eyes. Peterson failed to acknowledge that coins had yet to be invented. He was about five or six centuries before the date when coins are said to have first appeared in Greece. Ships and coins, along with out of place fifth and sixth century statues and Early Bronze Age jewelry, are minor inaccuracies, but since we lack solid historical evidence, it's easiest to compare *Troy*'s historical accuracy to the poem, the *Iliad*. Using *Iliad* as a reference, the movie is surprisingly accurate, but there are still some typical pieces of Hollywood magic.

Probably one of the biggest differences between the movie and the poem is the role of the gods, or the movie's glaring omission of Homer's most critical characters. What is Greek mythology without gods? Where would Hercules be without Zeus and where would Persephone be without Hades? Gods are a very important part of Ancient Greek mythology and Homer gave them lead roles in his epic.

Throughout the Greek wars, the Trojan War included, the gods' roles were to manipulate the people, and alter the course of the conflict. In fact, according to Homer, the goddesses Athena, Aphrodite, and Hera start the Trojan War after a quarrel over who was the fairest of them all; Poseidon stops the Trojan forces from conquering the Achaeans; Zeus helps the Trojans break into the Achaean camp; and the sea nymph Thetis dips Achilles in the river Styx, making him invulnerable (well, almost invulnerable) to any assailant.

However, unlike the 1980s cheesy, special-effects-challenged Greek tale *Clash of the Titans*, there are no gods in this film. Peterson wanted a movie the audience could buy wholeheartedly and the movie audiences prefer their victories from a buffed-out Brad Pitt and Eric Bana, not from a lightning bolt from Zeus' staff. In Peterson's defense, the characters do pray to the gods on more than one occasion, and it is Apollo's temple that is destroyed in Achilles' assault on the beach.

In addition, Brad Pitt's character, Achilles, and his story are portrayed differently than legend has it. Achilles is considered by some to be a god, or at least, immortal. The legend goes that his mother, Thetis, a sea nymph, wished to make him immortal so she held onto his heel and dipped him in the river Styx, the boundary between Earth and Hades (the Underworld). He was believed to have been left vulnerable in only one spot: his heel. However, in the *Iliad*, Achilles is not 'immortal' as he gets wounded several times. It isn't until Paris shoots an arrow (guided by Apollo) to Achilles' heel that the 'immortal' hero dies. None of Achilles' road to immortality is depicted in the movie, but that's not the problem.

The problem arises in the film version's death of Achilles, which comes after the climatic arrival of the Trojan Horse and during the destruction of Troy. In Homer's version, Achilles was killed before the horse was even built, but movie critic Steven Sailer noted that "Homer violated Screenwriting 101 by killing off his star before the [finale]." Subsequently, Peterson adjusted the "facts" a bit and made the wise cinematic decision to tweak Homer's version to satisfy his dramatic vision for an ending.

Important to Achilles' character is his cousin Patroclus. In the movie, Patroclus is played by a young actor with a striking resemblance to Pitt. The two appear to have a brotherly relationship where Achilles is always looking after the younger Patroclus. Historians have differed in their interpretation of this relationship. During the Classical Age of Greece through to the fall of Rome, it was seen as one of pederasty, a deep, sometimes sexual, relationship common to Ancient Greece where a boy would become the apprentice of an older man and would learn a variety of "skills" under his tutelage. In recent centuries, it was seen more as one of "war buddies" or possibly one of mutual homosexuality.

Peterson decided to keep the relationship neutral in order to avoid controversy with the public (a decision not made by Oliver Stone with the film *Alexander* to the detriment of that film's box office receipts). However neutral or homosexual the relationship, when Patroclus dies, Achilles is obviously deeply affected and decides to start fighting again for King Agamemnon. Patroclus, wearing Achilles' armor, was mistaken for Achilles and killed by Hector. In the movie, Patroclus stole the armor without Achilles knowing, while in the poem Achilles gave Patroclus the armor to use while fighting. Because of Patroclus's death, Achilles eventually challenges Hector outside the city walls, and Hector valiantly leaves the protection of the city to face his nemesis. In the *Iliad*, Hector actually is tricked by the goddess Athena to remain outside while every other Trojan sought protection. This alteration elevates the stature of Hector, making him appear more "manly" as he freely embraces the challenge. In Homer's version, free will rarely overpowers the will of the gods.

The one important "character" who adds to the mystery of the Trojan War is the horse. Built by Epideus, the massive wooden horse was filled with warriors and led by Odysseus. It is one of the most famous surprise attacks, but unfortunately the only evidence for the horse lies in the *Iliad* and several other minor Ancient literary resources. Some historians believe that the "horse" mentioned in the *Iliad* merely symbolized a sudden event that ended the war. Some believe siege warfare brought an end to the Trojan city, some believe it was disease brought over by the Greeks and others believe it was an earthquake. Recent accounts point to a fire. All of these are reasonable ends to the war, but by no means are they as interesting as thirty Greek warriors hidden in the belly of a giant wooden horse, emerging to eventually destroy Troy. Peterson did an excellent job depicting the majesty of such a horse, and the sack of the city showed the devious nature of the Greeks. What Peterson didn't show was that the Trojans were warned. He made it seem like the Trojans were completely unaware of what was going on and not a single citizen was smart enough to realize the nature of the horse. In reality, or at least according to Homer, two people, Laocoon and Cassandra, attempted to warn the Trojans of "Greeks bearing gifts." Of course, putting this in the movie would have complicated the plot and forced the director to introduce yet another character to the already crowded ensemble cast.

Apart from the character depictions, there are some other director's choices that invited criticism. One involves the length of the war. Homer's Trojan War lasted over ten years; Peterson's lasted a couple weeks.   Other critics believed Wolfgang Peterson chose the film to advance his own political beliefs. After Peterson publicly asserted, "just as King Agamemnon waged what was essentially a war of conquest on the ruse of trying to rescue the beautiful Helen from the hands of the Trojans, President George W. Bush concealed his true motives for the invasion of Iraq," one could see why critics scanned the dialogue for hints of bias.   Early on, Agamemnon is warned, "You cannot have the whole world, Agamemnon. It is too big, even for you," and later Brad Pitt's Achilles mocks the king, "Imagine a king that fights his own battle. Wouldn't that be a sight?" Although some might claim these comments allude to parallels between the Iraq War and the Trojan War, couldn't the same comparison be made between Agamemnon and hundreds of other political leaders over the centuries?

Aside from the political criticism, others saw the film as a Eurocentric, "white-washed" depiction of a multi-cultural conflict that omitted the contributions and impact of non-Europeans. Some believe the "Trojan War" was merely yet another conflict started by the "Sea Peoples" of the Mediterranean who scourged the coastal towns for centuries. These historians argue that it was only through Egyptian help and the lending of 10,000 troops that the Trojans were able to hold off the Sea Peoples' advance. However, like with other evidence for this time period, conflicting and scarce reports make one accepted interpretation nearly impossible.

Troy manages to create a relatively accurate recreation of Homer's tale, granted his tale is an epic poem and by no means a first hand historical account. However, instead of the poetry of Homer, Peterson brings us buffed bods, beautiful heroines, and such philosophically deep lines as Achilles' challenge, "Immortality! Take it! It's yours!" For those who like their historical movies light on the history, this is the tale for you.

Key Quotes

Menelaus: (*after discovering Paris has stolen his wife*) I want her back.
Agamemnon: Well of course you do, she's a beautiful woman.
Menelaus: I want her back so I can kill her with my own two hands, and I won't rest till I've burned Troy to the ground.
Agamemnon: I thought you wanted peace with Troy.
Menelaus: I should have listened to you.
Agamemnon: Peace is for the women, and the weak. Empires are forged by war.
Menelaus: All my life I've stood by your side, fought your enemies. You're the elder, you reap the glory. This is the war of the world. But have I ever complained brother? Have I ever asked you for anything?
Agamemnon: Never. You're a man of honour.
Menelaus: Will you go to war with me brother?

Achilles: (*to his men before storming the beach*) Myrmidons! My brothers of the sword! I would rather fight beside you than any army of thousands! Let no man forget how menacing we are, we are lions! Do you know what's waiting beyond that beach? Immortality! Take it! It's yours!

300

2007
Director: Zack Snyder
Starring: Gerard Butler, Lena Headey, Rodrigo Santoro
117 minutes – Rated R

By Eric Burnett

Synopsis:

In the 2006 blockbuster *300*, Zack Snyder retells the decisive battle of the Persian War, where 300 Spartans sacrificed their lives to thwart the Xerxes-led Persian army and save Western Civilization. The story picks up after King Leonidas of Sparta murders the Persian ambassador who entered Sparta encouraging surrender. Leonidas then takes his 300 battle-hardened soldiers to cut off the invaders, but after three days of heroic fighting and his betrayal at the hands of scorned hunchback Ephialtes, the Spartan numbers can no longer survive the onslaught. However, before the final Spartan falls, one half-blinded Spartan, Dilios, returns to Greece to tell the story of the brave men, and their sacrifice becomes the inspiration to unite the Greeks and subsequently send the numerically superior Persian force to its final defeat at Platea.

Historically Relevant Scenes

00:01:00>00:05:48	- Agoge
00:06:55>00:13:00	- King Leonidas murders ambassador
00:22:30>00:26:30	- Departing for battle
00:45:20>00:52:00	- Phalanx warfare
01:01:30>01:09:00	- Immortals
01:15:50>01:18:30	- Betrayal of Ephialtes
01:34:30>01:43:30	- Final Battle

Ratings:

Entertainment - ★ ★ ★ ★

Historical Accuracy - ★ ★ ☆ ☆

Historical Analysis:

When *300* first hit the screens, it immediately titillated its target audience - young men drooled at the heroically brutal battle sequences while the ladies exited the theaters drooling for entirely different reasons. Zack Snyder brought to life the vibrant vision of Frank Miller, taking the groundbreaking feel of Miller's *Sin City*, and applying it to one of the most critical events in Western history - the Battle of Thermopylae. Snyder immediately had to deal with criticism as the historical accuracy gurus set to work picking apart his masterpiece. To their criticism, Snyder responded that the film is "an opera, not a documentary" and "the events are 90 percent accurate. It's just in the visualization that it's crazy.... I've shown this movie to world-class historians who have said it's amazing. They can't believe it's as accurate as it is." Regardless of Snyder's admission that his film never intended to be true to history, in the diplomatically charged atmosphere we live in today, a film that pits the underdog Western force of liberty against the oppressive slave-wielding regime of the Persians will undoubtedly be looked at through a hypersensitive lens.

The Spartan's attempt to halt the invading Persian forces took place at the Thermopylae Pass in 480 B.C. In the movie, the Persian army invades Greece as retribution for Spartan King Leonidas' kicking of the Persian ambassador into a well after refusing to surrender because "THIS...IS...SPARTA!!!" In reality, the Persian invasion was anything but spontaneous. The Persian arrival of 480 B.C. came after King Xerxes had spent four years assembling a force that Greek historian Herodotus once numbered at 2.6 million combatants with an accompanying force of an additional 2 million (Recent historians peg the number at closer to 200,000, but regardless, this force had been unprecedented in the history of Mediterranean conflicts).

Xerxes was avenging the defeat of his father Darius, who ten years earlier succumbed to Athenian forces at Marathon (the battle where the Athenian messenger Pheidippides ran 26.2 miles back to Athens to report the climactic victory – he yelled "Nike" and then dropped dead). Darius entered Athens seeking to punish the Athenians for their earlier military support of the Ionians who attempted to break free from the Persian Empire on the landmass that today is known as Turkey. The Athenians felt affinity for these Ionian brothers, as they were once colonists of the expansive Greek empire. Eventually, the Ionians burnt down the Persian city of Sardis. So when Xerxes entered the peninsula of Hellas in 480, he came not to avenge the murder of one of his ambassadors, but to continue the punishment his father failed to inflict, and burn Athens to the ground.

But Xerxes' invasion was stalled by King Leonidas and his army of Spartans at Thermopylae, the only road between Thessaly and northern Greece, a passage known as the "hot gates" (thusly named due to the nearby hot springs). The movie depicts this passage as a narrow, rocky path lodged between a cliff and a water abyss. In reality, it was a narrow pass – probably only about 40 feet wide during the height of Ancient Greece (today, soil deposits have extended its coastal width to over two miles) that was wedged between the 5000 foot Mt. Kallidromon and the Aegean Sea. For any invading army, this was the only way to get through to Athens, and the Spartans knew it. They could negate the Persian numerical advantage by funneling their large numbers into a small front. Regardless of whether an army had 200,000 men or 300 men, only 15-20 could stand shoulder to shoulder at any one time on the narrow pass.

It was here that King Leonidas and his 300 Spartans made their final stand. In the movie, through their ferocity, determination, athleticism and combative skills, the 300 Spartans alone repel wave after wave of Persian advances. However, Sparta did not fight the Persians alone. On the first day, they were joined by over seven thousand other Greeks – among them Thespians, Phocians, and Arcadians. More importantly, their initial success and survival was assured by the role of a man whose importance has been lost through history – Themistocles.

Without Themistocles, there would have been no Battle at Thermopylae and the Persians probably could have conquered Athens and the Greek peninsula with minimal resistance. Born to a merchant and raised on ships, Themistocles rose through the political ranks and survived the first Persian invasion at Marathon. Leaving Marathon, Themistocles realized the key to defeating the Persians was not by expanding the Athenian land army, but by enhancing its navy, because the Persians could only resupply their vast army and hope to maintain an extended land campaign if they controlled the seas. Ironically, at the exact time Themistocles needed money, in 483 BC, vast amounts of silver deposits were discovered to the south of Athens. However, initially Themistocles' appeals to use this money for naval funding fell on deaf ears, and the Athenians were going to merely divide up the profits evenly among each of their citizens (each receiving about ten drachmas, or $1500 in today's dollars).

Here, Themistocles used his acquired political guile and manufactured a threat from the nearby island city of Aegina. Claiming the Aeginans intended to destroy Athenian maritime commerce, Themistocles secured funding for 100 additional Triremes, the boats that would eventually hold the Persian navy, preventing them from encircling

Leonidas' force. After employing this lie, or a "clever misdirection of the populace to achieve a greater end," Themistocles later coordinated the efforts of Leonidas' land army at Thermopylae and his 270 ships blocking the Artemesium Straits. These 270 ships frustrated and distracted the Persian navy (almost 1000 ships strong), delaying their ability to surround Leonidas' forces. Even when Xerxes attempted to circumvent this Athenian line of defense by sending 200 ships around the Eobea peninsula, his efforts were foiled by an even more powerful adversary – Mother Nature. As was depicted in the film, a massive storm did in fact strike the Aegean Sea, sinking all 200 ships.

Basically, the 300 Spartans received a lot of help from Themistocles' foresight, 7000 additional soldiers, and a fortuitous squall. However, historians (like film directors) are guilty of the time-honored tradition of exaggerating the role of an underdog force while underplaying the impact of supporting characters, all for the purpose of creating a more engaging tale. And what better tale to tell than that of incredibly overmatched heroes willing to give their lives for their country.

But all 300 Spartans did eventually die. That part can't be denied. After two days of fighting, Xerxes was humiliated that both his light infantry and his elite Immortals had done little damage to the Greek lines. Nearly 20,000 of his men lay dead on the battlefield, with no signs that the Spartans and their fellow Greeks would retreat. It is here that Xerxes tries option C – sending 10,000 of his troops around a "secret" path, thus surrounding the Greek forces. Not all historians agree on how Xerxes came to this knowledge, although some do direct blame to Ephialtes (yes a Greek, but not the revenge-seeking, perverted hunchback from the film).

This maneuver did not surprise King Leonidas. Knowing that the Anopaea Pass was the weak link to the Thermopylae defense, Leonidas stationed 1000 Phocians at the pass to prevent their outflanking of the Greek force. However, when Xerxes army appeared, the Phocians feared that the Persian army intended to attack their nearby city, so they chose to not stand and fight, but return to Phocia and defend their homes. This choice sealed the Spartans fate. Upon learning of the desertion, Leonidas relieved over four thousand Greeks of their duty, whereupon they all returned to their homelands, leaving the 300 Spartans and the 1000 Thespians to hold off Xerxes army of over 200,000.

On the third and final day, director Snyder has King Xerxes approach the battlefield to offer King Leonidas and his men terms of surrender. In the movie, Leonidas then removes his helmet and feigns surrender, only to leap to his feet and heave his spear at the unsuspecting

Xerxes. After the spear cuts his face, Xerxes launches the final attack and within moments King Leonidas and his Spartan warriors fall.

In reality, the only interaction between the Persians and the Greeks that third day came at a nearby stream where a Persian scout came across the Spartans bathing in the nude, combing their hair and taking care of their appearance. The Persians might have seen this as a testament to Greek vanity, but the truth was the Greeks knew this would be their last day and they were preparing for the afterlife. By the end of the day, all Greeks lay dead on the field and Xerxes ordered Leonidas' head to be mounted on a pike.

In the movie, this glorious defeat led to the downfall of Xerxes and his massive force, as the inspired Greek peninsula banded together to thwart the Persian invasion. Although the Battle of Thermopylae did become an Alamo-esque inspiring moment for Greek forces, the true defeat of Persia came not from this assembled force but from the massive Battle at Salamis where 378 Greek ships defeated over 700 Persian ships at a narrow pass (notice how the Persians keep losing at narrow passes?) that neutralized the Persian numerical advantage. It was this defeat, not the assembled land army, that forced Xerxes' withdrawal to resupply the bulk of his army. He did leave behind a smaller army, and this diminished force was defeated by the Greeks, but credit should be given more to the Athenian-led navy than to the Spartan-inspired army.

However, though Snyder and Miller might have exaggerated or downplayed the historical events of the three day battle, at least the major events are semi-grounded in fact. Once you begin to look past the critical military events, you'll begin to realize that Snyder and Miller took extensive liberties to give the audience a film where the flawless protagonists of Greece challenge the horrifically-vile antagonists from Persia. Any vice that might take away from Sparta's idealized status was ignored, as was any historical proof that might glorify the Persian forces.

In the movie, Sparta stands as a democracy, ruled by King Leonidas who reluctantly asks for advice from a council of Ephors, portrayed in the film as lepers. Although Greece was home to the only democracy (Athens) in the Mediterranean world, Sparta was far from a democracy, but more a military dictatorship run by two kings. The yearly elected Council of Ephors balanced the edicts of the two kings, and 37% of the population lived as slaves. Their entire society revolved around manufacturing men capable of combat. Subsequently, the Spartans widely practiced infanticide. On the day of every child's birth a city elder would decide if the child would live or be "exposed" on a hillside and left to die. Miller's creation of the Ephiliates character alludes to the notion that Sparta only banished the severely deformed, but in reality Spartans killed newborns for abnormalities as minimal as hairlines or birth marks.

Another choice made by the Miller/Snyder team dismissed the role of homosexuality in the Spartan world. In one scene, Leonidas jokingly disparages the Athenians as merely philosophers and "boy lovers" as if the practice of homosexuality was completely foreign to the Spartan male. In reality, Spartans engaged in pederastry, a formal bond between adult male soldiers and their adolescent pupils. In a world that eroticized the male form, even having athletes artistically depicted as nudes, it became natural to base true masculinity on the ability to attract the attention of a male suitor. Society expected the most dominant boys to have secured a lover by the age of twelve for "there was not any of the more hopeful boys who did not have a lover to bear him company."

Although some of these relationships remained chaste (historians such as Plutarch argued that any such behavior was as uncommon as a father molesting a son), others involved sexual relations. Regardless, Sparta did not create these relationships for sexual purposes, but more to militarily bond a youth with his mentor. Because all of the youth's military successes and failures directly reflected upon the worth of the adult mentor, these two developed an intimate relationship in which all skills passed down from teacher to pupil. These intimate relations, some of which involved homosexuality, definitely challenge Miller's depiction of Athenians as the sole practitioners of homosexuality, a condition actually quite common to the Greek world.

Not only could Miller not touch on the homosexual element of Spartan life, he also felt the need to hyper-exaggerate Spartan machismo. These exaggerations prove unnecessary when the real Spartans stood apart from their contemporaries as military machines able to dedicate their lives to defending the state. From the age of seven, Spartan boys began their military training – *agoge* - where they would box, wrestle, swim, run, learn gymnastics and even dance (needed for agility). They suffered through countless hardships - suffering beatings by superiors, surviving winters barefoot in the forest, or spending their every waking moment away from their family. They were given little to eat, encouraged to steal from neighboring villages. Once a year, they were taken in front of the Altar of Orthia Artemis, where they would be beaten bloody, all the while being watched to see if they would cry out in pain. Proud parents stood nearby crying out, "Don't you pass out! Don't you pass out!"

From the moment boys turned seven, Sparta was their only family, and they would defend it to their death. Spartan women needed to be strong, fertile and aggressive, for they would be the bearers of future Spartans. Mothers dared their boys to be fighting men, and this spirit is embodied by the oft-quoted Spartan mother challenge – "Come back with your shield, or on it." Only two types of Spartans ever had their names engraved on tombs – mothers who died during labor and men that died during battle. Only these two truly gave their life to the state.

Both in real life and in the film, King Leonidas embodies this sacrifice. Although the film plays loose with his agoge experience (he actually would have killed a slave, not a wolf), and his physical depiction (he was probably more a taunt 50 year old than the buffed-out 35 year old played by Gerard Butler), both the fictional and real life versions knew what this battle would mean. Prior to the battle, the Oracle at Delphi had foretold that a man would give his life for Sparta, and Leonidas knew he would be that man. Instead of retreating with the other four thousand Greeks when his fate was essentially sealed, King Leonidas remained on the battlefield, providing a covering force for the retreat, delaying the Persian advance into Greece, and securing for himself historical immortality.

Because of this training, Spartan soldiers became the most formidable fighting force in the Mediterranean. Miller and Snyder took the memory of these historic fighters and repackaged it for today's audience. From their clothing to their weapons to their fighting style, the Spartans seen on screen bare little resemblance to the true fighters. In the film, the men are bare-chested with only metal protection below their knees. They also don capes and lovely little loincloths to become "heroic classical-nude action figures." This recreation allowed the actors to showcase their freshly-formed physiques created courtesy of Mark Twight and his Gym Jones workout regimen. In reality, Spartan soldiers never entered battle with so little protection. True, they exercised and competed naked, but when it came to fighting, they actually realized the benefits of protection. In addition to chest armor (made of strips of leather, linen and bronze) and bronze shinguards, they hung strips of leather from their waist to protect their Spartan jewels, and their tunic covered their thighs to their knees. Also, in the movie, only King Leonidas wears a crested helmet, when in reality all Spartans wanted to look bigger, taller, and more intimidating by wearing crests plumed with horsehair. All Spartan men wore horsehaired helmets, although the officers would have worn their plumes across their helmet instead of from front to back. Their weapon of choice was the *dory*, the six- to nine-foot long spear used for thrusting, and their *xiphos*, the two- to three-foot long sword used only if the spear was to break or if the phalanx broke down.

When it came to fighting, the Spartan style was far more effective than it was entertaining. Audience members nurtured on *Matrix* fight scenes and the theatrics of professional wrestling enthusiastically embraced *300*'s battle scenes. The movie has the Spartans launch three thrusts against their enemy and then the Spartans break apart to engage in Jackie Chan-Neo-WWE mano y mano street brawls where each Spartan flies through the air while impaling foes or cutting off a variety of appendages. In reality, the Persians weren't such accommodating adversaries, and had a Spartan distanced himself from the pack, he would have died instantly. Spartan survival depended on a uniform attack. Carrying over seventy pounds of armor and weaponry, the front line of the Spartan phalanx would stand their ground while hundreds of their comrades pushed from behind. Those soldiers near the front thrust their spears at any piece of enemy flesh made available. This wasn't sexy, but it was effective. The phalanx made an impenetrable wall, and made it possible to defeat numerically-superior forces.

However, it wasn't Snyder's depiction of Spartan battle techniques or the superiority of Western culture that launched so much criticism of the film. It was the one-sided, demonic depiction of the Persians that so angered segments of the Iranian (modern day Persian) community that the Iran's motion picture board actually lodged a formal complaint to the United Nations Educational, Scientific and Cultural Organization (UNESCO) for the film's destruction of Iran's heritage. The film presents Xerxes as a sexually deviant "oversized drag queen," a sharp contrast to the macho ideal represented by the Spartan characters. His one million troops come across as monstrous disfigured barbarians, of which even the elite "Immortals" bare daggered teeth hidden behind Kabuki-esque Halloween masks.

Because of this one-dimensional representation of the entire Persian force and their leader, the final battle becomes a conflict between a dedicated, free Western army and an oppressive, barbaric slave-owning regime. Snyder recreated Miller's classic good vs. evil conflict where the victors went on to form the foundation of the superior Western civilization, while the losers retreated to their barbarism, subsequently dooming the Middle East to centuries of subservience to their superior neighbors to the West.

Unfortunately for the xenophobic audience members who need this tale to be true, the reality isn't so tidy. The Persians under the Achemenid Empire were historically tolerant and bestowed upon the world a human rights legacy unprecedented at the time. From Cyrus the Great onward, the Persian Empire created a bill of rights, while granting freedoms to women not seen elsewhere in the West. Cyrus, grandfather of Xerxes, proclaimed over 2500 years ago:

> "I will respect the traditions, customs and religions of the nations of my empire and never let any of my governors and subordinates look down on or insult them while I am alive. ...I will impose my monarchy on no nation. Each is free to accept it, and if any one of them rejects it, I never resolve on war to reign. While I am the king...I will never let anyone oppress others... I will never let anyone take possession of movable and landed properties of the others by force or without compensation. While I am alive, I will prevent unpaid, forced labour. Today, I announce that everyone is free to choose a religion...No one could be penalised for his or her relatives' faults..."

This declaration dealt with land claims, religious affiliation, women's rights, meritocracy, and personal freedoms. Although many historians trace the American Bill of Rights to English tradition or even Athenian democracy, in reality, one needs look further back to Persia, where the notion of individual freedoms was first protected by a political leader. And unlike the perception of Iran and the Middle East today, the Persia of Cyrus and Xerxes' time was highly tolerant of religions, and Cyrus the Great was responsible for releasing the Jews from their Babylonian Captivity. As for the Persians being slaveholders, no archaeological evidence exists to prove widespread acceptance of slavery, and in fact the Persian Empire became the "Promised Land" for slaves escaping captivity in Northern Africa and the Middle East. This is not to say that the Persian Empire was free of violence, corruption and inhumane treatment, but to say they were any more uncivilized than the rest of the classic world is an historical inaccuracy. As for much-maligned Xerxes, he was actually a bearded, heterosexual emperor married to Esther (a leading advocate for Jewish freedoms) – a far cry from the effeminate, ten-foot tall, body pierced beast that greets Leonidas in the film.

Why then has recent history depicted the Persian Empire in such a negative light? Much of this portrayal can be traced back to the Greek historian Herodotus, from whom much of our knowledge of early Greece comes. Prior to the 1850s, the primary historical texts (the Bible and the work of Greek author Xenophon) championed the role of Cyrus the Great and the Persian Empires, but toward the middle of the nineteenth century, Western historians felt the need to devalue the importance of monarchical rule. As the United States and France emerged triumphantly from imperial control, historians sought out historical interpretations that glorified the role of democracy. Enter Herodotus. His texts presented the Greeks in such a light - underdogs fighting insurmountable numbers, armed not only with determination and undying effort, but with firmly engrained democratic values leading their every movement. Since this time, future historians have followed this Eurocentric model established by the "Father of History" and subsequent Western texts have veered little from his analysis. Ironically, Herodotus, the champion of everything Greek, chose the Persian Empire to live, write and publish his texts, for it was here that he was granted the artistic freedom to express his views without fear of retribution.

Many point to the Battle of Thermopylae as the beginning of Western Civilization. The Persian invasion and subsequent burning of Athens forced the Greek city-states to unite and abandon their centuries-long tradition of infighting. The subsequent alliance known as the Delian League brought great riches to Athens, creating an unprecedented flowering of culture that produced some of the West's greatest philosophers, political thinkers, playwrights, artists, poets, scientists and historians. When Philip II later came down from Macedonia and united all the remaining city-states under the banner of Greece, he had created the beginnings of an empire that his son, Alexander the Great, would one day share with the entire known world.

However, some might argue that this exchange of ideas could have happened regardless, and earlier, with less carnage and without the legacy of East/West tension. Would not the Persians have been equally accommodating to the Athenians as they were to the other regions under their realm? Would not the flowering of Greek culture been shared with the Persian world nearly two centuries before the campaigns of Alexander the Great? And how would have Eastern/Western relations developed had the Persians controlled Eastern Europe through antiquity? Before hastily dismissing these oversimplified hypothetical scenarios, maybe the audience should reconsider that the Persian Empire truly wasn't the domain of demonic barbarians depicted in the film *300*, and just because Western Civilization went on to such great heights after Themopylae, does not mean that Thermopylae alone and the subsequent repulsion of the Persian invasion sparked the dominance of the Western world.

300 is an exceptionally entertaining film, but also an extremely important film to analyze objectively. Because director Zack Snyder and graphic novelist Frank Miller created a tale that so obviously distorts the historical accuracy of both the protagonists and antagonists, it stands as a perfect example of how Hollywood manipulates history to satisfy the box office reliance on a good guy/bad guy conflict. Instead of condemning the film, historical advocates should recommend it. Its alterations are easy to recognize, as are its creator's motivations. Only by learning from such over the top films as *300* can an average filmgoer begin to learn the "tricks of the trade," thus enabling them to be cognizant of the less obvious alterations that exist in all Hollywood historical films.

Key Quotes

Persian Messenger: (*challenging Queen Gorgo*) What makes this woman think she can speak among men?
Queen Gorgo: Because only Spartan women give birth to real men.

King Leonidas: (*after Persian ambassador requests Spartan surrender*) You bring the crowns and heads of conquered kings to my city steps. You insult my queen. You threaten my people with slavery and death! Oh, I've chosen my words carefully, Persian. Perhaps you should have done the same!
Persian Messenger: This is blasphemy! This is madness!
King Leonidas: Madness...? THIS... IS... SPARTA!

King Leonidas: (*preparing for the final battle*) Spartans! Ready your breakfast and eat hearty... For tonight, we dine in hell!

King Leonidas: (*predicting the battle's impact*) The world will know that free men stood against a tyrant, that few stood against many, and that before this battle is over, even a god-king can bleed.

Persian: (*threatening Spartans with annihilation*) A thousand nations of the Persian empire descend upon you. Our arrows will blot out the sun!
Stelios: Then we will fight in the shade.

Dilios: (*discussing the legacy of the Spartan sacrifice at the Battle of Thermopylae*) Long I pondered my king's cryptic talk of victory, but time has proven him wise, for from free Greek to free Greek, the word was spread that bold Leonidas and his 300, so far from home, laid down their lives... not just for Sparta, but for all Greece and the promise this country holds. Now here on this ragged patch of earth called Plateaea, let his hordes face obliteration!

Alexander

2004
Director: Oliver Stone
Starring: Collin Farrell, Angelina Jolie, Anthony Hopkins, Val Kilmer,
Jared Leto
167 minutes – Rated R

By Patrick Bousky

Synopsis:

Following the life of the greatest general and conquerer to have lived, Oliver Stone's *Alexander* gives us insight into the life and dreams of Alexander the Great. Taking place after the Peloponnesian Wars, it follows the life of the son of King Philip II of Macedon - Alexander. Alexander is taught from a young age by Aristotle, and those lessons and exposure to Greek culture followed him throughout his future conquests. After the assassination of his father, Alexander vows to fulfill his father's dream of conquering the Persian Empire, and killing King Darius, the man Alexander holds responsible for his father's death. After a series of epic battles, Alexander conquers the Persian Empire, and then sets his sight on taking his Greek army to a world where no Greek man had gone before. As Alexander moves into India, he must try to appease an army desiring a return to Greece, integrate the conquered peoples into his vision of a united world, and defeat foes that are becoming increasingly belligerent. Eventually, Alexander loses those closest to him and is forced to face his own mortality.

Historically Relevant Scenes	
00:26:30>00:47:52	- Battle at Gaugamela
00:50:00>00:51:32	- Alexander's Entrance to Babylon
01:07:42>01:11:00	- Protest of Alexander's Marriage to Roxana
01:41:00>01:42:28	- Depiction of Bisexuality
01:44:16>01:48:47	- Protest of Alexander's Transfer of Culture
01:49:37>01:55:47	- Assassination of King Philip II
02:04:20>02:14:17	- Battle at Hydaspes

Ratings:

Entertainment -   ★ ★ ☆ ☆

Historical Accuracy - ★ ★ ★ ★

Historical Analysis:

Oliver Stone's highly anticipated film *Alexander* was to many a gigantic let down. Whether it was Colin Farrell's portrayal of Alexander as a whiney, neurotic boy living under his father's shadow, or Oliver Stone's emphasis on Alexander's bisexuality, or the poor casting of Angelina Jolie as Alexander's mother, or the lack of any truly original battle scenes, the movie failed to interest the American market. At a cost of over $160 million, the film only recovered $34 million in US box office revenue. But take heart, Stone did recover his money with overseas tickets and DVD sales. Despite the overall failure of the film, there are still important facts to be learned from this movie that delved into the history of Macedon and, more importantly, into the life of one of the greatest generals in the history of Western Civilization – Alexander the Great.

Before looking at the content of the movie, let's first return to the time leading up to Alexander's rule. Before Macedonia was the great empire it was when Alexander took rule, it was seen as a small city-state filled with drunken brawlers. Even after its attempt to integrate the Greek way of thinking, "most Macedonians much preferred their traditional rough pleasures – hunting, gambling, drinking, and philandering." When King Philip II eventually conquered and unified Greece, he was never fully accepted by the Greeks because of his heritage. The Greek orator Demosthenes mocked Philip II asserting that "not only he is not a Greek, but also he does not have anything in common with the Greeks. If only he would have been a barbarian from a decent country - but he is not even that. He is a scabby creature from Macedonia - a land that one can not even bring a slave that is worth something from."

Now during the time of Philip II's rule, from approximately 359 to 336 B.C., there was a massive civil war destroying Greece. This Peloponnesian War pitted the alliance of the Delian League, led by the Athenians, against the Peloponnesian League, headed by the Spartans. City-states in Greece had been fighting each other for centuries over political power, economic influence and territorial expansion across the peninsula of Hellas. This recent conflict resulted from the steps Greeks took to repulse the Persian invasion of Xerxes in 480 BCE.

King Xerxes had entered Greece in 480 BCE looking to avenge the Athenian support of the Ionians who tried to revolt from Persian authority by reducing the city of Sardos to ashes. After being momentarily stalled by the King Leonidas-led Greek force at the Battle of Thermopylae (think *300*), Xerxes took his army to Athens and burned the vacated city to the ground. However, his forces were eventually driven back to the East by the Athenian navy at the Battle of Salamis. After this retreat, Xerxes never returned to Greece, but the Athenians realized the need for military protection, so they started the alliance known as the Delian League.

The purpose of this coalition was to defend Greece against future Persian invasions. Athens, at this time, had the most powerful navy in Greece, which allowed them to call the shots. The thing about this "League" was that membership was not always voluntary. One Greek city-state Thasos, tried to pull out of the Delian League over a conflict over gold deposits, but after a two year war with Athens, they were brought to their knees by the Athenian general Cimon. Thasos was forced to tear down their fortified walls, turn over their navy and pay reparations to Athens. Eventually most of the coastal city-states joined the Delian League, except for the ever-so-resistant Spartans who thought the maintenance of an alliance was pointless since Greek unity was no longer needed once the Persians had been forced back across the Aegean Sea.

As the Delian League expanded, Sparta found additional faults with the Athenian power structure. Firstly, instead of putting the collected taxes into the military for an improved defense, the Athenians simply put a large chunk of it toward works projects (like the Parthenon and the Acropolis). Secondly, Sparta felt it was a bad idea to have all of Greece essentially controlled by one city-state. So Sparta started the Peloponnesian League – an alliance of the city-states on the eastern Peloponnes peninsula. Within a few decades, the newly formed Peloponnesian League rivaled the Delian League for supremacy in the region, and war became almost inevitable.

The Peloponnesian War began because simply, Sparta didn't want Athens controlling everything. The war itself was fought in three main stages. First, the Archidamian War, which was Sparta, attempting to invade Attica, the region in which Athens lies, while on the other end of the war, Athens was hammering the coast of the Peloponnese with their superior navy. Eventually they both decided to sign a truce known as the Peace of Nicias. This lasted about six years. Everything was going well until city-states within the Peloponnese League started to revolt and pressure the Spartan king to go to war, which like the good Spartan he was, he did. The second part of the war was when Nicias and Syracuse went to war and called upon their allies, Sparta and Athens to aid them. Athens first sent an enormous fleet consisting of more than 5,000 infantry, 100 ships, and about 30 cavalry. Winter soon came, so Athens waited until it was over. In the meantime, Syracuse sent word to Sparta of Athenian involvement and requested Spartan aid. Sparta sent over a fleet of men and eventually destroyed the entire Athenian and Nician fleet. The final stage of the war saw Athens surrendering after a series of naval defeats. Sparta installed an oligarchy of thirty men to rule Athens, and after surviving this rule of the "Thirty Tyrants," Athens reestablished democracy and started to rebuild itself.

So, after centuries of fighting off the superior Persian forces and surviving a civil war, how did an army of drunken barbarians defeat Greece? The answer is simple. King Philip II was smart. He only resorted to military force when needed; he felt that military combat should always be avoided when possible. He mainly used his power of persuasion and bribery. Many of the Greek city-states merely succumbed to the bribes of wealth and alliance to Macedonia, except of course Sparta and Athens. With Sparta, King Philip didn't see them as much of a threat due to the fact they were in complete disarray after the financially and militarily draining Peloponnesian War. Athens however, was high on his threat meter. They were forming resistances against Macedonia with surrounding city-states and were starting to rebuild their regional empire. However, this Athenian force was no match for King Philip's Macedonian war machine.

With their superior military strategy and training, Macedonia easily plowed through Athens and her allies. How did he do this? With his modified phalanx. The original phalanx used by the Spartans employed shields and spears. They would also still wear their heavy bronze armor. The problem with this was that they were slow. They could not maneuver very well due to the fact that they were holding a heavy shield and spear on top of their already heavy armor.

King Philip modified the armor by combining the body armor with the shield. He put a shield, no more than 18 inches across and put it on the shoulder of the body armor (which was lightened by making it leather and bronze). This made the infantry able to carry a larger spear, approximately 18 feet long – more than twice the length of the Greek dory. This enabled the Macedonians to stop the Greeks before they could even get within stabbing distance of the Macedonian phalanx. What was more genius was how King Phillip protected his sides by stationing men there purely to defend the flank. It was these political manipulations and military adjustments employed by King Philip II that his son Alexander later utilized to conquer the known world.

Now this is where we delve into the facts presented in the movie. We will start with the childhood of Alexander. Alexander grew up with all the material and philosophical benefits his newly-crowned father could provide. He was educated by Aristotle (who was taught by Plato, who was taught by Socrates) in the teachings of philosophy, physics, and mathematics. During his childhood, he also met his lifetime friend and the person he loved most, Hephaistion.

However, although he had some of the fringe benefits of wealth and power, Alexander also had a pretty dysfunctional family. Many of the problems erupted because his dad liked to gain alliances through marriage. King Philip married the Illyrian princess Audata, then the Elimean princess Phila, and then the Epirian princess Olympias – all marriages were made more for political gain than for love. In the film, Alexander's mother, Olympias, seems to be at the center of many conflicts with Philip as she constantly plots to try to gain for his son more power. In the film, Olympias, played by Angelina Jolie, is a snake-yielding schemer with a confusingly sultry accent and a sometimes awkward affection for her son. Many historians had trouble with the casting of Jolie, only a year older than the man (Colin Farrel) depicting her son. As for Olympias' obsession with snakes, she was in fact a snake charmer and would have been quite comfortable around the creatures.

One story that stands out in the movie and in his childhood was the story of how Alexander tamed his horse – Bucephalus. A Thesssalian horse breeder brought a black stallion to King Philip. After both he and his generals failed to tame the beast, King Philip ordered the horse to be taken away. However, Alexander, only nine years old, proclaimed that he could ride the horse. King Philip and his council laughed, but Alexander persisted even wagering that if he was unsuccessful, he would pay back to the king the cost of the horse. After Philip accepted his son's wager, Alexander noticed that the horse was frightened at the sight of his own shadow, and Alexander approached the horse, turning it to face towards the sun as to not cast a shadow, and stroked and calmed the horse, and at the right moment, mounted him. They rode off out of the arena and upon their return, they were greeted by a tearful King Philip, who out of pride, surprise and fear, announced, "You'll have to find another kingdom. Macedon isn't gong to be big enough for you." Although the quote is pure Hollywood, this event did signal a warming in the relationship between Philip and Alexander.

In 336 B.C., after finally conquering the Greek peninsula, King Philip began preparations for his long-awaited invasion of Persia. In the movie, a festival is arranged to honor the Greek and Macedonian union and the ensuing Persian offensive, but in reality this festival was to honor the marriage of Philip's daughter Cleopatra to another Alexander, Prince Alexander of nearby Epirus. In the film, during this festival, Philip enters an arena unguarded to prove his fearlessness, only upon entry to be stabbed by an assassin. As Alexander stands over his dying father, he vows revenge against Darius, ruler of the Persian Empire, the man he presumes was the mastermind of the assassination.

In reality, a young nobleman by the name of Pausania killed Philip, and was immediately killed by Alexander's friends. This killing without a trial has led some historians to believe that Alexander and Olympias plotted the murder. Although Stone alludes to this theory by flashing to Angelina Jolie's emotionless Olympias, sitting amongst the crowd in a red dress and a wicked smirk, the true culprit behind the murders is never truly revealed.

Now in control of the Macedonian empire and army, in 334 BC, Alexander implemented his father's plan for the invasion of Persia. A large part left out by Oliver Stone involves the first three years of this campaign, including Alexander's foray into Egypt. Although some might argue Alexander invaded Egypt merely for personal gratification, Egypt provided a key trading port to supply his continued expeditions. Alexander's campaign started with the takeover of Tyre, in which it took Alexander eight grueling months to conquer. After Tyre fell, most of the Egyptian cities merely bowed down and accepted him as their pharaoh. All except Gaza. He marched to Gaza and eventually took the city after employing siege towers with constructed platforms between them to allow his troops to storm the city, thus making him crowned pharaoh of all of Egypt. He then founded Alexandria in 331 B.C., making it the largest sea port in Egypt. Stone does allude to Egypt's role by having the narrator of the movie, Anthony Hopkins' Ptolemy, recount the story to an Egyptian scribe, who undoubtedly will include the information in the famed Library of Alexandria.

After three years of fighting, in 331 B.C. Alexander put his Macedonian led force of 50,000 against Darius's 100,000 troops. Darius had chosen this battlefield because it was a flat plain which would hypothetically allow the Persian army to use their size to the greatest advantage. The Battle at Gaugamela became the turning point in the fight against Persia. Regardless of their numeric disadvantage, the Macedonia army had one key advantage - strategy.

In addition to the Macedonian phalanx, Alexander performed another brilliant move by taking a large amount of cavalry and riding away from battle. Thinking Alexander was trying to escape, Darius sent his cavalry after Alexander. Eventually, this enabled Alexander to flank the Persians and slice through their mass of soldiers forcing Darius to flee from the battle and hide in the deserts of Persia. All of this is historically accurate, and historians for the most part agree that "its recreation on film has some spectacular moments, and is heavily based on recorded history." Some Macedonian contingencies find fault with the film, noting that Alexander's motivational speech before the battle in which he claims that they were fighting for the "glory of Greece" was false, and that in reality, they were fighting to "subdue all races on Earth [so that] Bactria and India would become Macedonian provinces." This example exemplifies how on several occasions Alexander is referred to as Greek, when in reality he would have had pride in his Macedonian roots. Some Persian historians also point to the depiction of the Persians as an unorganized mass of barbarians who can easily be defeated in one short battle with a leader who flees at the first sign of distress. They contend that the Persians were a well-trained, uniformed army who took years to suppress and that Darius never actually fled, but instead was abandoned by his troops. This criticism piggy-backed the complaints made against *300* where Persians again got the short end of the historical stick.

After the Battle at Gaugamela, Alexander enters Babylon and his obsession of conquering the world begins. He is driven by the idea of going further than the gods ever went and bringing Hellenistic culture to a united kingdom. Alexander takes his reluctant men all the way to India, where he is eventually forced to retreat.

The scene in the film that shows Alexander in India is known as the Battle of Hydaspes River, where Alexander faced off against King Porus in what is now modern day Pakistan. This became Alexander's last major battle. His horse Bucephalus was killed (he later founded a nearby town in the horse's honor - Bucephela). His men fought valiantly against charging war elephants, a sight that could have left the men paralyzed with fear. And Alexander was wounded by a spear that penetrated his breastplate. All in all, although the battle was a victory, it signaled the beginning of the end. Exhausted and homesick, his men lobbied for a return to their homeland. Eventually, Alexander fell sick with fever and died at the age of 33.

One topic Stone repeatedly touched on was Alexander's attempts to adopt local customs of the conquered people while sharing Greek culture. Alexander started to eventually dress in typical Asian royal garb and even changed his royal title to "Shahanshah" meaning "King of Kings." He even borrowed a page from his father's skills of diplomacy by marring Darius' daughter Statira and Roxanna of Bactria. In both of these cases, Alexander endeared himself to the native peoples by embracing the local marriage rituals and not taking the women by force. With his marriage to Statira, Alexander also encouraged the intermarriage of his Macedonian soldiers with the best of the local Persian women.

This issue of Alexander's romantic relationships brings us to another topic that surrounded the film – his perceived bisexuality. After the numerous embraces, jealous glances, and whispered terms of endearment, the audience can only assume Alexander and his childhood friend Hephastion were lovers. Most historians concur that this relationship was probably sexual, but Stone's decision to include it almost guaranteed the movie's failure. Americans like their historical movie heroes to be heterosexual, and it's even better if they spend the bulk of the film avenging the death of their wives (see *Gladiator*, *Kingdom of Heaven*, or any movie starring Mel Gibson). As for how one should perceive Alexander's liaisons, historian Dr. Cathy Schulz remarked "the context of the times must also be considered. Bisexual behavior was typical for elite Greeks and Macedonians, including Alexander's own father, Philip. Greek philosophers, like Alexander's famed tutor, Aristotle, taught the Greek conventional wisdom: that intense relationships-sexual or otherwise-were most appropriate between men. There was little concern in the Greek world for the 'hetero' and 'homo' labels our society adheres to."

So, despite complaints from critics, historians and movie goers, Oliver Stone actually does a pretty good job staying true to the life of Alexander. What he fails at was creating a film anyone wanted to see. Although it contains a few minor historical inaccuracies or omissions, it is a great source to get a real life visual of the life of Alexander the Great. Though it is grueling and dull during some parts (mostly just the beginning, middle and end), if you are looking for a historically accurate film that's one step more entertaining than a Ken Burns' documentary, *Alexander* is the film for you. If you're looking for an action film, you probably just want to look for the latest "Die Hard" at your local Blockbuster.

Key Quotes

Alexander: (*trying to alleviate his best friend's jealousy*) It is you I love Hephaistion, no other.

Alexander: (*inspiring his troops*) Conquer your fears, and I promise you, you will conquer death!

Cassander: (*concerned about Alexander's policy of intermarriage*) Alexander, be reasonable! Were they ever meant to be our equals? Share our rewards? You remember what Aristotle said. An Asian? What would a wedding vow mean to a race that has never kept their word to a Greek
Alexander: Aristotle be damned! By Zeus and all the gods what makes you so much better than them?

Olympia: (*encouraging his son to continue his campaign*) The world is yours, take it!

Gladiator

2000
Director: Ridley Scott
Starring: Russell Crowe, Joaquin Phoenix, Connie Nielsen
155 minutes – Rated R

By Eric Burnett

Synopsis:

Supposedly taking place during the 180 A.D. transfer of power between Marcus Aurelius and his son Commodus, *Gladiator* tells the story of how famed Roman general Maximus, the chosen heir to the throne, survives a murder plot only to find himself exiled to a foreign land where he reinvents himself as a gladiator. At first hesitant to embrace this superficial role, Maximus eventually changes his mind when he realizes he can use the bloodsport as a means of returning to Rome and exacting vengeance on the man who took his life. Meanwhile, back in Rome, the insecure, deluded, sexually-inappropriate Emperor Commodus attempts to distract his suffering citizens by restoring the defunct gladiatorial game. Eventually, Maximus has his revenge as he squares off against Commodus in the arena for one final battle.

Historically Relevant Scenes

00:01:00>00:12:35	- Battle: Roman Legion vs. Germanic tribe
00:58:30>01:02:00	- Senate Debate
01:04:20>01:06:05	- Daily life in Roman market
01:21:16>01:33:00	- Gladiator Match: Re-enactment of Punic War

---

Ratings:

Entertainment -   ★ ★ ★ ★

Historical Accuracy -   ★ ★ ☆ ☆

Historical Analysis:

Ridley Scott's 2000 Roman epic hit *Gladiator* wowed audiences at the box office and equally impressed critics, later earning an Oscar for Best Picture. Though it will forever remain at the top of every 14-year old boy's top movie list (due in large part to its virtual bevy of sword-induced amputations), historians have a bit more trouble giving it top honors. It's not that there weren't in fact gladiators. There were. It's not that there wasn't a sexually deranged emperor named Commodus. There was. And it's not even that this same emperor didn't have an affinity for gladiatorial combat. He most certainly did.

Before ripping in to where the story swayed from reality, let's begin with its premise that at one point in Roman history gladiators fought to the death to entertain bloodthirsty audiences. This is true.

These gladiatorial fights started out at funeral rituals where slaves fought to the death over the buried corpse in hopes that the lost blood would benefit the newly-departed in the afterlife. As onlookers gradually realized the entertainment value of such contests, the arena expanded until eventually these slave warriors found themselves fighting at the Flavian Ampitheatre (anachronistically labeled the Coliseum in the film). Eventually, they became part of a larger "bread and circus" campaign by Roman Emperors who believed that through chariot races, public executions, and gladiatorial combat, the citizens would forget about less curable societal problems. Though they still occurred illegally from time to time throughout the Roman Empire, Emperor Constantine banned gladiators in 325 A.D.

In the film version, gladiators are all slaves who fight at the whim of the Emperor. In reality, many gladiators were not slaves, and some even reached a near-celebrity status while earning a comfortable income. Also, Ridley Scott has Maximus and his slave cohorts arriving in Rome from a North African province to fight in front of the emperor and Rome's citizens. However, enslaved gladiators were not allowed into Rome. And finally, slaves never fought in groups, so the notion that Maximus could rally them together to defeat a well-coordinated onslaught was entirely fabricated.

So, slaves and freemen fought. But did women fight? From the experience of historical advisor Kathy Coleman, it appears Scott was more concerned with quenching the appetite of those voyeuristic young lads needing to see Amazonian women in action. In her criticism of the filmmaking process, Coleman noted that in one instance she was told, "Kathy, we need to get a piece of evidence which proves that women gladiators had sharpened razor blades attached to their nipples. Could you have it by lunchtime?" Some might argue that films should be based on history. In Scott's case, history needed to be "found" to justify his imagination. However, regardless of Scott's motivations, proof of female gladiators does exist. Aside from their appearance in Roman texts, female gladiators probably did exist because in 200 A.D. Emperor Severus felt it necessary to outlaw them. Rarely are things outlawed that never existed. In addition, in 1996, in a Roman cemetery in London, archaeologists exhumed the corpse of a 20 year old female buried with two lamps. These two lamps were adorned with a fallen gladiator and Anubis, the messenger god of Mercury whose role was to carry the souls of gladiators from the arena. In addition to this relatively suspect evidence, the British Museum houses a Roman relief found at Halicarnassus that depicts two women –*Amazon* and *Achillia* – locked in a gladiatorialesque struggle.

Now that we've established that there were in fact gladiators - some of which were slaves and some of which might have been women – let's look at the major plot events and the role of the two main characters – Maximus and Commodus.

The film starts off near the height of the Roman Empire when a General Maximus leads his forces against some Germanic tribe that grunts a lot, rarely shaves, and looks like they all shop at a the local Rags R' Us department store. Though Marcus Aurelius, the last of the Five Good Emperors, did in fact push the Roman borders northward into direct contact with the Germanic peoples, no General Maximus ever existed. From this initial scene onward, Ridley Scott makes choices to appeal more to the audience's perception of Roman reality than to reality itself. The audience is told this battle takes place in Germania and at one point the Germanic leader cries out, "Ihr seid verfluchte hunde" (you are cursed dogs). In reality, this battle did not take place in Germania but instead Pannonia (modern day Austria) and this "cursed dog" declaration could not have ever been shouted since it is a contemporary German phrase originating centuries after the end of the Roman Empire. Also in this battle, Maximus leads a cavalry charge on horseback, with his feet firmly locked into stirrups (an invention not brought to Europe until the 600s) and then dismounts his noble steed to fight mano y mano against his Germanic He-Man adversary. This is quite implausible. Romans rarely broke formation, especially not for the sole reason of showcasing their general's swordsmanship, and if they would have done so against the Germanic tribes they would have been torn to pieces.

Though these anachronisms in the initial battle can be written off as merely attempts to acquaint the audience with the power of Rome and the prowess of Maximus, the altered depiction of the antagonist, emperor-to-be Commodus, stems from an entirely different motivation. The real life Commodus was just too weird. His antics would easily warrant an X-rating, and if only 12% of his behaviors were put on the screen, cries for censorship would reign down from soccer moms across the land. In one of the few exceptions to the rule, the antagonist in *Gladiator* is rather sweet compared to his namesake.

Born Lucius Aelius Aurelius Commodus, Commodus had some rather interesting hobbies. Possibly making up for his father's insistence that he take an academic path, or maybe even making up for a lack of machismo, Commodus felt the need to prove himself as a fighter. He had mini-gladiator arenas built in his palace. He trained against some of the finest disabled people, chained aggressors and injured animals he could find. Later, he took his suspect skills to the big stage, where he embarrassed himself all the way to a 735-0 record. Granted most of his opponents were either given outdated weapons, restrained, or merely confused at the site of their opponent. Most of these 735 "losers" merely surrendered before putting up a fight. These obvious gladiatorial farces were scorned by the aristocracy who couldn't believe one of their own would lower himself to be at an equal footing as a slave. The lower classes were equally disturbed by the sight of their leader going head-to-head in staged combat. It's fair to say that Americans today would likewise cringe if George W. Bush stepped into a Steel Cage Deathmatch pitted against a prison convict.

Rome's Commodus didn't merely dispatch human foes, he also reveled in slaying beasts. Not only did he duel giraffes, rhinoceroses, and hippopotamuses (or is it hippopotami?), one afternoon he felled 100 chained bears, and on another day he used his better-than-average archery skills to decapitate an ostrich (a feat that most assuredly entertained the audience as the torso and legs continued to scamper around the arena). Alas, as his combat record revealed, Commodus did not die the movie-version death in the arena, but instead he was murdered at the hands of his best friend Narcissus after being drugged by his favorite concubine, and cousin, Marcia. It says a lot about your character when your lover and your best friend conspire to kill you in a bathtub.

It wasn't the first time someone close to Commodus had tried to assassinate him. His sister Lucilla was eventually exiled and killed herself after failing to kill dear-old brother. After viewing *Gladiator,* you might think she was justified, seeing how she had to deal with the constant incestuous advances of her younger brother. However, there is no proof that Commodus ever came on to his older sis. That isn't to say he didn't force his other sisters down an incestuous path - he did. While we're on the subject of depravity, Commodus also kept a harem of 300 boys and girls and enjoyed walking through town wearing lion's fur while human blood dripped from every inch of his bared skin.

Needless to say, Commodus wasn't a stable leader, and in fact his reign can be seen as the beginning of the end of the Roman Empire. Not only did he severely tax the Roman coffers by charging one million sesterces for the honor of seeing him fight, but he also left the majority of the day-to-day affairs to his prefects (many of whom were later killed if they performed too much work). When he did make decisions, they were usually to the detriment of the Roman Empire, like when he ceded the lands gained by his father back to the Germanic tribes, or when he destroyed an entire city because one of its citizens looked at Commodus with a mean face.

Maybe Ridley Scott was correct in adorning his Commodus in virginal white throughout the film. Compared to the real-life version, Joaquin Phoenix's interpretation comes across as almost saintly.

It must be noted that Ridley Scott never claimed he was making a documentary. In fact, his vision of Rome and its gladiators stems less from historical research and more from an 1872 Pollice Verso painting titled "Thumbs Down" and Scott's own film library. Maximus embodies Charlton Heston's *Ben Hur*, a slave who rose through society to eventually square off against his tormentor, and Kirk Douglass's *Spartacus*, a gladiator who organizes his fellow fighters to attack the aristocracy. Some might even argue that Maximus was in fact Narcissus, Commodus's wrestler friend who became his murderer. Even Commodus's royal parade through Rome reminds the viewer of a similar scene where Hitler emerged in *Triumph of the Will*, a Nazi propaganda film.

When it comes to set design, Scott was equally blasé about the facts. From Scott's perspective, his perception of the past holds as much weight as that of historians. When questioned about a few of his inclusions, Scott replied, "I'd say, 'How do you know? You weren't there.' What we do is jump back in time into our own imaginations, and that is the most important thing to do. Historians say, 'I'm not sure that they did that.' And we say, 'Well, they bloody well do now.'" This assumption led to his inclusion of a sidewalk café that he declared was the "first coffee bar in history," and a slew of other architectural designs that mimicked British, American, and German "classic" architecture. Real Rome was not a white-washed world of stone pillars and glowing temples. Much of the architecture was either vibrantly painted, strewn with vulgar graffiti or stained by floods and fires. But Scott's version falls in line with the Hollywoodized version of Rome the audience has come to expect.

Regardless of its historical inaccuracies, *Gladiator* single-handedly revitalized the historical epic genre, launching a slew of copycat films – *Troy*, *Kingdom of Heaven*, *Alexander*, and *The Patriot* to name a few. Unlike those wannabes that followed, Ridley Scott created in *Gladiator* the perfect balance between an ultramacho protagonist, an engaging vengeance story, and a modified version of history that kept the audience enthralled from beginning to end.

Key Quotes

Lucilla: (*after Maximus had a fairly successful day at the arena*) Today I saw a slave become more powerful than the Emperor of Rome.

Maximus: (*prior to the battle against the Germanic tribes*) At my signal, unleash hell.

Commodus: (*after finding out that Commodus is still alive*) It vexes me. I'm terribly vexed.

Proximo: (*instructing/motivating his gladiators-in-training*) Sadly, we cannot choose when, but...we can decide how we meet that end, so that we are remembered...as men.

Gracchus: (*discussing Commodus' decision to bring back gladiatorial combat*) He will bring them death, and they will love him for it.

Kingdom of Heaven

2005
Director: Ridley Scott
Starring: Orlando Bloom, Eva Green, Jeremy Irons
145 minutes – Rated R

By Eric Burnett

Synopsis:

Taking place during the 12th century siege of Jerusalem, this Crusades-era epic follows the transformation of Balian from a lowly blacksmith who inherits a noble title to the knight that eventually saves Jerusalem from destruction. Balian flees France and joins his father on the Crusades after his wife commits suicide and he murders the corrupt town priest. Unfortunately, on the way to Jerusalem, his father dies, leaving Balian the Lord of Ibelin (a kingdom outside Jerusalem). Once in Jerusalem, Balian finds himself in the midst of a deadly drama between a king trying to maintain peace while dying of leprosy, a band of bloodthirsty Christians bent on starting a war, and a Muslim force led by the feared Saladin that controls the surrounding area. One by one, the saviors of Jerusalem abandon Balian, leaving him alone to defend the Holy Land.

Historically Relevant Scenes

00:33:30>00:45:00	- Life in Jerusalem/Political Conflict
01:27:00>01:39:00	- Battle of Hattin
01:39:00>02:09:00	- Siege of Jerusalem - Medieval Siege Techniques

---

Ratings:

Entertainment -   ★ ★ ★ ☆

Historical Accuracy -   ★ ★ ☆ ☆

Historical Analysis:

Today, Jerusalem (and the Middle East to a greater extent) stands out in most American's eyes as one of the most violent, unstable regions in the world. To many unfamiliar with the region, Jerusalem only exists to cause conflict between Muslims, Christians and Jews. In 2005, Ridley Scott attempted to make sense of this seemingly unwarranted chaos by creating the film *Kingdom of Heaven*, a 21st century retelling of the Second Crusade and the Christian defense of Jerusalem. Although many of the characters from the film actually existed and most of the events mentioned did occur, Scott took great liberties in exaggerating the role of each character and the specifics surrounding each event.

In the film, when the lead character, Orlando Bloom's Balian, arrives in Jerusalem, the region stands on the edge of war, and only Tiberias, the kingdom's regent, can maintain a delicate truce between the bloodthirsty Christian Crusaders and Saladin's Muslim forces.

The history of Jerusalem stretches back over five thousand years, making it one of the oldest cities in human history. According to the Jewish Torah, in the 11th century BCE, after Moses led the Hebrew exodus out of Egypt, David established the United Kingdom of Israel and Judah. Later, Solomon built the Temple Mount which became the holiest of Jewish sites. Over the next fifteen hundred years, Jews tried to maintain autonomy under the constant pressure of Greeks, Romans, Persians and other regional powers. Under control of the Romans, Jews were banned by Emperor Constantine from returning to Jerusalem. However, in 637 Caliph Omar's Muslim forces defeated the Byzantine army ushering in a four century reign where Christians, Jews and Muslims lived together in relative religious harmony.

This period of religious toleration forever changed with the coming of the Turks in 1076. Their capture of the city and subsequent murder, kidnapping and robbing of Christian pilgrims sent European zealots into a fury. Pope Urban II, responding to an appeal by the threatened Eastern Orthodox city of Constantinople as well as the seemingly unprovoked attacks on Christian pilgrims, inspired a generation of Europeans to embark on a Holy Crusade to recapture Jerusalem for the Christian world. This call to action sparked two centuries of Islamic-Jewish-Christian conflict that over the course of nine crusades saw Jerusalem change hands back and forth between the warring factions, each claiming control of the holy land of their prophets.

For the Muslims, Jerusalem is not only the home to David, Solomon, and Jesus, but also, it was here that Mohammad "was taken on a momentous journey from Makkah to Jerusalem and then from there to the heavenly celestial abodes" where he met with the prophets and messengers of Allah. Upon his return to Mecca, Mohammad made Jerusalem the direction all Muslims must face during their five daily prayers. After seventeen months, Allah commanded that this direction be changed to Mecca, but because of its early role, Jerusalem will always be held as one of Islam's holiest sites.

Right now, you're wondering, why the religion lesson? Well, without this lesson you'll have no idea why hundreds of thousands of men and women risked their lives. In our contemporary world, killing for control of a symbolic object or place might seem irrational, but to the 12th century religious follower, this was the greatest motivation. You could fight for no one higher purpose than God. It was the ultimate calling.

It was this motivation that brought hundreds of thousands of knights, religious zealots and riff-raff down to the Holy Land where in 1099 the Christians captured Jerusalem and brutally murdered all Jewish and Muslim women and children. One observer noted that the massacre "was so great that our men waded in blood up to their ankles."

After this capture, the Kingdom of Jerusalem was created and was ruled like the European fiefdoms. Christian crusaders took control of the Muslim kingdoms, becoming vassals to the King of Jerusalem. Due to the fact that most lords lived in the city of Jerusalem and ruled as absentee landholders, the Syrian, Jewish and Muslim peasants of these kingdoms maintained a level of freedom unknown in the European world. These lords thought numerous Europeans would be attracted to the newly-conquered Holy Land, but the expected mass migration of Europeans down to the Middle East never materialized, thus leaving the military defense of Jerusalem in the hands of the Pope-controlled Knights Templar and Knights Hospitaller.

And this is where *Kingdom of Heaven* begins. According to Ridley Scott's interpretation, Balian, the illegitimate French blacksmith son of Godfrey, escapes poverty, his wife's suicide and his inevitable prosecution for murder to join his father on a quest to maintain peace in Jerusalem. After briefly joining his father and surviving a fifteen minute sword lesson, Godfrey's band of crusaders is hijacked on the road, and Godfrey suffers what will become a fatal blow. Godfrey then hands over to Balian the keys to his kingdom of Ibelin, and commands him to protect Jerusalem, the Kingdom of Heaven. After surviving a shipwreck, a duel with a Muslim swordsman and a long walk across the desert, Balian arrives in Jerusalem where there is a fragile peace between the king, the Crusaders, and Saladin – the Muslim leader of a nearby army.

In reality, Balian was in no way a peasant or a blacksmith. He was a noble whose ancestors fought a century earlier in the First Crusade. The casting of Orlando Bloom made it seem as if Balian was somewhere in his early 30s when the conflict broke out. In reality, he was closer to fifty and as for his chivalrous manners, philanthropic spirit, and charismatic way with Princess Sibylla, the real Balian was described by his contemporaries as "more false than a goblin" and "cruel, fickle and faithless." In the movie, Balian takes control of Ibelin and immediately sheds his noble garments to work side by side with his peasants as they search for water. This ridiculous scene never happened. Not only did Balian never work alongside his peasants, it is quite insulting to assume that the Syrians, Jews and Muslims under his control never thought to dig a hole in the ground to search for water. It's fair to say that as one of civilization's oldest cities, the residents of Jerusalem didn't need a French blacksmith to teach them how to irrigate.

The romantic love triangle that Bloom's Balian walks into is equally preposterous. First, Sibylla didn't hate her husband or plot his assassination, but instead she did everything within her influence to acquire more power for her husband. Second, as for a relationship between Balian and Sibylla, this never happened. Balian was in fact married to Maria Comnena, Sibylla's ex-step mother-in-law, King Almaric's first wife, mother of Isabella.

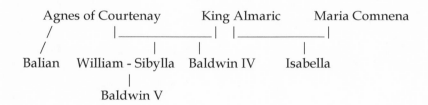

I just lost you. At this point, it might be a good idea to give you a bit of a Kingdom of Jerusalem family tree. King Almaric and Agnes of Courtenay had two kids – Baldwin IV (leper king) and Sibylla. Almaric later divorced Courtenay and married Maria Comnena, and they had a daughter – Isabella. When King Almaric died, the throne was handed over to his leper son at the age of 13 – King Baldwin IV – and Maria Comnena married Balian. So, did Balian ever have an affair with Sibylla? No. They both had their own spouses, and Balian was twenty years her senior. Some historians say that Raymond III (the character Tiberias in the film) tried to set Sibylla up with Balian's older brother (another guy named Baldwin), but this wasn't for romance, it was a power play to gain control of the throne.

If you think this family tree is confusing, wait until you learn about what happens when the leper king dies. In the film, when King Baldwin IV dies, Sibylla goes to Balian and offers her hand in marriage if he will kill her husband – the crusader Guy de Lusignan. Even though

Balian had already tasted the forbidden fruit of this married woman, to this offer, he courteously declines. This ethical decision puts Sibylla in a bind. She then returns to her husband and tells him that she will support him as king, if he super promises to defend Jerusalem and not become a sadistic dictator. In his Hitleresque way, Guy de Lusignan agrees to the deal and in a formal ceremony the heir to the throne – Sibylla – officially crowns her husband King of Jerusalem. And as did Hitler when he conquered Czechoslovakia, Austria and Poland after promising to never, ever invade another country again, Guy de Lusignan immediately links up with his buddy Reynald de Chatillon, and they launch a campaign against Saladin and his forces.

These events of succession bare little resemblance to what actually transpired. As Baldwin IV slowly succumbed to the effects of leprosy, it was initially unclear which of the two sisters – Sibylla or Isabella - would take the throne. A key character left out in the film was little Baldwin V – Sibylla's son with her first husband William of Montferrat. As a preemptive measure, when he was five years old, Baldwin V was made co-king with his uncle Baldwin IV. When Baldwin IV (remember Baldwin IV = leper king; Baldwin V = 5 year old king) eventually died in 1185, his nephew assumed the throne. At the crowning ceremony, our fateful protagonist Balian carried little Baldwin V on his shoulders, declaring his support of the child-king. Unfortunately this great plan for succession went awry when the little kid died just a year later. Now that both Baldwins were dead, the throne was up for grabs again.

Here's where the movie again departs from reality. In real life, Sibylla was offered the throne only if she publicly announced the annulment of her marriage to Guy de Lusignan and took another husband. She initially agreed, but in a stunning turn of events, at the moment she was too announce her annulment, she instead crowned Guy de Lusignan King of Jerusalem. So, not only did she not try to have Balian kill her husband so that she could marry the humble blacksmith, she actually fully supported Guy's ascension to the throne.

Aside from the political intrigue within Jerusalem, the film also explores the conflict between the Western Crusaders and the Muslim caravans. The film has the demented, bloodthirsty Reynald de Chatillon continually attacking these defenseless caravans to try to incite war. In reality, Reynald did time and again ignore the truce with Saladin, regularly plundering the caravans. He also commissioned ships to pirate the waters of the Red Sea. Some claim Reynald's hatred for the Muslims stemmed from his 17 years in Syrian captivity. Regardless, Reynald's continued assault on defenseless caravans could not be overlooked. In the film, the final straw comes when Reynald attacks a caravan and brutally murders Saladin's sister. Although historians disagree on whether or not Reynald captured Saladin's sister, she definitely was not killed.

Whether it was due to the personal attack on his family member, or the blatant disregard for the Muslim-Christian truce, or pressure from internal factions to reclaim Jerusalem for the Muslims, Saladin prepared to attack Jerusalem. In the film, Saladin sends a messenger to the new king of Jerusalem – Guy de Lusignan – demanding justice for the murder of his sister. Guy's response is reminiscent of King Leonidas's response to the Persian messenger in the film *300*. However, instead of kicking the messenger down a well after yelling, "This is SPARTA!" the drunken King Guy responds to the question - "What answer do you return to Saladin?" by slitting the messenger's throat and sneering, "This!"

The inspired Guy and Reynald then round up an army of crusaders and head out to battle, but first they send out three Templar Knights to kill the pesky Balian. In a costume discrepancy, these "Knights" wear white and black, when true Templar Knights wore red crosses on white mantles. The white and black knights of the day were the Teutonic Knights, but this group wasn't created until years after the alleged attack. Regardless, the entire scene of a lowly blacksmith defeating three trained knights is utterly ridiculous. How can a young man who has had a couple hours of sword training defeat three soldiers who have led a lifetime of warfare? Bottom line – he couldn't. But in Hollywood, Balian survives and then returns to Jerusalem to fulfill his pledge to Baldwin IV to defend the city.

Meanwhile, Guy and Reynald drag their men across the desert, and at the point of exhaustion, face off against Saladin's forces. The movie doesn't show this battle in detail, instead saving the main event for the siege on the Balian-defended Jerusalem. In reality however, this was the key battle – The Battle of Hattin. On July 4, 1187, Saladin crushed the defenders of Jerusalem and captured Guy and Reynald. In the film, the two leaders are brought to Saladin's tent where he offers King Guy a goblet of water. In Muslim tradition, this offering symbolized the safety of King Guy's life in Saladin's hands. When Reynald takes the goblet from Guy to quench his thirst, Saladin immediately knocks it from his hand, showing that Reynald would not receive the same treatment from Saladin. In real life, Reynald went on to mock Mohammad and the Muslim faith, to which Saladin immediately hacked off his arm and a Muslim soldier entered and decapitated him. In the movie, his throat is merely slit. Following this, King Guy sat trembling, stricken with fear, and to assuage his panic, Saladin said, "Have no fear. It is not the custom of kings to kill kings." Instead, King Guy was imprisoned and held captive for over a year. Unlike in the movie where before the siege of Jerusalem he is dragged out naked and paraded on a donkey in front of the mocking Muslim army, in real life he served out his imprisonment in Nablus (what today is known as the Palestinian West Bank). After this captivity, he returned to Jerusalem politics, only to lose an election to Isabella's husband Conrad de Monterrat. He eventually was given control of Cyprus where he ruled for two years until his death in 1194.

With Jerusalem's army defeated, Saladin set his sights on Jerusalem, a walled city at this point in the film only defended by Balian. In reality, Queen Sibylla was forced to organize the defense of the city that was short on men but long on refugees. Due to the monumental losses at the Battle of Hattin and the thousands of refugees that fled to Jerusalem from the countryside, over 60,000 inhabitants filled a city only able to hold 30,000 (and at the time of the Siege of Jerusalem there were fifty women and children for every one man). At the commencement of the battle, Balian was in nearby Tyre (not fighting Templar Knights seeking his assassination) and was summoned back to Jerusalem to assist with the surrender of the city. After assuring Saladin that he needed to return to secure the safety of his family in Jerusalem, Saladin "granted him permission to go to Jerusalem on the condition that he not bear weapons against him and that he spend only one night there."

In the movie, once within the walls Balian gives one of his "can't we all just get along" speeches and then knights every man in the city. The real life Balian did in fact knight 100 city officials, not everyone of the 1,200 random male citizens (however he did pass out all available arms to the able-bodied men). In keeping with Scott's policy of portraying Christians as cowards or murderers, the Bishop of Jerusalem pleads for surrender, imploring that they all could "convert to Islam [and r]epent later." The real Patriarch Heraclius of Jerusalem actually helped organize the defenses and stayed until the end.

The siege that follows has Balian defending against a *Lord of the Rings* type assault with fireballs flying from the sky and siege towers allowing Muslims to take the walls. In reality, the battle did not take the mere minutes shown in the film; it took over a month to knock down one wall. And as for the flaming fireballs and siege towers, again, these follow more the accepted Hollywood script for castle sieges, as stones were used as projectiles and the wall was not toppled by siege towers, but were instead mined from beneath.

Eventually, Saladin's vastly superior army force Balian to ask for terms of surrender. In the film, Saladin allows every inhabitant to leave without punishment, but in reality only those that could afford the ransom were granted leave. At this point in the film, Saladin enters the city and places a fallen cross back on a table, showing his tolerance to all religions.

It was this depiction of Saladin and the subsequent depiction of Muslims and Christians that resulted in so much scholarly criticism of the film. Time and again, Ridley Scott tried to incorporate modern day themes of open-mindedness and religious acceptance, while branding Christians as hedonistic murderers and Muslims as heroic pacifists. Professor of Medieval History at the University of Notre Dame Paul Cobb noted, "To have religious tolerance as the central theme of a movie about the Crusades is like having lasers in a movie about the Civil War. It's a modern concept being imported into the film." And as for his depiction of Muslims, Scott probably went too far in the other extreme, because during the Crusades "cruelty was not on one side but on all." However, Dr. Parvez Ahmed of the Council on American-Islamic Relations (CAIR) noted, "Perhaps *Kingdom of Heaven* will do for Muslims what Kevin Costner's *Dances with Wolves* did for Native Americans — humanize a perceived 'other.'"

As history has shown us, the conflict over the "Kingdom of Heaven" did not end here. When word of the Muslim capture of Jerusalem reached Europe, another Crusade, this one led by Richard the Lionheart, headed east to again regain the Holy Land. After years of fighting, the two sides reluctantly agreed to the Treaty of Ramla in 1192 which allowed Muslims to maintain control of the city as long as Christians were granted safe journey on their pilgrimages. This agreement lasted until the 20th century, but with the creation of Israel and the resulting Palestinian/Israeli conflict, it appears the "Kingdom of Heaven" will be a battleground for centuries to come.

Key Quotes

Bishop, Patriarch of Jerusalem: (*when surrounded by Muslim forces*) Convert to Islam, repent later.
Balian of Ibelin: You have taught me a lot about religion, Your Eminence.

King Baldwin: (*upon meeting Balian*) You see, none of us choose our end really. A king may move a man, a father may claim a son. But remember that, even when those who move you be kings or men of power, your soul is in your keeping alone. When you stand before God you cannot say "but I was told by others to do thus" or that "virtue was not convenient at the time."

Reynald: (*after unprovoked slaughter of caravan*) I am what I am. Someone has to be.

Sibylla: (*after Balian refuses to marry her*) There'll be a day when you will wish you had done a little evil to do a greater good.

Balian of Ibelin: (*inspiring the citizens of Jerusalem before the final siege*) It has fallen to us, to defend Jerusalem, and we have made our preparations as well as they can be made. None of us took this city from Muslims. No Muslim of the great army now coming against us was born when this city was lost. We fight over an offence we did not give, against those who were not alive to be offended. What is Jerusalem? Your holy places lie over the Jewish temple that the Romans pulled down. The Muslim places of worship lie over yours. Which is more holy? The wall? The Mosque? The Sepulchre? Who has claim? No one has claim. All have claim!

Braveheart

1995
Director: Mel Gibson
Starring: Mel Gibson, Sophie Marceau, Catherine McCormack
177 minutes – Rated R

By Eric Burnett

Synopsis:

Set in the 13th century, *Braveheart* charts the rise of William Wallace, a Scottish knight who struggles to free Scotland from the control of Edward I's England after his wife is brutally killed by an English lord. Though outnumbered and technologically inferior, William Wallace and his band of marauders eventually stage a series of successful revolts against the English feudal lords, ultimately stretching their assault into English territory. After being captured, tortured, and beheaded, William Wallace becomes the symbol of the Scottish independence movement.

Historically Relevant Scenes	
00:25:37>00:28:00	- Medieval town life
00:39:00>00:42:00	- Medieval town life
01:58:00>02:09:30	- Battle of Falkirk
02:36:00>02:46:00	- Medieval torture

Ratings:

Entertainment - ★ ★ ★ ★

Historical Accuracy - ★ ☆ ☆ ☆

Historical Analysis:

As in his other historically-based films (*The Patriot* and *We Were Soldiers*), Mel Gibson has proven quite adept at transforming historical figures into mythical supermen void of vice, but able to summon courage and strength to overcome any foe. William Wallace is the hero every boy wants to become, and the man every woman wants to marry. Gibson has a habit of taking roles that portray him as the über protagonist and because little was known about the Scottish legendary hero, Gibson was able to play loosely with the truth.

The movie takes place during the late 13th century when the throne of Scotland was under dispute. In 1286, when the king of Scotland, Alexander III, died after falling off a horse, numerous candidates stepped forward to claim the crown. For the next four years, power passed between the respected nobles and the heir to the throne – Margaret of Norway – but when Margaret died, conflict arose again. In stepped King Edward I of England to mediate the conflict between the two most likely heirs – Robert Bruce and John Baliol – to try and prevent a civil war. Edward I quickly used his newfound position to rule over Scotland, and imposed taxes, procured troops and implemented laws. Even though John Baliol eventually was crowned King of Scots, because it was Edward I that granted this power, the king of England acted as if he was the ultimate ruler.

Here is where tensions rose. The Scots made an alliance with France, to which Edward I responded harshly. His troops invaded Scotland and his legacy of brutality was firmly entrenched after his sacking of the border town of Berwick. One witness recounted, "When the town had been taken in this way and its citizens had submitted, Edward spared no one, whatever the age or sex, and for two days streams of blood flowed from the bodies of the slain, for in his tyrannous rage he ordered 7,500 souls of both sexes to be massacred...So that mills could be turned round by the flow of their blood." Returning to England, Edward I expressed his disgust for the Scottish people when he allegedly proclaimed, "A man does good work when he rids himself of shit."

Although not directly mentioned, the film alludes to these incidents. The Baliol and Bruce factions squabble over control of Scotland, the characters comment on Edward I's earlier atrocities, and at one point the film version of Edward I jokes, "The trouble with Scotland is that it's full of Scots." Although the details were omitted, Gibson does do an acceptable job introducing the tension within Scotland and between the Scottish lords and King Edward I of England.

It is to this era of tension and oppression that William Wallace enters the scene. However, based almost entirely on a 1722 translation of the Blind Harry popular poem *The Wallace* (a poem that remained for centuries the most popular book next to the Bible in Scotland), *Braveheart* rests on the flimsiest of evidence. Although Wallace did in fact play a substantial role in the Scottish independence movement and was subsequently a hero for centuries to come, the Mel Gibson directed tale whitewashes the truth surrounding William Wallace.

Gibson conveniently forgets the five years of banditry Wallace spent while roaming the countryside, as well as his tendency to decapitate or dismember those who fell out of his favor. Instead, Gibson creates a Christ-like figure that on two separate occasions is brought through a hostile crowd in a crucifixion-esque posture. Likewise, Gibson's Wallace abhors violence, and it is only after the defiling and murder of his wife that he is able to summon his inner executioner. To make the eventual confrontation even more dramatic, this Wallace comes from a peasant upbringing – whereas in reality his father and grandfather were landowners of some considerable import in the community.

The yang to Gibson's yin comes to us as the "genocidal psychopath" King Edward I of England, Edward the Longshanks. It isn't enough that Wallace is a male angel; Longshanks must be the devil. When first introduced, he is referred to as a "pagan" (a blatant inaccuracy), and with each subsequent scene, his behavior makes him seem more the antichrist. Not only does he frequently belittle his diminutive, effeminate son, he murders his son's male "friend," and (of greater significance to the Scots) enacts the policy of *prima nocte*. Under this policy, English lords hypothetically had sexual privileges with any maiden on her wedding night. Though urban legend would later encourage this notion of Fornication Under Consent of the King (figure out the acronym yourself), the reality is that *prima nocte* never existed during the Medieval Era and there is minimal evidence of its existence in later centuries. However, Gibson was never one to quibble over historical accuracy, especially when its inclusion would later give Wallace the motivation needed to avenge the deflowering of his people.

Aside from the alterations made to the two key characters, the film also distorts the role of other figures from the era. In keeping with the Christ theme, Robert Bruce becomes Wallace's Judas, though in reality he never could have betrayed William Wallace at Falkirk because Bruce was simultaneously involved in another battle just a few miles away. Eventually, the film has Bruce inspiring a group of Scottish troops who eventually defeat the far superior army at the famous June 23, 1314 Battle of Bannockburn. However, the movie erroneously has Bruce deciding on the spur of the moment to fight the English instead of passively accepting terms of surrender. In reality, Robert Bruce had spent nearly a decade surviving a civil war and leading guerilla warfare attacks against the English. Although he doesn't die a martyr's death like the more famous William Wallace, it was Robert Bruce who should receive a substantial amount of credit for Scotland's independence.

Another key character in the film is the Princess of Wales – Isabelle of France. According to the film, Isabelle is sent to Wallace as a sacrificial ambassador, and she later develops a schoolgirl crush on the Scottish crusader. This crush leads to a night of passion, which in turn sets up the dramatic climax where Isabelle reveals to her devil of a father-in-law that she is impregnated with Wallace's son. In Gibson's version, this lovechild later becomes Edward III. Unfortunately, this lovely liaison and its fortuitous fruit are biologically impossible. At the time of William Wallace's death (1305), Queen Isabelle was six years old and living in France. Also, Edward III was not born until 1312. So...for the studio version to be accurate, you would simply need to accept the possibility that a six year old girl living across the English Channel could birth a child after a 2500 day gestation period.

At the time of its release, the character depiction that garnered the greatest criticism was the homosexual son Edward II. Though in reality he was a tall, athletic man who was an accomplished rower, Gibson felt the need to portray him as a sappy, diminutive pretty boy who embodies all the negative stereotypes of a homosexual male. The movie even implied that daddy Longshanks' services would be needed to impregnate Queen Isabelle. It is true that no one would mistake the Edward II-Isabelle union as a romantic ideal, but they did however produce four children after Longshanks' death.

The uproar amongst the gay community almost mirrored the reaction of the Jewish community ten years later when an intoxicated Gibson claimed that Jews were "responsible for all the war(s) in the world." It's fair to say that Mel will not be winning any lifetime achievement awards for tolerance.

Fortunately, Gibson did save the audience from the horrific realities of death – 14th century style. Edward II was eventually murdered and disemboweled, only to later have a hot poker rammed up his derriere. Sir Thomas Moore recounts how the future king "was suddenly seized and, while a great mattress... weighed him down, a plumber's iron, heated intensely hot, was introduced through a tube into his secret parts so that it burned the inner portions beyond the intestines."

Equally disturbing is the death of Wallace. Gibson has Wallace brought in on a wagon, hung, stretched, disemboweled and then beheaded. The truth was that he was pulled through London naked, hung, castrated, disemboweled and then forced to watch as his organs were cooked in front of him. Eventually he was beheaded, but it is fair to say that lacking genitals and intestines, it would have been quite difficult to shout out "FREEEEE-DOMMMM" for all to hear.

Even many of the included props are anachronisms – the swords, cottages, kilts (philabegs) and bagpipes used all date to the 16th century and the face paint used for the battles is more representative of 20th century football hooligans or 1st century Celtic warriors.

Though this movie is undeniably one of the more entertaining movies of all time – it has gore for the boys, a love story for the girls, and enough wet eye inducing moments to sway even the most hardened heart – it is historically a joke. True, there was a man named William Wallace who led some rebels in some skirmishes against the British, but the other points are ridiculous, distorted or outright wrong.

Key Quotes

Edward I: (*prior to issuing prima nocte edict*) The trouble with Scotland is that it's full of Scots.

William Wallace: (*motivational speech prior to Falkirk*) Aye, fight and you may die, run, and you'll live... at least for a while. And dying in your beds, many years from now, would you be willin' to trade ALL the days, from this day to that, for one chance, just one chance, to come back here and tell our enemies that they may take our lives, but they'll never take... OUR FREEDOM!

William Wallace: (*final line shouted out while his intestines were dangling on the floor*) FREEEEEEEE-DOMMMMMMM!!!

Pocahontas

1995
Directors: Mike Gabriel and Eric Goldberg
Starring: Mel Gibson, Irene Bedard and Christian Bale
84 minutes – Rated G

By Allie Lesiuk

Synopsis:

The movie takes place during the creation of the Jamestown colony in Virginia as Pocahontas, a young Indian maiden, struggles to keep peace between the two hostile groups living in the Jamestown area: the recently-arrived English settlers and her own Powhatan Indian tribe. While doing this she falls madly in love with the leader of the English settlers - John Smith. The English settlers leave London with a grand farewell in hopes of finding gold, riches and freedom in the new land. Upon arrival, the settlers are quick to find that they are not the only ones occupying this new land and that they are most certainly not welcome. The Powhatan Indians and the English settlers become very hostile towards each other and by the end are prepared to fight till the death for this New World.

Historically Relevant Scenes	
00:35>01:50	- Leaving London for Jamestown
06:35>07:00	- Powhatan Town
34:10>35:00	- Indian and Settler Warfare

Ratings:

Entertainment - ★ ★ ☆ ☆

Historical Accuracy - ★ ☆ ☆ ☆

Historical Analysis:

Many laugh at the idea of a Disney movie being considered historically accurate, and even the producer of *Pocahontas* Sarah Green, stated that they "were definitely not doing a historical piece." Critic James Berardinelli wrote, "Anyone who expects historical accuracy from a Disney animated feature should be ashamed of themself." Trying to make a movie appealing to young children and adults is definitely a challenge, but that was a task that Disney proudly achieved. If you look past the main inaccuracy of the relationship between Pocahontas and John Smith, the movie provides some accurate details of what life was like back in 1607, although it is sometimes hard to trust a piece that so blatantly invents a fictional romance between two real life characters. If you are going to judge a movie's accuracy purely on if there is a fictional romance or not then you might as well ignore every element of the cheesy flicks *Pearl Harbor* and *Titanic*.

The story picks up after over a century of exploration in the New World. After Christopher Columbus's discovery of the Americas in 1492, a wave of Spanish, Portuguese, Dutch, British and French explorers set out to explore these lands, looking for riches and a Western shortcut to Asia. Along the way, the Europeans established settlements up and down the coast, many of which came in direct conflict with the indigenous people.

By 1600, the Spanish and Portuguese were firmly entrenched in what is now called South America, and North America had yet to be carved up by the opportunistic Europeans. Because there were numerous conflicting land claims in this early period, the best way to truly control a piece of land was through settlement.

The Spanish were first to "settle" land that today is known as the United States of America. The Spanish failed at their first attempts to colonize the region, but eventually succeeded in 1565 with the founding of St. Augustine. In the film, the Spanish settlements and their stories of gold and glory can be seen when Governor Ratcliffe takes out his map and talks about the mountains of gold the Spanish supposedly found.

The British attempted to enter the America sweepstakes with a colonizing effort at Roanoke Island, off the coast of present day North Carolina. Sir Francis Drake brought 117 settlers to Roanoke Island in 1587, but after being delayed in England for three years while Spain and England fought, Drake returned to an abandoned settlement. The only hint to where these early settlers went came from the engraving "CRO" on a tree and "Croatoan" on a nearby rock. Although some believe this group was killed by the locals, others believe these engravings hint that the settlers left behind the failed island settlement and joined a neighboring tribe on the island of Croatoan.

Two decades passed and the British thought they would give this whole settlement thing another try. The London Company, commissioned by King James, was sent off into the New World in hopes of discovering a new shorter route to the Orient and finding gold and riches-- basically the same reason anyone else voyaged there. The movie alludes to these motivations in the opening song:

> In sixteen hundred seven
> We sail the open sea
> For glory, God, and gold
> And The Virginia Company
> For the New World is like heaven
> And we'll all be rich and free
> Or so we have been told
> By The Virginia Company
> For glory, God and gold
> And The Virginia Company
> On the beaches of Virginny
> There's diamonds like debris
> There's silver rivers flow
> And gold you pick right off a tree

This group was made up of 104 men (which started off as 144 but 40 died on the voyage from starvation and sickness) who ventured over on three boats - *Godspeed, Discovery*, and *Susan Constant*. These boats contained the equipment needed to start their life in the New World. These men were volunteers who agreed that if they gave seven years of labor to the company they would in turn be rewarded with food, lodging, protection and land ownership. In the movie however, they depict the crew coming over in only one boat.

The London Company left for the New World in December of 1606 and arrived four months later in Jamestown, named after King James. Jamestown appeared to have perfect conditions for starting a new colony, such as the deep harbors that as said by John Smith in the movie allowed them to "pull right into the shores." In the movie you see Pocahontas standing on the edge of a cliff by a waterfall and John Smith scaling the side of the cliff to get a better view of the New World. In reality, Virginia is relatively flat with the exception of a few hills, but it certainly does not have the towering cliffs depicted in the movie. The settlers found that this area was in fact not as ideal as they had imagined. Jamestown is an isolated island right by the Virginia mainland. Because of its isolation, it was very bad for hunting, so crops were their main source of food.

Diseases started to spread very quickly because of two main problems: unsanitary water and mosquitoes that spread disease quite rapidly. This significant detail of history was never depicted in the movie.

In fact, the movie never even depicted life as being hard in any way for the settlers. Also, the group flies their flag proudly for all to see. This would all be well and good if the flag they were flying actually existed, but unfortunately, the Union Flag of Great Britain which is depicted in the movie was not adopted until 1801.

Another glitch that the men faced was their lack of food. Initially, the men prioritized finding the promised gold, and they subsequently chose to not plant crops and prepare for the coming winter. The movie leaves out the depth of despair these men faced in what became known as the "Starving Time." Men resorted to eating belts and clothing, grubs, insects, dead animals, and they even started digging up graves of their own men and those of the neighboring Indians. One settler even recounts how a man murdered and ate his wife. He wrote:

> "And one amongst the rest did kill his wife, powdered her, and had eaten part of her before it was known, for which he was executed, as he well deserved; now whether she was better roasted, boiled or carbonado'd, I know not, but of such a dish as powdered wife I never heard of."

The entire settlement would have probably succumbed to the same fate as the Roanoke settlers if not for the leadership of one man – Captain John Smith. He was an experienced explorer and had previous skills in leading and defending groups. His combat skills were admired by all and his leadership techniques set an example for many after him...at least according to the journal that he kept, which can't always be taken seriously. You see, John Smith is what we like to call today a "conceited braggart." John Mohawk, a director of indigenous studies, says that "John Smith was one of those guys who used to go around writing stories that made himself look glamorous." Because of this, it is believed that many of his stories are greatly exaggerated.

John Smith, born in Willoughby, England in 1580, was a good choice by King James as leader, due to his previous combat experience. At the age of twenty he fought in the Long War with the Austrian Forces. While fighting in Hungary he was promoted to Captain because of his deft battle skills. In 1602 he then started fighting in Transylvania. He was wounded and then captured and sold into slavery to a Turkish man who then gave him as a present to his love in Istanbul. Smith escaped by traveling through Russia and Poland and returned back to Transylvania. After he was done with service he voyaged all through Northern Africa and Europe until 1605; his next voyage was going to be his infamous journey to Virginia.

Upon arrival to the New World the English settlers were welcomed by the Algonquian Indians, or Powhatan Indians. The leader of these thirty tribes was Wahunsonacock (you're not allowed to giggle at his name), a man approaching sixty years old, who had over a hundred wives and numerous children, one of which was the legendary Pocahontas. These nearly 13,000 Indians were divided into villages, some having over one hundred homes, most of which were "longhouses." The name "longhouse" was not given without reason--these houses were usually anywhere from 60 to 100 feet long. They held multiple families (meant to house around 20 families) and had holes at the top to let smoke escape from the home (the number of holes usually corresponded to the number of families). Their houses were so well-made that according to Smith "notwithstanding wind, rain, or weather they are as warm as stoves." While Disney did make an attempt to create these houses accurately (not the stereotypical teepee of most Hollywood films), they still were not completely accurate because their size in the movie was much smaller than reality.

The film also inaccurately depicts the early relations between the Powhatan Indians and the Jamestown settlers. The movie has them almost immediately coming into violent conflict over control of the land, building up to the climatic scene in which both sides prepare for war. Although there were episodes of violence between the two groups, for the first decade of settlement, the groups realized the mutual benefits of a peaceful relationship. The settlers needed food and guides to explore the surrounding area, and the Powhatan leaders benefitted from the finished products that made their daily lives easier. However, in 1622, the heir to the Powhatan throne, Opechancanough, launched a pre-emptive attack against the expanding settlement, killing over 400 settlers. Obviously, this attack was met with British retaliation, and two decades of war ensued. Eventually, outnumbered and technologically at a disadvantage, the Powhatan Indians signed a series of treaties that restricted their movement and by 1722, the tribe no longer existed in Virginia.

However, instead of showing how this conflict evolved over a century, Disney condenses numerous events into a two week period, much of which revolves around the alleged relationship between Pocahontas and John Smith. In the movie, Pocahontas and John Smith meet each other while the majestic Pocahontas frolics through fields, and within a few minutes, thanks to the incredible Grandmother Willow language translation tool of "listening with your heart," they understand each other. They fall in love almost immediately and after a tragic accident that takes one of Pocahontas's tribe mates, the Powhatan tribe seeks revenge by taking John Smith's life. Hearing the fate of their leader, the Jamestown settlers prepare for war. In the movie, it is here that Pocahontas steps in and convinces the Powhatan tribe to not hurt her beloved – John Smith.

This scene has absolutely no historical truth, although many believed it to be true because John Smith's interpretation of the event is the one that has passed down through the ages. According to Smith, he was captured by the Powhatan Indians and brought to their village where he was then ordered to stretch across two stones. At this point, obviously overtaken by his charming personality, a little girl (Pocahontas would have been eleven years old at the time) jumped in and took Smith's "head in her arms and laid her owne upon his to save him from death." Even if this oft-repeated story did happen, there is a strong chance that it was merely an elaborate ritual for accepting outsiders into the Powhatan tribe. However, in his memoirs, John Smith "spun this fancy tale about how this beautiful maiden saved his life, but it was all bunkum." Disney took the legend to an all new level by portraying Pocahontas as a young, strikingly beautiful woman with brown skin and European features, who falls in love with an equally handsome and dashing John Smith. Although the real life John Smith would have probably approved of his depiction, Chief Roy Crazy Horse of the Powhatan tribe warned, "Euro-Americans must ask themselves why it has been so important to elevate Smith's fibbing to status as a national myth worthy of being recycled again by Disney."

In reality, Pocahontas did have a relationship with a Jamestown settler, but that settler was tobacco farmer John Rolfe. After being held captive by the English settlers for almost a year, John Rolfe fell "in love" with her and in 1614 they were married after she was baptized and took the name Rebecca (her actual name was Matoaka…Pocahontas was a nickname meaning "little playful one"). Although Rolfe might have had romantic feelings toward her, at the time he admitted that the marriage was "for the good of the plantation." Whether or not the marriage was made to forge a peaceful alliance between the two factions or if was based on mutual love is unknown, but Rebecca moved into the Jamestown settlement and began the process of acculturation into British ways. Rebecca adopted European dress and mannerisms, and they eventually had a son in 1615. The following year they went to London, where, acting as an ambassador, Lady Rebecca met numerous members of London society. After seven months, John Rolfe planned their return to Virginia, but before the voyage departed, she contracted an illness – probably pneumonia or tuberculosis – and died in 1617.

At the end of the movie John Smith is shot and has to return to England for medical treatment. This is partially historically accurate. In

October 1609 he was injured, but not by trying to protect the Powhatan Chief, but by an accidental gun powder explosion. While in England, John Smith actually ran into Pocahontas (Rebecca) one last time, and their meeting revolved around sharing stories of life in Virginia.

Because of the cheesy love story between Pocahontas and John Smith, it is easy to discount this movie as pure Disney fluff. However, the filmmakers did explore life in the colonies, and although much of the historical truth was either altered or omitted to create clear good guys and bad guys, it is a good introduction to life in early America and relations between the settlers and the Native Americans.

Key Quotes

Pocahontas: (*when father is about to kill John Smith*) No! If you kill him, you'll have to kill me too.
Powhatan Chief: Daughter, stand back.

Lon: (*searching for John Smith*) What if we run into savages?
Governor Ratcliffe: That's what guns are for! Now arm yourselves and get moving!

Grandmother Willow: (*talking to Pocahontas about her dream*) Sometimes the right path is not always the easiest one.

Governor Ratcliffe: (*trying to bring back John Smith*) This is my land! I make the laws here. And I say anyone who so much as looks at an Indian without killing him on sight, will be tried for treason…and hanged!

Governor Ratcliffe: (*giving a pep talk to his crew*) Remember what awaits us there. Freedom, Prosperity, the adventure of our live.

National Treasure: Book of Secrets

2007
Director: Jon Turteltaub
Starring: Nicolas Cage, Diane Kruger, Jon Voight
124 minutes – Rated PG

By Eric Burnett

Synopsis:

National Treasure: Book of Secrets picks up where the 2004 hit left off. Treasure hunter Benjamin Franklin Gates, popular and wealthy due to his discovery of a long-lost treasure in New York City, now must try to clear his family's name after a mysterious character, Mitch Wilkinson, claims to have proof that Gates' great, great, great grand-father was involved in the assassination of Abraham Lincoln. After decoding a fragment of John Wilkes Booth's diary, Benjamin Gates enlists the help of his ex-girlfriend and technological geek side-kick to follow a treasure trail that will eventually take them to Paris, London and Washington D.C., all in hopes of finding the legendary Lost City of Gold and bringing back honor to his maligned ancestor.

Historically Relevant Scenes	
00:01:13>00:08:32	- Assassination of Abraham Lincoln
00:43.56>00:45:02	- Background of the Lost City of Gold

Ratings:

Entertainment -   ★ ★ ★ ☆

Historical Accuracy -   ★ ☆ ☆ ☆

Historical Analysis:

Although the movie *National Treasure: Book of Secrets* is a contemporary tale, its band of treasure hunters continually allude to events from America's (and even England's and France's) past. Taking a page from Dan Brown's *The Da Vinci Code*, director Jon Turteltaub and the producers of *Book of Secrets* bring history alive by tapping the audience's interest in conspiracy theories that hint at hidden messages in famous artifacts. To say this movie is historically accurate would be like saying that another Disney tale, let's say Aladdin, is historically accurate because it mentions a Sultan and has a few street scenes with characters dressed in traditional Arabic attire. The fact is Disney is known as a "Dream Factory," and this film is yet another in its extensive library that merely mentions a smidgen of history and then elaborates upon it to craft an engagingly far-fetched tale for all ages.

However, that's not to say that the events and historical figures mentioned in this movie were all figments of the writers' imaginations. The majority of the movie revolves around events that occurred during and after the American Civil War. There is an additional event concerning the discovery of Cibola, the Lost City of Gold, but even this historical reference is put in the context of the Civil War.

According to the movie, the Civil War started to unite the states, and once and for all create a country instead of a confederation of independent units. As Nicolas Cage's character Benjamin Gates reflects, before the Civil War people always said, "The United States are..." but after the Civil War, we then said, "The United States is..."

However, this simplification only touches on the numerous causes of the Civil War which lasted from 1861 to 1865 and cost more than 600,000 American lives. Although most Americans would state that the war started to end slavery (a point never touched on in the movie), in reality there were numerous issues that were creating a wedge between the North and the South. One of the issues involved tariffs, in which the North's fledgling industrial economy wanted to protect their budding industry by setting high tariffs on foreign goods, while the South (based almost exclusively on the staple crop of cotton) wanted foreign goods at the cheapest prices possible. Another issue involved the role of the federal government. Whereas many Northern states believed the law of the United States was the ultimate authority, Southern states believed that states and local governments should have full autonomy. However, because slavery was such an integral part of Southern society, it played a critical role in bringing the two sides to arms.

After decades of compromise in which both sides maneuvered to determine the role of slavery in America and in the acquired territories, the 1850s saw a series of violent episodes that made both sides fear the other would attempt to completely alter their way of life. From the publication of *Uncle Tom's Cabin,* to the planned invasion of the South by John Brown, to the caning of Senator Sumner while in Congress, to the civil war already decimating the Kansas territory, a series of catalysts put both sides on edge, and when Abraham Lincoln was elected in 1860, the Southern states seceded and created the Confederate States of America. Starting with South Carolina, one by one the Southern states left the union, believing the newly elected president, representing the recently founded anti-slavery Republican Party, would abolish slavery, destroying their livelihood.

Four months after South Carolina seceded, war broke out. The United States armory at Fort Sumter refused to surrender to the CSA forces, and was subsequently bombed into oblivion. Lincoln met this blatant attack with force, calling for thousands of soldiers to come to the aid of their country and put the South in its place. What was initially thought by both sides to be a quick war gradually bogged down into a war of attrition in which both sides attempted to destroy the other's will to fight.

This is where *Book of Secrets* steps in. According to the film, the South was at an extreme financial disadvantage (which they were) and Queen Victoria of England hoped to even the odds by delivering to General Pike instructions on how to find Cibola – the Lost City of Gold – and return the military advantage to the Southerners. In the film, the Queen hypothetically wanted to assist the Confederacy both to weaken the growing United States and also to ensure the flow of cotton to their garment mills. In reality, the Confederate States of America never even received recognition from England as an independent sovereignty, let alone financial assistance. Granted, the CSA tried time and again to send diplomats such as James Mason to England, hoping the British reliance on Southern cotton would sway their hand. Unfortunately for the South, England's flow of cotton went relatively uninterrupted as Egypt and India stepped up to fill the demand. Also, after 1863 and Lincoln's Emancipation Proclamation that made the Civil War a war to end slavery, it was doubtful if England would have officially recognized a nation directly linked to slavery, an institution outlawed by England in 1772. Another story that surfaced from time to time was that Queen Victoria even cried after reading the slavery tale *Uncle Tom's Cabin* (although the Queen also refused to meet the book's author Harriet Beecher Stowe, so this story's validity is called into question). Regardless, the notion that Queen Victoria would somehow aide the Confederacy is quite preposterous and is antithetical to her nation's actual policy of neutrality adhered to throughout the war.

In addition to suggesting a conspiratorial role of Queen Victoria in the Civil War, *Book of Secrets* also proposes that there was much more to the assassination of Abraham Lincoln than merely the actions of the enraged Southerner John Wilkes Booth. In the film, John Wilkes Booth

NATIONAL TREASURE: BOOK OF SECRETS

and his co-conspirator Michael O'Laughlin enter a bar, open Booth's diary and share a coded message with Thomas Gates. While Thomas Gates deciphers the code, Booth excuses himself, rides off, enters the theater and assassinates Abraham Lincoln. Once Gates realizes what he is holding is a treasure map and the man who solicited his services is the man who killed the President, he discards the coded message only to be shot by O'Laughlin. Part of this coded message was salvaged by O'Laughlin and because Gates's name was on the diary entry, 150 years later, Thomas Gates is implicated in the assassination of Abraham Lincoln. This information is revealed within the first few minutes of the film, and Ben Gates along with his techie buddy and cleverly beautiful ex-girlfriend crisscross the Atlantic searching for proof to vindicate his ancestor.

In history, John Wilkes Booth did in fact enter Ford's Theater on April 14, 1865 and, during the play *Our American Cousin,* shoot Abraham Lincoln in the head before jumping to the stage, breaking his leg and shouting "Sic Semper Tyrannis!" to the shocked audience. However, the film either embellishes or leaves out key elements of the assassination attempt. First, there were at least eight co-conspirators who hatched an elaborate plot to take down the United States government by killing the top three executives - the President, the Vice-President, and the Secretary of State. In 1860, the actor John Wilkes Booth joined the Knights of the Golden Circle, referred to in the movie as a treacherous Northern group dedicated to toppling the federal government. In reality, the Knights of the Golden Circle was a secret society of men who "were committed to the preservation of slavery in the lands bordering the Caribbean" and who one day wanted to annex the nations surrounding the Caribbean to create a "Golden Circle" of slavery. From this initiation, Booth dedicated himself to overthrowing the government and even discussed killing Lincoln at his inauguration or even kidnapping him and bringing him to the South as a bargaining chip to secure an equitable prisoner exchange. The group of conspirators eventually settled on simultaneous assassinations that would kill President Abraham Lincoln, Vice-President Andrew Johnson, and Secretary of State William Seward. On the night of April 14th, both Johnson's and Seward's would-be assailants proved unsuccessful. Andrew Johnson's intended killer, George Atzerodt, chickened out, got drunk and staggered down the street, whereas Seward's attacker Lewis Powell did actually stab Seward while he laid in bed, but his inflicted wounds were not fatal (Seward had on a neck brace, due to another injury, that prevented the fatal blow).

Whereas his accomplices failed, Booth proved successful. Like in the movie, the actor came in through the back doors and because of his professional recognition, he was allowed to walk unquestioned through the corridors. However, unlike in the movie where only Lincoln and his wife are watching the play in their private suite, in reality, they were accompanied by Major Henry Rathbone and his fiancée Clara Harris. After Lincoln was shot, Rathbone immediately tried to restrain Booth, but after being stabbed several times, Rathbone released his grip, allowing Booth to jump to the stage. At this point, he uttered the now famous words "Sic Semper Tyrannis" – "Thus Ever to Tyrants" – which was the state motto of Virginia as well as the words supposedly uttered by Marcus Brutus at the assassination of Julius Caesar. Whereas most historians believe Booth shattered his leg due to the fall, others state that he only injured it later due to an accident involving his horse.

The eight accomplices to the assassination conspiracy were all tried and convicted, four of which were hung, including Booth and Mary Surratt, the first woman executed by the Federal Government. In the film, the names of Atzerodt and Powell were seen in Booth's diary (alongside the fictional Thomas Gates), as well as another conspirator – Dr. Samuel Mudd. In an attempt to demonstrate how anyone linked to the assassination would forever have their name soiled, character Benjamin Gates discusses the origin of the phrase, "Your name is mud." In real life, Dr. Samuel Mudd was the doctor who treated Booth's injured leg, and was later convicted for his complicity in the crime (even though he probably did not know the crime had been committed). Gates relates that although Mudd might have been innocent, his name was forever attached to a phrase that translates roughly to "You are a naïve, bumbling idiot." In reality, this term predates Mudd's action by thirty years, but that is irrelevant since it is forever linked to the alleged co-conspirator. However, although many of the key facts are omitted, for the most part, the individuals and events introduced regarding the assassination attempt are fairly accurate.

Back in present day, when the treasure hunters gain possession of the fictitious diary entry, they then journey across the Atlantic to find the next clue. Their four main stops will eventually be the Statue of Liberty, Buckingham Palace, the White House, and Mount Rushmore. Each of these locations does in fact exist, but the facts surrounding them were of course not pursued thoroughly in the film.

The first clue facing Benjamin Gates and his plucky little band of treasure hunters involves "Laboulaye's Lady" – a reference to Edouard Rene Lefebvre de Laboulaye, the mastermind behind the creation of the Statue of Liberty. However, Gates quickly reminds his faithful little sidekick Riley Poole that there were actually three Statues of Liberty created, and the only one Laboulaye would refer to as his "lady" rests in the Seine River in Paris, France. In reality, there are hundreds of Liberty replicas around the world, not merely the ones mentioned in Ellis Island, New York, the Jardin de Luxembourg in Paris, and the aforementioned Seine River version. Laboulaye came up with the idea and discussed it as his 1865 dinner party where he and a group of French intellectuals mused over the American and French shared history of liberty and how it would be remarkable if they could honor the Americans on their centennial anniversary. He pondered, "Wouldn't it be wonderful if people in France gave the United States a great monument as a lasting memorial to independence and thereby showed that the French government was also dedicated to the idea of human liberty?"

Although Laboulaye never lived to see his vision brought to reality, sculptor Frédéric-Auguste Bartholdi spearheaded the project, which after nearly two decades of planning and fundraising (which required a series of Parisian lotteries), the Statue of Liberty was completed and installed in New York in 1886. In addition to the difficulties raising money to construct the elaborate sculpture, the Americans struggled to raise the funds necessary to pay for the pedestal. The U.S. government failed to pass a law appropriating funds, the newly wealthy Robber Barons refused to support the project, and most Americans outside New York showed little interest in the creation of the local landmark.

Enter the brilliantly cunning newspaper mogul – Joseph Pulitzer. Over a series of months, he promised to print the names of every individual who donated money. He even wrote that the statue came as a gift from "the masses of the French people. Let us respond in like manner. Let us not wait for the millionaires to give this money. It is not a gift from the millionaires of France to the millionaires of America, but a gift of the whole people of France to the whole people of America." This strategy, coupled with a little taunting of the apathetic upper class, led to over 120,000 individual donations, easily reaching the $100,000 goal (and increasing Pulitzer's circulation by over 50,000 copies).

When America finally caught its first glimpse of "Lady Liberty" on October 28, 1886, those in attendance cast their gaze on the symbol of America that would come to promise freedom to millions of immigrants who journeyed west across the Atlantic hoping to make America their home. However, this New York version was not the focus of *National Treasure*. Instead, Gates travels to Paris to investigate a secret phrase written on the 1889 replica (gifted to the French by the Americans) that sits on the man-made Île des Cygnes (Island of the Swans). After using his buddy Riley Poole's remote controlled, camera-enabled helicopter to take up-close images, Gates finally deciphers that the inscription on the torch reads, "Across the sea, these twins stand resolute – 1876." Granted, in real life, no such inscription exists, but for the 247 IQ'd Ben Gates, he quickly realizes that this clue must be referring to two desks made out of the decommissioned ship – the HMS Resolute. And of course, where are these two desks? One is in Buckingham Palace, while the other resides in the Oval Office.

Neither location will deter our fearless band of thrill seekers, for not only do they have PhD's in random trivia, they also know how to outsmart the top security agents in both Great Britain and the United States. In Buckingham Palace, they gain access to the Queen's office by feigning a marital spout, while in D.C. they use the assets of Gates's ex-girlfriend Abigail Chase to tease and then distract a helplessly smitten White House curator into helping them enter the Oval Office. Once inside each locale, they find that hidden inside the Resolute desks are Native American maps that only become available after entering a special code. Fortunately, for the Gates' clan, Benjamin's mom just happens to be an expert in Native American languages.

This little series of plot events raises a few questions. What was the HMS Resolute? Was the wood of the boat turned into desks? Are the desks currently in Buckingham Palace and the White House? Could a Chinese Puzzle have been installed in the desks, and if so, what are the odds of a Native American message finding its way into its hidden compartments?

The HMS Resolute was in fact a British vessel that was abandoned at sea in 1854 after getting stuck in the Arctic ice, ironically while on a rescue mission itself. Oddly enough, the following year, an American ship came across the HMS Resolute which had drifted crewless over 1200 miles. Eventually the Americans repaired the ship, and returned it to England, where it remained until it was decommissioned in 1880. Queen Victoria then had her carpenters use the wood from the ship to create a desk, the Resolute desk, that was then gifted to President Rutherford B. Hayes, and since 1880, the desk has been used by every president except Presidents Johnson, Nixon, and Ford. As mentioned in the movie, Franklin D. Roosevelt did add a front panel with the presidential seal to hide his leg braces, and also little John F. Kennedy Jr. was photographed hiding inside the desk. Ronald Reagan had the desk raised a few inches so that his Californian chair could fit comfortably underneath. Today, for the low, low price of $6,000, you too can own your very own Resolute desk (replica that is). As for the Queen having a replica, this is true Hollywood fiction. Although Queen Victoria did commission the creation of small writing table from the boat's timbers, a twin table never existed.

However, according to the film, a Chinese puzzle box maker altered the desks to store a clue to a sacred Native American treasure. There is no such thing as a Chinese puzzle box, but because Japanese puzzle boxes were sold in Chinatowns across America in the 1960s and 1970s, the misnomer became accepted. In reality, Japanese craftsman began designing these elaborately decorated, finely engineered boxes in the 1830s. More decorative than practical, these Japanese Rubik's Cube-like boxes can only be opened after sliding panels in a specific order. Although they can be as tall as ten inches and have up to 125 different moves, the average box measures seven inches and has six to eight moves. Subsequently, though the technology might have existed to create a puzzle box, no craftsman actually utilized the Japanese art form to hide a treasure in a national icon.

Fortunately for Ben Gates' clever crew, the movie version did have a map and it pointed to the fabled Lost City of Gold. However, yet again, our friends at Disney chose to play loose with the historical facts. According to the movie, in 1527, a Spanish vessel sunk off the coast of Florida and of the four survivors, one named Esteban was taken to the City of Gold, but he could never find it again. This search for the City of Gold would cost the lives of thousands of men, and even General Custer would die in pursuit of the riches, and his "Last Stand" meant that "nobody would ever find it." Yet, according again to the movie, the Olmec people wrote clues to the treasure which were then discovered and passed on by the British to the Confederates in hopes that the riches would tilt the balance of power in their favor.

In reality, first, the Olmec people lived in Mexico and never would have known of a treasure in South Dakota, and because gold was barely known by the Olmecs, they wouldn't have cared anyway. Second, although four men did survive a Spanish shipwreck and walk for eight years through the American Southwest, it was a man named Cabeza de Vaca, not Esteban, who passed on the stories of the seven lost Cibola cities of gold. The fanciful stories of Mr. "Head of the Cow" set off a flurry of expeditions led by Spaniards such as Marcos de Niza and Vasquez de Coronado. It was on Niza's expedition that Esteban (one of the four hired to be a guide) was killed by the Natives, offering proof to those in power that the Indians must be hiding something. In the century that followed, the Spanish crown funded numerous failed expeditions, but it wasn't until our fearless archaeologist Benjamin Gates enters the scene that the treasure was finally discovered – beneath Mount Rushmore.

Now, this is an easy one to debunk, because I have a strong feeling that if there was in fact a treasure of gold beneath Mt. Rushmore, their attendance rates would have increased significantly in the past year. Alas, it was not to be. However, you too can visit this historic monument, built from 1927 to 1941 to draw tourists to the Black Hills area. Originally, this monument was to house head to waist carvings of the four greatest presidents in America's history, as well as engravings of the most critical territorial acquisitions in America's past. However, when the funding ran out in 1941, the building project ended. As for the Olmecs hiding treasure in the hills, that would be fairly difficult considering the land was controlled by the Lakota tribe who continue to protest the creation of the monument, considering the sacred mountain was granted to them by the U.S. Government in the 1868 Treaty of Fort Laramie. In response to Mt. Rushmore, the Lakota currently are building a stone monument of Crazy Horse that will eventually dwarf the presidential cut-out.

As we come to the end, you must be wondering, "But what about the 'Book of Secrets' – the President's Secret Book? Although President's do have access to classified information not known to the common man, the fact that there is a book that has all the information on such theories as the existence of Area 51, the other shooter in the JFK assassination, and the authenticity of the moon landing is complete rubbish. This "Book of Secrets" exists in the film as an all-encompassing conspiracy theory handbook, and now that it is in the hands of Benjamin Gates, countless adventures (aka "sequels") await.

So, although Disney spun a clever tale, it appears that historical accuracy wasn't a priority, but considering its eventual $441 million gross, the producers must have caught on to a fairly successful recipe for success – a bit of history, a smidge of conspiracy, a few national monuments and a treasure worth billions buried right under our noses. It's worked twice before, and knowing the powers-that-be at Disney, you can bet you'll be seeing National Treasure 3 before the decade is over.

Key Quotes

Benjamin Gates: (*discussing his philosophy of life*) The past is filled with incredible mysteries. The clues to solving them are all around, hidden in plain sight. But this story begins with the most famous assassination in history. Abraham Lincoln's killer, John Wilkes Booth, kept a diary. A diary that was found the night Booth was killed, with 18 pages missing. Concealed in those pages is the key to something much, much bigger. A conspiracy that crosses the globe, and a discovery that the world isn't ready to believe.

Benjamin Gates: (*planning how he will gain access to the "Book of Secrets"*) I'm gonna kidnap him. I'm gonna kidnap the President of the United States.
Riley Poole: Wouldn't it just have been easier to make an appointment?

Riley Poole: (*realizing they were probably going to continue their illogical quest*) The last time I checked, we make our living off crazy.

U.S. President: (*talking about why there will probably be a sequel*) Even if something like that really did exist, why do you think I would actually just give it to you?
Benjamin Gates: Because it will probably lead us to the discovery of the greatest Native-American treasure of all time; a huge piece of culture lost. You can give that history back to its descendants. And because you're the President of the United States, sir. Whether by innate character or the oath you took to defend the Constitution or the weight of history that falls upon you, I believe you to be an honorable man, sir.
U.S. President: Gates, people don't believe that stuff anymore.
Benjamin Gates: They want to believe it.

Gangs of New York

2002

Director: Martin Scorsese

Starring: Leonardo DiCaprio, Daniel Day-Lewis, Cameron Diaz

160 minutes – Rated R

By Wanwen Wu

Synopsis:

During the Civil War era in New York City's Five Points, Amsterdam Vallon, an Irish youth, plans to avenge his father's death at the hands of Bill 'the Butcher' Cutting. *Gangs of New York* begins in 1846, with a battle between the Dead Rabbits and the Nativists. After his father is killed, Amsterdam returns sixteen years later to the Five Points and works under Bill. While serving as Bill's right hand man, Amsterdam simultaneously plans his assassination; however, Bill 'the Butcher' was forewarned and scars Amsterdam instead, leaving him to live on disfigured and in shame. After recovering, in the midst of a city-wide riot over the newly passed Conscription Act, Amsterdam resurrects the Dead Rabbits and plans one final battle against Bill and his Nativists.

Historically Relevant Scenes	
00:01:10>00:12:51	- Gang war: Dead Rabbits vs. Nativists
00:18:12>00:22:14	- Boss Tweed/ introduction to the Five Points
00:24:18> 00:25:57	- Overview of the Five Points' gangs
00:27:42>00:30:42	- Fire in the Five Points
02:09:30>02:12:20	- Election day for sheriff
02:17:53>02:36:20	- Civil war New York Draft Riot/ gang war

Ratings:

Entertainment -   ★ ★ ☆ ☆

Historical Accuracy -   ★ ★ ☆ ☆

Historical Analysis:

Based mainly on Herbert Asbury's 1927 book *The Gangs of New York*, written from gang histories and pre-Civil War New York City journalism, *Gangs of New York* depicts New York City during a time of transition where gangs, bosses, immigrants and Nativists all struggled to survive in a world coming to grips with the chaotic impacts of industrialization. Nominated for ten Academy Awards and winning one Golden Globe, audiences have equally praised and criticized the film. Its extremely long running time of over two and a half hours and underdeveloped characters stand out as its major flaws. Also, historians claim the film inaccurately portrays gang warfare and gender and race relations of the time, especially reducing the actual racism of the era. On the other hand, the historian Tyler Anbinder, who wrote the book *Five Points*, considers the film relatively accurate, especially in its depiction of the persecution and discrimination of Irish immigrants and the immigrants' fight for a better life in America. He recognized that Scorsese made a "dramatic statement not a documentary." And as Scorsese himself admits, "This is based on history. There's no doubt about it. But it is still a film that is more of an opera than history."

Although characteristic of the Gilded Age, the film isn't set during the actual Gilded Age of 1870 through 1900. Coined in 1873 by Mark Twain, the term "Gilded Age" refers to a time when things appeared to be in a good condition in America, but beneath this gilded layer sat deep-rooted problems. While America looked to be prospering, by taking a closer look one could easily spot the internal problems: corrupt government institutions and businesses, sweat shop labor, an abundance of slums due to the influx of immigrants, and massive discrimination of both these immigrants and African-Americans. While the few rich, including the Robber Barons (industrial leaders like John D. Rockefeller, J.P. Morgan, and Andrew Carnegie who often employed "questionable" practices to increase their wealth), remained largely unaffected by issues of the time, 90% of the population lay below the poverty line, living in slums.

Of the many slums in America during the time, one of the most well-known was New York City's Five Points, named for being at the intersection of five streets: Mulberry, Orange, Little Water, Cross, and Anthony. Built over the drained, putrid smelling Collect Pond, the area retained its stench so only the poorest lived there. The areas of lower Manhattan's Five Points mentioned in *Gangs of New York* – Paradise Square, Murderer's Alley and Brickbat Mansion – existed in the actual Five Points of the mid 1850s. Although many who visited the Five Points noted the decaying conditions, such as Charles Dickens who called it a "world of vice and misery," the crime rate, for instance, may not have been as bad as the film suggests, and regardless, the rest of New York City suffered from similar conditions. In reality, the slums gained notoriety not for its soaring crime rates but for its congestion, widespread disease, terrible sanitation, alcoholism, prostitution, horrific tenement conditions and sometimes deadly and dangerous work environment.

It was no wonder that the conditions of the Five Points harbored disease and death. For example, meat and milk from diseased cows killed 70% of the children under two each year. While those living in the Southern part of New York City lived in decent houses, inhabitants of the Five Points lived in frame houses which were sometimes originally barns or stables, with both people and animals running around. The cave-like underground quarters shown in the film would have been impossible because the drained area consisted of swamp land, which caused buildings to actually sink into the ground, adding more to the slovenliness.

Tenements, with names such as the Old Brewery, Jacob's Ladder and Mulberry Bend, crammed many families together into dark rooms without a bathroom. That resulted in people using the streets as bathrooms to do their business while pigs ran around in the streets - not helping the already disgusting living conditions in a stinky swamp land. Some "old" immigrants even opened boarding houses to accommodate the newly arrived immigrants, providing them with an alternative to the regular tenements.

Also, widespread prostitution caused Five Points missionary Lewis Pease to write, "Every house was a brothel, and every brothel a hell." As depicted in the film, those from higher classes traveled to the Five Points, "some holding camphor-soaked kerchiefs to their noses to ward off the stench," to "go 'slumming' in Five Points–escorted by police–to see if the lurid tales given by reporters and missionaries were true." The way people in the Five Points lived appalled many of those who visited, including Davy Crockett, Charles Dickens, Herman Melville, Walt Whitman, and even Abraham Lincoln.

By the time of the Civil War, citywide conditions had gradually improved, although the lowest on the economic ladder, the Irish immigrants and freed slaves, continued to be the main inhabitants of the area. Unlike the film's portrayal though, not that many of them wore rags. And by that time, they began "moving up the economic ladder" as well.

The film depicts a variety of forms of entertainment, many of which accurately represented the interests of the era. Those living in the Five Points enjoyed boxing matches, cockfights, and matches between dogs and rats. People also commonly attended plays, especially those by Shakespeare or those with violent themes, and PT Barnum's Museum of Wonder did provide a source of entertainment during its time in the area.

Immigrants arriving daily contributed largely to the culture of the Five Points. In general, immigrants moved to America in search of a better life, fleeing from overpopulation, disease, famine, or religious or political persecution. The immigrants in the Five Points made the best of what they had and their work as shoemakers, tailors, masons, grocers, cigar makers, liquor dealers, and laborers (not merely gang members loitering the streets) afforded them three decent meals a day. While the film focuses on the 1.8 million Irish immigrants who arrived in America due to the Great Potato Famine of the 1840s, the film fails to explore the role of other immigrant groups such as the Germans, Welsh, Scots, Italians and Polish.

After being accustomed to a rural lifestyle, the Irish who moved to America lacked the city skills to survive and so formed many little communities, but they still couldn't afford to not live in the slums of the Five Points. The Protestant Americans of the era saw Irish Catholics as religiously and racially inferior. Many employers of the era preferred the newly freed Blacks to the Irish, and even paid Blacks more than they paid an Irishman for the same job.

What about other immigrants? Well, although the film shows quite a lot of Chinese, the only Chinese who would be in New York City at the time would be the very few sailors (no women at all). The majority of Chinese immigrants arrived later, in the 1880s, so Sparrow's Chinese Pagoda, which the characters in the film visit often, could not have existed. Quite a lot of German Jews did immigrate at around the same time as the Irish, but because they were more prosperous, they settled in the better living conditions of the South of New York City. As for other groups such as Italians, Welsh and Polish, fewer immigrated than the Irish, yet they suffered discrimination similar to what the Irish faced.

While the film primarily depicts immigrant men in gangs, it unfairly portrays immigrant women as thieves, pickpockets and prostitutes. Although many women and even children resorted to crime in order to survive, most women actually made their living as seamstresses or servants, two occupations not depicted in the film at all. Sometimes women took small roles in gang fights, throwing things out windows at opponents, but the majority of Irish immigrant women served as seamstresses. As for children, some sold matches or newspapers, some swept the streets, some joined gangs, and some became pickpockets or succumbed to child labor, but seldom did they become prostitutes.

With the huge amount of immigrants flooding in, a method of dealing with all the people needed to be devised – enter the Boss System and specifically Boss Tweed. A city "boss" could either be an electd political leader, or the man who pulled the strings of all the involved parties that made the city work. Bosses would assist the newly arrived immigrants who in turn would vote for the boss's elected leader of choice. Once he controlled the political system, he could appropriate funds to build and control public works projects so that he could both improve the city's efficiency while padding his own pocketbook. Historian Tyler Anbinder described Boss Tweed as "ambivalent about the immigrants" but aware of the critical importance of immigrant votes (as is accurately depicted in the film). William Tweed began his rise to political power by joining a volunteer fire company, a common profession at the time. From there, he joined Congress, became the face of Tammany Hall by the early 1850s, and created the "Tweed Ring" in 1857.

During its political reign, the Tweed Ring plundered New York City's coffers of at least $30 million (about $500 million today), through fake expenditures and tax favors. Tweed worked alongside gangs to steal elections, and he especially worked with Irish gangs and appointed Irish as "minor ward bosses" in order to gain Irish votes for the Democrats of Tammany Hall. By controlling Irish policemen, Tweed avoided punishment. Besides gaining Irish votes by providing them with aid, Tweed used "repeaters" in elections, getting people to vote multiple times by changing their appearance for each vote, similar to what occurs in the film's depiction of election day.

Besides elections, Boss Tweed and his Tweed Ring also concerned themselves with civic duties such as the construction and the maintenance of public facilities. Although projects such as the New York County Courthouse, or Tweed Courthouse, plundered New York's treasury by purposely using the most expensive building materials, the Tweed Ring actually improved the water supply and sewage disposal of the city. Because of those little improvements which manifested and mattered to the everyday immigrant, Tweed remained popular. He provided Irish immigrants with jobs and food in an unfamiliar land and even attempted to help poor New Yorkers buy their way out of the draft from the first Conscription Act.

By the 1860s Tweed controlled New York's state and city nominations and served as a state senator. In 1870 Tammany Hall itself unsuccessfully attempted to oust the Tweed Ring. But Tweed's eventual demise came from Thomas Nast's cartoons which revealed his unscrupulous behavior. Upon arrest, Tweed's first trial ended with no verdict and the second trial resulted in only one year of jail. After fleeing to Cuba and then Spain, the American government finally got a hold of him, sending him back to jail in the United States in 1876, where he remained until his death in 1878.

Because of the corruption, vice, and violence of New York City, an official police force called the Municipal Police was created in 1850. Despite the official police force, gangs still thrived and continued working with and for corrupt politicians. Under the mayor Fernando Wood, the Municipal Police grew so corrupt that the state created the Metropolitan Police in 1857 in order to combat the corruption of the Municipal Police. Eventually, with both police forces fighting gangs and each other, more chaos erupted and the two police forces even freed each other's prisoners.

In the same way that the multiple police forces created disorder, the multiple volunteer fire companies, which existed because of no singular public fire department, also caused more problems than they solved. With the streets crammed with buildings, fire spread easily. Because of their prevalence, insurance companies paid the first fire company that arrived, causing even more mayhem since the first person from a fire company at the scene sometimes placed a barrel over the hydrant in order to prevent others from using the hydrant, as shown in the film during a fire. That act resulted in the gang name "plug uglies" because the barrel they used was an "ugly" "plug" over the hydrant. By doing that they left the fire to rage on while waiting for the rest of their fire company to show up.

In total, thirty to forty fire companies existed, comprised mostly of men who wanted to be heroes, but like the two police forces depicted in the film, the many fire companies ended up fighting with each other while the fire destroyed the city. In the process of fighting the fires and each other, some volunteer firefighters looted the houses or shops being burnt, prompting many to join the fire companies so their own homes would not be looted if it ever caught fire. The same way the police forces grew corrupt due to corrupt politicians and government officials, the fire companies revolved around political and gang-related issues and linked themselves with gangs since the insurance money and looting financed the gangs.

Aside from the turmoil caused by the New York fire companies, New York also suffered from the preponderance of gangs. In the political arena, by beating up opponents, gangs brought votes, causing "the lines between gangs and political parties [to become] very blurred." For immigrants though, ethnic-based, territorial gangs formed to ensure their own safety since the police concerned themselves more with protecting the rich from the poor than protecting everyone. By 1855, an estimated

30,000 people had an "allegiance" to gang leaders, such as Bill 'the Butcher,' and through them to politicians such as Boss Tweed.

Numerous gangs existed during this era, some of which escaped recorded history. Many of the gangs mentioned in the film might have actually represented real gangs such as the Daybreak Boys, Frog Hollows, Nightwalkers or Broadway Twisters. With the boatfuls of Irish arriving day by day, it should be of no surprise that many, many Irish gangs formed. Before moving to America due to the Great Potato Famine, the Irish already had a history of violence and gangs, which they brought with them to America. With many immigrants receiving police or fire company jobs, they invariably became linked back to gangs and politics. Of the Irish gangs portrayed in *Gangs of New York*, all have some written evidence, either in journalism or gang history, to prove their existence, including the Shirt Tails, Plug Uglies, O'Connell Guard, Chichesters, Forty Thieves, and most important to the film, the Dead Rabbits.

Several different theories exist to explain the origin of the Dead Rabbits. One of which is that it split from the Roach Guards after someone threw a dead rabbit in the middle of the room during a meeting. While the Roach Guards used a blue stripe to identify themselves (unlike in the movie where a Nativist gang uses a blue stripe), the Dead Rabbits used a red stripe to identify themselves (correctly shown in the movie). The two became enemies, although they still united against common foes, such as Nativist gangs like the Bowery Boys. Another theory to the creation of the name comes from the Gaelic "dead ráibéad" which translates to "very big lug" or "tough guys." The Dead Rabbits, consisting of thugs and thieves, were also called the Black Birds.

Although the film shows the members of the Dead Rabbits carrying an actual dead rabbit into battle with them, that fact is questionable. Some sources claim it to be true, while others regard it as a myth. As accurately depicted in the film, the Dead Rabbits worked for Tweed's Democratic Party of Tammany Hall; however, the Irish opposed Blacks so the film inaccurately portrayed the Dead Rabbits as having a Black member. However, in the same way the film has members of the Dead Rabbits switching sides to support the Nativist gang after defeat, gang members did in fact switch sides, sometimes even multiple times.

Several of the characters portrayed to be in gangs actually existed. For example, the character of Walter 'Monk' McGinn was based loosely on Monk Eastman, a Jewish gangster of the late 1800s who ran the Eastman gang and was eventually killed by a corrupt Prohibition enforcement agent. Jack Mulraney, who in the film worked as a corrupt policeman for Bill 'the Butcher,' ran with the Gophers, and his nickname "Happy Jack" resulted from the permanent grin across his face caused b a form of facial muscle paralysis. As mentioned earlier, women sometimes took part in gang fights by throwing things at opponents, but probably none became as involved as Hellcat Maggie. The depiction of Hellcat Maggie in the film accurately shows a woman who filed her teeth to fangs and attached brass nails to her fingers in order to scratch people's eyes out or cut their ears off in fights. And similar to the film, she collected the ears of opponents in a jar.

For the large array of Irish gangs who often fought each other, their common enemy remained the "Nativists" or "Native American" gangs like the Bowery Boys, American Guard or Slaughter Housers. The most famous of which, the anti-Catholic and anti-Irish Bowery Boys, often fought the Dead Rabbits and O'Connell Guard. While the Bowery Boys actively took part in the New York Draft Riots, looting buildings and fighting opposing gangs, by the end of the 1860s the gang split up into many other groups and soon enough, the Bowery Boys ceased to exist.

Although the Bowery Boys originally worked with Tammany Hall, they ended up associating themselves with the Know Nothing Political Party, named because its members acted dumb and pretended they "knew nothing" when questioned. The Bowery Boys decided to align themselves with the Know Nothings because they too saw the Irish immigrants as scum and held the same anti-Irish and anti-Catholic spirit. A Detroit Know Nothing recommended true Americans to "carry your revolver and shoot down the first Irish rebel that dare insult your person as an American!" Another called Catholics "mindless 'emissaries of bloody and bigoted Rome,' bishops' pawns incapable of voting their individual consciences." In the film, Bill Cutting reflects this belief when he comments, "[the Irish] vote how the archbishop tells 'em. And who tells the archbishop? Their king in the pointy hat that sits on his throne in Rome."

Similar to how Boss Tweed influenced Irish gangs to help him steal elections, the Know Nothings and their gangs messed with elections by attacking immigrants, the largest group of voters in the Five Points. Nationwide, Know Nothings received support from many Republicans, running on a "xenophobic platform," asking for the "purification of the ballot box" and aiming to protect Americans from foreign influence, seen in the film with the Nativist flag that states, "Native Americans beware of foreign influence."

Because of their disparaging attitude towards the Irish, many gang fights broke out between the Protestant Nativist and Irish Catholic gangs. But a lot of the time fights broke out between Irish gangs themselves. In general, the depiction of gang fights in the movie exaggerates the events. Not many brought weapons into fights and not as many died as shown. Fists remained the most common weapons, not axes and knives as depicted in the film, while bats and clubs sometimes appeared, but not handguns until the late 1850s. As for the battle between the Dead Rabbits and Natives at the beginning of the film, historians claim it to be "reasonably true to history" except for the death toll. An actual battle of the Dead Rabbits and Plug Uglies against the Bowery Boys did occur in 1857 (not 1846 as in the film), with 800 to 1000 involved, resulting in twelve deaths, far less than the exaggerated casualties shown in the film.

Although the history of the Bowery Boys remains vague, several members of the gang have become relatively well-known, with the most famous being Bill 'the Butcher' Poole. As it can be assumed by the name, the character of Bill 'the Butcher' Cutting in the film reflects the life of the actual Bill 'the Butcher.' The actual 'Butcher' was of English descent, had a wife and a son, and lived from 1821 to 1855 and not in the Five Points. He took part in gambling, bare-knuckle boxing, street fighting, worked in the Red Rover fire company, and participated in many gang activities as a member of the Bowery Boys. Unlike the character in the film, William Poole did not have a glass eye. As can be assumed by his name, he was an actual butcher. He learned the trade from his father, and although no proof exists of whether he actually murdered people with his "knife handling" skills, he did injure people and became known for the "bloodiness of his actions," similar to Day-Lewis' character in the film who believes "[fear] preserves the order of things."

Because of his tactics, those in the Five Points and lower Manhattan area feared him, but Poole did not hold as much power as 'the Butcher' depicted in the film. In actuality, he worked for political bosses and used violence in order to ensure votes, and with his hatred of Irish immigrants, he joined the Know Nothing political party, and as some sources say he became its leader. Similar to the issues between the characters of Bill 'the Butcher' and Amsterdam Vallon, the real 'Butcher' faced many issues with John Morrissey, an Irishman who worked for Tammany Hall, which led to 'the Butcher's' death in 1855, when he was shot by Morrissey's friend, a fellow Irishman, Lew Baker. Strangely, Poole survived for nearly two weeks after initially being shot, and supposedly, with his last breath he said, "Goodbye Boys, I die a true American" and "what grieves me most is thinking that I've been murdered by a set of Irish." Although he uttered similar last words in the film as in real life, Bill 'the Butcher' Poole died eight years before the New York Draft Riots even occurred.

As issues between gangs tore New York City apart, the United States simultaneously tore itself apart with the Civil War, which serves as a backdrop to the issues in New York City's Five Points in the film. New Yorkers largely opposed the Civil War and often blamed and persecuted Blacks, causing Blacks to be placed under federal protection. The Civil War itself added to the mess of New York, but the first Conscription Act intensified the mess. Issued on March 3, 1863, the Conscription Act called for 300,000 soldiers, requiring men from ages 20 through 45 to put their names in for the July 11 drawing that would determine who would go to battle. With the numbers killed in battle published in newspapers, civilians feared being drafted into the Civil War. But by paying a "commutation fee" of $300 (around $5000 today), or by finding a substitute, one could avoid being potentially drafted. These realities led to intense backlash from immigrants. From the Irish immigrants' perspective, first off, they disliked the Blacks who earned more than they did for the same jobs and they refused to fight for them. Secondly, they could afford nowhere near the commutation fee. And lastly, Union army members recruited Irish to fight fresh off the arriving boats, which undoubtedly made the Irish dislike the Union even more.

Leonardo DiCaprio's character stated, "they read out the draftees names' like they was already dead." Subsequently, the Conscription Act led to four days and nights of rioting, in what came to be known as the New York Draft Riots. In Scorsese's depiction of the Draft Riots, several inaccuracies arose. First, Scorsese made the riots seem to occur at the same time as the gang wars of the 1830s and 1840s. Second, while the riots occurred during the summer, the film shows it occurring during winter. Third, in the film, the navy fires canons from the harbor (a completely erroneous depiction). The idea of placing candles on windowsills to demonstrate support for riot was not done for this conflict, but instead for an anti-Black riot that occurred thirty years earlier. In spite of these errors, Scorsese accurately conveys the essence of the Draft Riots: the belief that the Civil War was a "rich man's war" but a "poor man's fight." Because most of the rioters were Irish, they refused to fight for Blacks after having to compete with them for jobs, and they subsequently lynched or beat many Blacks and burned Colored churches and orphanages. Started by the Black Joke fire company, rioters first attacked draft offices, robbing and looting buildings in their path and targeting any Blacks and abolitionists they passed.

Rioting raged on for four days and nights from July 13 through 16, until Lincoln sent in the Federal Army, who arrived in New York City straight from the Gettysburg battlefield. Although the army eventually restored order, by the end of the riot, with 50,000 to 70,000 involved, between 100 and 1000 were killed or wounded, including rioters, and $1.5 to 2 million worth of damage was inflicted (equivalent to $25 to 35 million today). Despite the rioting, by August the drawing of draftees' names continued.

After suffering through the Civil War and then decades of the Gilded Age, America welcomed the arrival of the Progressive Era, which lasted from 1902 to 1920. During the Progressive Era, muckrakers finally exposed the terrible living conditions of the Five Points in works such as Jacob Riis' book *How the Other Half Lives*, which brought to light the reality of tenement living and child labor in the Five Points. By the 1920s, the Teddy Roosevelt-led Progressive Era had enacted numerous reforms at the federal, state and local levels to reduce the influence of bosses while improving the working and living conditions of urban dwellers.

Although *Gangs of New York* met criticism, historian Anbinder argued that the film showed "that the making of the multi-ethnic America we know today was a lot more difficult than we remember. We tend to think that our ancestors were not like immigrants today, but in almost every way they were." With the overall accurate sense of the plight of immigrants and by showing the World Trade Center at the end of the film even after the September 11th terrorist attack, Scorsese's decision "to make a film about the ones who built New York, not the ones who tried to destroy it" rings true. However, as the film concludes, Amsterdam Vallon predicts, "And no matter what they did to build this city up again for the rest of time, it would be like no one even knew we was ever here." Fortunately for a generation of Americans, Scorsese rebuilt the world of 19th century America, and the lives of those founders of urban America will never be lost again.

Key Quotes

Boss Tweed: (*while talking to Bill 'the Butcher' about an alliance*) The appearance of the law must be upheld, especially while it's being broken.

Bill the Butcher: (*when Johnny claims he's with the Natives not the Irish*) A Native is a man what's willing to give his life for his country.

Jenny Everdeane: (*after bumping into people*) I leave you in the grace and favor of the Lord.

Bill the Butcher: (*walking down the streets with Amsterdam after beating up McGloin*) Now everything you see belongs to me, to one degree or another. The beggars and newsboys and quick thieves here in Paradise, the sailor dives and gin mills and blind tigers on the waterfront, the anglers and amusers, the she-hes and the Chinks- everybody owes, everybody pays because that's how you stand up against the rising of the tide.

Amsterdam Vallon: (*sitting eating with Jenny, Johnny and other Irish after his recovery*) Get all of us together, and we ain't got a gang. We got an army. And all you need's a spark, right? Just one spark, something to wake us all up.

Bill the Butcher: (*sitting with an American flag draped over him while talking to Amsterdam the night he is shot in the theater*) Civilization is crumbling.

Boss Tweed: (*after the draft riots*) We're burying a lot of votes down here tonight.

From Hell

2001
Director: The Hughes Brothers
Starring: Johnny Depp, Heather Graham, Ian Holm
122 minutes – Rated R

By Stevie Day

Synopsis:

Set in London's Whitechapel District, *From Hell* follows the sadistically horrific events surrounding the Jack the Ripper murders of 1888. Fighting against the clock, Scotland Yard Inspector Frederick Abberline uses his immense investigative knowledge and supposedly drug-fueled psychic ability to solve the case as the Ripper slowly picks off the prostitutes of Whitechapel including Mary Kelly and her companions. Delving deeper and deeper into the sinister underworld of London, Abberline discoverers the true nature of the grisly murders.

Historically Relevant Scenes	
00:02:02>00:04:05	- Views of 1888 London
00:52:21>00:53:10	- More Views of 1888 London
00:10:43>00:12:59	- Opium Den
00:38:11>00:41:16	- Ripper's methods of luring the victims
01:12:16>01:14:04	- Freemason Initiation
01:15:01>01:15:20	- "From Hell" Letter
01:50:35>01:52:00	- Freemason's trial of Gull

Ratings:

Entertainment - ★ ★ ★ ★

Historical Accuracy - ★ ★ ☆ ☆

Historical Analysis:

The Hughes Brothers 2001 film *From Hell*, their fourth big screen outing, offered a stylized, "MTV Generation" retelling of the legendary Jack the Ripper murders. The movie is partly based on the graphic novel of the same name by Alan Moore and Eddie Campbell, and on Stephen Knight's *Jack the Ripper: The Final Solution* (1976). The Brother's film is a splash of fact watered down by fantasized conspiracies of Knight's work and ghastly amounts of gore.

The movie is set in London's Whitechapel District and in order to portray the ten week atrocity, they created what is hailed as one of the most accurate and "authentic sets ever designed" in Prague and London. They successfully rebuilt Whitechapel in all its grime-coated, filth-ridden glory, rather than using CGI or other new age techniques.

In this infamous district, "The Ripper," who "vanished into London fog just as readily as he appeared," managed to slaughter at least five prostitutes, but is believed to have killed more. Five other victims suffered deaths that resembled that of the five confirmed murders – slashing of the throat and assorted mutilations.

Soon after mutilating and murdering his last victim, the Ripper was never heard from or ever stepped into the history books again. During the murders, many letters claiming to be written by the Ripper himself, all of which boasted the horrific acts and alluded to further gruesome deeds, were sent to newspapers and police. Almost all of these are thought to be spurious (apart from one which was attached with half a kidney and signed "From Hell"). Seen as one of the first true serial killers, the Ripper gave birth to tabloid journalism, as journalistic scavengers competed for their audience. Before his horrific killing spree, only a few hundred papers were published in London but after him "a thousand papers emerged."

Even though the identity of the Ripper still remains a mystery, *From Hell* offers a slew of possible killers before settling on the movie's chosen killer – Sir William Gull. Gull in the movie, and in real life, was one of the key physicians for Queen Victoria and the Royal Family of England at the time. Seen in the movie as a member of the Freemasons, he initially is used as their puppet of destruction, although he sort of breaks free and goes on an insane, homicidal rampage slicing out women's "money-makers" left right and centre, not exactly what the Masons had in mind when they first employed his services.

While in popular fiction and in the film the Ripper is seen as a well-dressed man in a top hat and long coat who carries a surgeon's bag, according to some historians and Ripper experts this is not how the Ripper would have looked. He was most likely lower class and would have been dressed in average pauper clothing of the period. As for the bag, it is possible that he had access to one, but this is unsubstantiated as he only used one type of knife for all the murders. The methods used by Gull in the movie are completely embellished, hardly reflecting those of the real Ripper. Firstly, he worked alone by trapping his victims in back alleys rather than using carriages or sub-intelligent peons to ship him around London's backstreets as the movie's faux-Ripper did. Nor did he lure them with grapes or alcohol as the only grape stalks found during the murders were on one victim and it was believed to be dropped by a reporter. All the real Ripper's victims were random, most likely being picked from whoever he saw along the streets. Also, unlike in the film, he did not move their bodies from where they were killed. But it is true that the Ripper obviously had some anatomical knowledge as he did remove organs with great precision and in very little time.

In the film, the murder victims are depicted as a circle of friends, all hard working prostitutes, banding together to survive the harsh London streets. As Mary Kelly says, "England doesn't have whores, just a great mass of really unlucky women." The real victims had no connection to each other apart from the fact they were all prostitutes. Each of them was also cast inaccurately by replacing the disgusting Victorian women of the night that they were, with young attractive Hollywood starlets. Although Mary Kelly was described as being better looking than your average prostitute, she was not Heather Graham better looking (no prostitutes had teeth THAT minty clean). Kelly's friends would have definitely been older and less easy on the eyes. Two of the Ripper's victims, Annie Chapman and Martha Tabram, were overweight at the time and another, Polly Nichols, had grey hair and reportedly was missing teeth (an occupational advantage perhaps?) In addition, Elizabeth Stride, the fourth of the five victims, was not a verified lesbian as seen in the film, although there are accounts of her being a little friendlier with females than was normally accepted.

The murders themselves are reasonably accurate, with the gore factor being pretty spot on, if not a tad excessive. However, Polly Nichols, her real name being Mary Nichols and the first victim of the Ripper, was missing no organs when killed and Martha Tabram had 39 stab wounds rather than the 'vagina-ectomy' and cut throat shown in the film.

The protagonist played by Johnny Depp in the film was in fact the actual inspector for the Ripper case. Frederick Abberline was in charge of solving the Ripper murders and hopefully apprehending the killer. He is the source of almost all our knowledge of the Ripper. If anyone knew who the Ripper might have been, it was Abberline. The actual primary suspect Abberline believed to be the Ripper - George Chapman, a Polish immigrant who had murdered his wives and had surgical knowledge - was left out of the film, replaced instead by Gull and the Royal Conspiracy.

The Hughes brothers paint a very different picture of the real life Abberline, transforming him from a humble English police officer to the "Victorian equivalent of a crack addict." To begin, he was not a drug addict; he was by no means addicted to "chasing the dragon," inhaling pipe after pipe of opium while pouring himself the highly hallucinogenic alcohol absinthe. Abberline was also not the young, ruggedly charming man Depp happens to be. Abberline was in fact much older, around 45 at the time of the murders, and was described to be "portly with the general appearance of a banker." Unfortunately we have no photos of what Abberline looked like so his true visage is as mysterious as the Ripper himself.

To some critics, almost as horrific as the portrayed murders, is Depp's pathetic *cockney* (the accent of lower class Londoners) accent, dubbed by the critics 'mockney'. Abberline was upper middle class and wouldn't have had such an accent in the first place. Removed as well from the film was the fact Abberline had both a wife and two children. Apparently, this reality was less marketable than having Depp's character engage in a fling with saucy Miss Graham's sultry prostitute. Historically speaking, Abberline and Kelly never met prior to the murders and there is no evidence for anything more than a professional relationship between them. Abberline actually died in 1929 from natural causes at the age of 86, not due to an opium overdose, as depicted in the film.

The character of Abberline shown in *From Hell* is more a composite creation, combining the character described in Moore and Campbell's graphic novel and the 1800's psychic Robert Lee James, who at the time claimed to police to have solved the Ripper case. Abberline's partner Godley, played by Robbie Coltrane, also was not cast correctly. The real Godley was 13 years younger than Abberline and more 'streamlined' than Coltrane has been in years.

The few historical accuracies that managed to survive the Hughes brothers' gory interpretation end here. Taking over are the composite reflections of conspiracy theorists and fiction writers, who together proposed a completely inaccurate conclusion to the murders.

The film's grand conspiracy has the reigning Prince Albert marry prostitute Anne Cook and they subsequently have a child. In order to prevent this child from being heir to the throne of England, the Queen contracts the Freemasons to kill all the witnesses (Mary Kelly and her filthy friends), lobotomize Cook, haul Albert off somewhere, and dispose of the child in some undisclosed location.

To begin with, the concept of Albert getting jiggy with a prostitute is, according to film critic Richard Scheib, "akin to say our Prince Charles having an affair with a $5 crack whore." It just didn't happen. Albert was actually a homosexual and had no interest in women, eventually dying alone of influenza in 1892. There is no proof of Anne

Cook ever having an affair with any member of the Royal family or having a child.

The crown employed the Freemasons to oversee the killing. They are a real organization that have been seen as a "secretive cult-like establishment" for centuries, but have never been linked to any murders, especially not those of Jack the Ripper. The Freemasons were founded in 1717 and rose to popularity in the late 18th and early 19th century. They existed as more of a gentlemen's club across America and Europe. Many famous figures were Freemasons such as American presidents George Washington, Andrew Jackson, and Franklin D. Roosevelt. The Masons once wielded significant political influence on governments across Europe and the Americas, but this influence has long since died out. The latter half of the movie reveals the Freemasons as the guiding hand behind the Ripper killings, using Sir Gull as their pawn. Due to the overstepping of his duties, and the ensuing chaos caused, Sir William Gull is condemned to an insane asylum and lobotomized.

Sir William Gull was certainly never a knife wielding maniac who chopped up prostitutes and the Freemasons most definitely did not oversee the mafia style executions on the streets of London while forwarding citizens to the local asylum for lobotomies when they became a tad embarrassing.

Although *From Hell's* version of the Jack the Ripper murders and the Royal Family/Freemason cover-up behind them is quite entertaining, it certainly never happened. Instead the movie exists only as a 21st century horror flick built around a cult legend with some historical truths thrown in from time to time.

Key Quotes

Sir William Gull: (*During a speech to Abberline after being confronted and called out as the Ripper*) One day men will look back and say that I gave birth to the twentieth century.

Masonic Governor: (*during Gull's trial before the Masons*) You stand before your peers, masons and doctors both.
Sir William Gull: I have no peers present here.
Masonic Governor: What?
Sir William Gull: No man amongst you is fit to judge... the mighty art that I have wrought. Your rituals are empty oaths you neither understand nor live by. The Great Architect speaks to me. He is the balance where my deeds are weighed and judged... not you.

Mary Kelly: (*While explaining her background to Abberline*) England doesn't have whores, just a great mass of really unlucky women.

Flyboys

2006
Director: Tony Bill
Starring: James Franco, Martin Henderson, Jean Reno
139 minutes – Rated PG-13

By Eric Burnett

Synopsis:

Flyboys tells the story of a group of American young men who, in the early years of World War I, head to France to join a newly-created military squadron of fighter pilots. Coming from a variety of socioeconomic backgrounds, this hastily-assembled group learns to overcome individual character flaws while uniting to defeat the Germans in aerial dogfights that break out over the French countryside. The main character, Blaine Rawlings, leaves behind a bankrupted farm in Texas and becomes a hero of the air and a lover of a local French farm girl.

Historically Relevant Scenes	
00:03:30>00:07:50	- American enlistment
00:35:30>00:44:00	-Dogfight
01:17:45>01:24:40	- Dogfight and Trench Warfare
01:41:10>01:48:30	- Attack on the Zeppelin

Ratings:

Entertainment -   ★ ★ ☆ ☆

Historical Accuracy -   ★ ★ ☆ ☆

Historical Analysis:

On June 28, 1914, Gavrilo Princip, a member of the Serbian nationalist organization the Black Hand, assassinated Archduke Frans Ferdinand of Austria and set in motion a series of events that would lead to the greatest war in human history (until of course World War II), costing over 40 million casualties. The leaders of both the Entente Powers (France, England, and Russia) and the Central Powers (Germany, Austria-Hungary and the Ottoman Empire) painfully learned that in the age of industrial warfare, the reliance on outdated Napoleonic military tactics would only lead their troops to senseless slaughter. Within a few short months, the conflict bogged down to what would become years of trench warfare where thousands of men would race across no-man's land hoping to escape the ceaseless onslaught of machine gun fire and artillery bombardment. As the war progressed, each side developed new methods of warfare to break through the opposition's line. One of these methods employed a technology created only a decade earlier - the airplane.

Just a few short years after the Wright Brothers' successful testing of an airplane at Kitty Hawk, North Carolina in 1903, the European powers looked at how best to adapt this civilian invention to military combat. In 1910, the French created the Aéronautique Militaire, the French Air Service, where pilots gained the training necessary to conduct military reconnaissance. Credited as being the world's first air force, the Aéronautique Militaire developed several escadrilles (squadrons), one of which was the Escadrille Americaine.

Created in 1916, the Escadrille Americaine was formed to both assist the French effort against the Germans, but also as a method of putting political pressure on the Americans to enter the war. The logic being that if the French could attract American boys to fight for and die for the allied cause, the American people would lobby their government to enter on the side of the French and British. Almost immediately, the Germans demanded that the French change the name or else risk the allegedly neutral status of the United States. Eventually, the group settled on the symbolic name Lafayette Escadrille, in honor of the Marquis de Lafayette, a Frenchman who fought for the Americans during the Revolutionary War.

This is where *Flyboys* takes off. The movie starts off with a brief montage showing the diversity of young men drawn to the Western Front - the pampered, lost aristocrat, the military legacy, the crass mid-westerner, the oppressed black man, and the rebellious Texas rancher. These men finally meet on the French airfield and are subsequently warned that the "life expectancy for pilots around here [is]…three to six weeks." Although a bit exaggerated, the casualty rates of these first pilots far surpassed that of the average infantryman. For World War I, approximately 110,000 enlisted men died out of a total of 4,700,000 American soldiers - about a 1:43 ratio. For members of the Lafayette Escadrille, that ratio soared to 1:4 (63 out of 265).

In spite of the inherent danger in this new form of warfare, the Americans still found success, scoring 159 enemy kills and seeing eleven members of the squadron awarded with the title of "flying ace" (having five or more enemy kills). Part of the reason for their success was their cocky, reckless demeanor. In this world of death and danger, the

American pilots survived by creating for themselves a safe haven with a party atmosphere back at base camp. *Flyboys* illustrates this wild, at times juvenile, environment through the frequent bar scenes and even through the squadron's adopted mascot - a lion named Whiskey. In reality, the Lafayette Escadrille did have a raunchy reputation for carousing and hitting the bottle. And as for the mascot, there was a lion named Whiskey. There also was Whiskey's lion companion - Soda.

When the men weren't hydrating themselves in the local pub, they were up in the skies destroying the German enemies. However, it is these combat scenes where the movie veers from reality. At times the aerial theatrics look more like the Death Star scene from George Lucas's Star Wars, than actual 1916 aerial combat. When one considers the previous works of producer Dean Devlin - the *Patriot*, *Independence Day*, and *Godzilla* - should it really be a surprise that the final edit leaned more toward excitement than historical accuracy? Through the miracle of CGI, the French Nieuport 17s and the German Fokker Dr. I tri-planes perform feats that are, and were, gravitationally impossible. Also, when eventually shot down, both planes explode as if their entire crafts were filled with a portable nuclear device. Reality would have had produced dramatically less pyrotechnics. Speaking of being shot down, the movie depicts Germans as possessing anti-aircraft artillery with accuracy and power that would not actually enter the world of combat until thirty years later during World War II.

One of the most obvious historical deviations was the type of planes used by the Germans. The movie has the Germans almost universally using red, Fokker tri-planes (and yes...a few film critics had fun throwing a few "Meet the Fockers" puns into their reviews). In reality, the Germans were far more apt to fly the two-winged Albatross. And as for the color red, *only* the famed German ace pilot Manfred von Richtofen, the "Red Baron," adorned his plane in red. In a far more interesting twist of fate than what was explored in the film, von Richtofen's fellow pilots followed their leader's precedent and painted their planes a variety of flamboyant, vibrant colors. Some even nicknamed this aeronautic spectacle the "Flying Circus." Of course, the director chose the red Fokkers so that the audience could readily distinguish the good guys from the bad guys. You can almost imagine a 13 year-old in the audience whispering to his buddy, "Oh...so the red planes with three wings are the evil Germans...and that black plane is the really bad guy." This was one of those instances where in an attempt to clearly delineate the protagonist from the antagonist, the director dropped a perfect opportunity to bring history alive.

One fascinating element of air combat the director did insert was the dreaded, awe-inspiring zeppelin. Longer than a football field and as tall as the Statue of Liberty, these inflated machines could reach speeds of 65 miles per hour and could bomb targets hundreds of miles from their takeoff. For many in the audience whose knowledge of the zeppelin extended to a rock band from the 1970s and possibly the Hindenberg, seeing the zeppelin as a military machine was quite a surprise. In reality, for civilians, the zeppelin was the most feared technological beasts of World War I. Invented by Ferdinand von Zeppelin at the turn of the century after seeing balloons used during the American Civil War, the zeppelins were initially used for bombing and reconnaissance. For the first few years of the war, they were indestructible because they flew too high and anti-aircraft artillery was harmless. Their greatest threat was weather and transport. Almost as many zeppelins were destroyed being moved from hangers to airports than were destroyed in the air.

When the zeppelins began targeting civilians in 1915, war changed forever. The Germans initially meant for the zeppelins to attack military installations, but because they had to fly at night and high above the clouds, their bombing accuracy couldn't be guaranteed. This was made worse by the nighttime blackouts demanded by the British. Subsequently, on January 19, 1915, two zeppelins cruised across the London skies, carrying close to 20,000 pounds of cargo and dropped a series of bombs on the unsuspecting civilians below. Although only four civilians died and less than a hundred thousand dollars in damage was incurred, the psychological and military repercussions would be felt for decades. Civilians were now targets. The battlefield had extended to the city. Civilians panicked and military and political leaders rushed to assuage their fears. In England alone, twelve fighter squadrons and over ten thousand men were diverted from the front to defend the homeland from these "giants of the air."

Eventually, technology would end the reign of the zeppelins as incendiary bullets and anti-aircraft fire advanced to the point that zeppelins could be destroyed. Because the zeppelins traveled almost exclusively at night, the British developed a successful strategy of downing the craft where they would point three searchlights at the target while allied aircraft attacked the undercarriage with machine gunfire.

One of the more dramatic scenes in *Flyboys* deals with the downing of a zeppelin. However, in a historical improbability, the movie zeppelin attacks during the daylight, and its target is Paris. It is only destroyed after the American squadron leader, after being riddled with a virtual bevy of bullets, points his Nieuport 17 toward the zeppelin and with kamikaze courage flies his ship directly into the heart of the zeppelin. The ensuing explosion sends the beast to its death, but not before a German gunner uses his superhuman speed of 12 miles per hour to outrun the hydrogen fire. Movie enthusiasts almost immediately noted that the kamikaze scene seems quite similar to Devlin's climax in *Independence Day,* and the zeppelin running incident looks remarkably like one from the 1991 film - the *Rocketeer.*

Not only did the filmmakers borrow heavily from plot points of previous films, they also employed the tried-and-true method of only offering one-dimensional stereotypical characters. The English soldiers are boring, emotionless automatons, the French are culturally elitist pushovers, the Germans are cruel, heartless heathens, and the Americans are young, cocky nonconformists. The Americans at least receive a bit more character development, though each character was seemingly given a maximum of two personality traits to avoid confusing the audience. Reed Cassidy is the wise, angry mentor who does things his own way. Blaine Rawlings is the Texas cowboy who at first despises Reed, but realizes that he actually wants to be like him. Briggs Lowry is a rich kid who wants to impress his dad. Eugene Skinner is a black boxer with a chip on his shoulder due to the racial injustice back home. And William Jensen is the farm boy just wanting to carry on the family's military tradition. These characters were obviously chosen to drive home the point that Americans volunteered for a variety of reasons and came from diverse backgrounds.

Although all of these characters are fictional and the movie claims to be only "inspired by a true story," three characters bear remarkable resemblance to real life World War I pilots. Cassidy resembles the American pilot Raoul Lufberry, one of the oldest pilots in the Lafayette Escadrille, and a man known for borrowing planes and shooting down Germans. Whereas in the movie, Cassidy makes many of these additional trips, each time shooting down German pilots, in reality Lufberry only got away with one such escapade. Also in the movie is the Black Falcon, and because the Black Falcon is widely recognized as the deadliest German pilot and because he too flies a plane with a distinguishing color, one can only assume the director was channeling the spirit of the Red Baron. Unlike the movie death that sees the Black Falcon shot to death by Blaine Rawlings' handgun, the actual cause of the Red Baron's death has proven inconclusive. During a low flying dogfight, either he was shot dead by a single bullet from ground troops or from a pursuing Canadian pilot.

Whereas the true identity of Cassidy and the Black Falcon are only hinted at, it is quite obvious that the black boxer turned pilot, Eugene Skinner, was created specifically from the life of Eugene Ballard, the first African-American pilot in the world. Nicknamed the "Black Swallow of Death" for his two enemy kills, Ballard, like the Skinner character, was also a boxer with a fierce temper. Born and raised in Georgia, Ballard eventually fled the racist oppression of America and spent the next four decades in France, first as a member of the French Foreign Legion and later as a pilot in the Lafayette Escadrille. In the closing moments of the movie, Skinner's epilogue states that he returned to America to fly mail carrying air planes. In reality, Bullard tried to continue his career in the military, but after being denied entry into the American Air Force due to race, Ballard eventually joined the French infantry and then spent his post-war years running nightclubs around Paris. During World War II, he was forced to flee France, but was later injured in the back while in Spain. At the tale end of the war, he returned to America and spent the remaining years of his life in relative obscurity doing odd jobs as an elevator attendant, security guard and perfume salesman. He died alone in anonymity of stomach cancer in 1961, but in 1994 he was posthumously commissioned as Second Lieutenant in the US Air Force, a recognition of his success that unfortunately came eighty years too late.

Eugene Ballard and the rest of the Lafayette Escadrille will forever hold a place in America's military history. Although the movie *Flyboys* might have glazed over some of the facts, they did succeed in demonstrating how a small group of American men, coming from all corners of society, sacrificed their lives while showing how the rest of the 20th century would need to take notice of the battle for the skies.

Key Quotes

Reed Cassidy: (*revealing to Rawlings the senselessness of the war*) Some day it'll just end. Everyone will go home, get on with their lives. Tall grass will cover the battlefields. And all the pilots we've lost won't mean a damn thing.

Eugene Skinner: (*speaking of France*) This country has been good to me. Better than my own. I owe them something.

Captain Thenault: (*advising Rawlings on how he should respond to German atrocities*) Reports can be filed. But you want "justice"? You're the man in the air. You're the man with the gun!

Lawrence of Arabia

1962
Director: David Lean
Starring: Peter O'Toole, Alec Guinness, Anthony Quinn
216 minutes – Rated PG

By Jack Pitfield

Synopsis:

This is a movie about the life of T. E. Lawrence who used his knowledge of Arab culture to play a major part in the war against the Ottoman Empire during WWI. Although he began with a mundane job with the British intelligence, Lawrence quickly became the liaison between Prince Feisal – leader of the Arab revolt – and General Alenby – commander of the British forces in the Middle East.

Historically Relevant Scenes

00:00:00>00:01:00	- Lawrence's Death
00:06:40>00:10:40	- Lawrence's Job at Cairo
00:42:00>00:44:30	- Bedouin Justice
00:45:00>00:47:30	- Attack on Aquaba
01:29:00>01:32:00	- Raid on Turkish train
02:44:00>02:51:00	- Lawrence's Punishment by Turkish Troops
03:10:00>03:17:20	- Slaughter of Turkish Troops
03:23:40>03:31:00	- Damascus under Arab Control

Ratings:

Entertainment -   ★ ★ ★ ☆

Historical Accuracy -   ★ ★ ☆ ☆

Historical Analysis:

The movie *Lawrence of Arabia* discusses the fall of the Ottoman Empire during World War I, and the role played by British soldier T.E. Lawrence in leading the Arab Revolt against the Ottoman forces. The Ottoman Empire is one of the world's longest running empires, spanning from the 13th century to its dissolution after World War I in 1918. At its height it controlled territory in Europe, Asia and Africa, and although it was toward the end labeled the "sick man of Europe" due to its crumbling power, its ability to control the diverse groups in the volatile Middle East has in recent years gained more acclaim.

World War I started in Europe in 1914 after the assassination of Archduke Franz Ferdinand, the heir to the throne of the Austro-Hungarian Empire, set in motion a series of alliances whose members had pledged to defend each other in military conflict. Tension in Europe had been rising for decades with the growing German nation threatening to economically and militarily diminish the worldwide role of the British, French and Belgium nations. After the rise of nationalistic fervor in the first part of the 20th century, coupled with the industrialized arms race, the key nations in Europe seemed to look for an excuse to hastily defeat their competition in military combat. This illusion of a quick defeat quickly evaporated after the reality set in that Napoleonic tactics in the age of industrialized warfare would only lead to astronomical casualty reports.

Three primary fronts emerged during the war – 1) the Western Front in France where the French, British and later American forces squared off against the Germans, 2) the Eastern Front where Russia attacked the Austro-Hungarian and German military, and 3) the Middle Eastern Theatre where the Western European nations worked with the Arab kingdoms to end control of the Ottoman Empire. It is this third front that provides the backdrop to the film *Lawrence of Arabia.*

Between 1916 and 1918, with the Ottoman Empire firmly aligned with Germany and Austria-Hungary, the Sharif of Mecca, Sayyid Hussein bin Ali, took this period of military conflict to attempt to dislodge the Arab region from Ottoman control and create an independent Arab nation in the Middle East. The French and British quickly picked up on the strategic benefit of supporting a third front, and sent in Captain T.E. Lawrence, a graduate student who had extensive first hand knowledge of Middle Eastern topography due to his many travels. It would be his task to encourage and support the types of asymmetrical (non-traditional – usually involving sabotage and other attacks on infrastructure) warfare needed to draw away resources from the European theaters.

T.E. Lawrence had gained his expertise prior to the outbreak of the Great War. After 1,100 miles of walking in the hostile Ottoman Empire, carrying only a camera, revolver, notebook, and socks, Thomas Edward Lawrence returned to Oxford University in England in 1909 to complete his thesis on how the Crusades affected European military architecture (this emphasis replaced his earlier interest in medieval pottery). The journey, which lasted over three months, was an important step for Lawrence. Not only did the trip show his ability to successfully plan and undertake trips that most people believed were irrational, it also demonstrated Lawrence's uncanny ability to pick up and adapt to foreign cultures. While working on his post-graduate work, Lawrence participated in archaeological excavations in Syria and the Mesopotamia region, all the while sharpening his skills in Arabic.

Lawrence returned to the Middle East in 1914, after the beginning of World War I, as a member of the British Army intelligence. This is where the 1964 movie *Lawrence of Arabia* begins. The three hour movie, directed by David Lean, stars Peter O'Toole as Lawrence. The six foot three actor stands ten inches higher then the real Lawrence - one of the many inaccuracies in the movie. However, the problem with *Lawrence of Arabia* goes much deeper than this casting error. Arnold Lawrence, Lawrence's youngest brother, believed the film swayed far from reality, accusing the director of "[using] as psychological recipe...[taking] an ounce of narcissism, a pound of exhibitionism, a pint of sadism, a gallon of blood-lust and a sprinkle of other aberrations and [stirring] well."

In an opening scene of the movie, Lawrence is portrayed as slightly "different." In front of an amazed audience, he puts out a match by slowly smothering it with his fingers. When asked how he did it, Lawrence replies that "The trick... is not minding that it hurts." This scene implies that Lawrence has masochistic tendencies, and in reality, though he might not have gotten pleasure from pain, he did make some interesting choices as a child. As a boy, instead of playing rugby or cricket with the other children his age, Lawrence spent his time "hardening his body and spirit for some future ordeal." At Oxford University, Lawrence even ate only bread and water for lunch – every day.

These Spartan habits eventually enabled Lawrence to have little difficulty on his 1,100 mile journey across the Middle East and he was easily able to keep up with his Bedouin friends – members of the Arab Revolt – during their arduous treks across inhospitable deserts.

The Arab Revolt became blessed with Lawrence's subtle leadership in 1916 when he was sent on a secret mission with Ronald Storrs, the Oriental Secretary of the British Agency, to meet with Sheif Hussein. Later Storrs asked Lawrence to stay behind as a liaison and to keep an eye on the situation.

Lawrence then met Feisal, one of Hussein's four sons and the one who, according to Lawrence, brought "the Arab Revolt to full glory." Although Lawrence's charisma was not conducive to Arab culture, Feisal accepted Lawrence as an advisor and liaison to the British military and government. Lawrence realized that "the trick [was] not to give orders but to work as an adviser to one who [could]." Many of his fellow officers would have scorned such a seemingly passive role; however, his lack of military experience and reputation as a loose cannon allowed Lawrence to behave against the norm. Unlike in the movie where Lawrence acted an as ad-hoc general during the Arab Revolt, "in councils of war he [would] feed in his idea, then let the Arabs debate it until it appear[ed] their own." This type of diplomacy required far more patience and tact than what O'Toole demonstrated in the film.

Although the movie had some spectacular shots of the desert, the action and warfare in it was not completely accurate. Lawrence's "miracle" – the attack on Aquaba – was almost entirely fictional. It was true that Lawrence and a party of Arabs crossed a desert, and Lawrence even had to save one of his companions along the way. Aquaba was an important port, but the big guns that supposedly threatened a land attack were not facing towards the desert but rather the sea. It would have been impossible for the Turkish soldiers to turn the guns around. In the film, this "big victory" was a critical victory for the Arab Revolt. In reality, it was a rather hollow victory – Aquaba had minimal defenses and would have easily fallen to British soldiers.

In the movie it appears as though Lawrence makes an alliance with Ali ibn el Kharish following his difficult trek through the desert, but Ali had been with Lawrence since the initial planning of the attack. This anachronism had been inserted by the director so that it would appear as though Lawrence had used political savvy to unite various Arab factions.

This need to unite the Arab tribes accurately reflects the situation. The Arab Revolt was made up of numerous tribes who constantly squabbled over honor. In addition Arab soldiers were free to come and go as they pleased. "Their only contract [to the Revolt] was honour." However, the Arabs made up for their lack of discipline in their impressive ability to "reduce the Turks to helplessness."

This was accomplished by a "war of detachment." Because any Arab casualties were devastating to morale and too many dead or wounded would have caused the Arab Revolt to fall apart, the united Arab tribes could not attempt to meet the Ottoman forces in traditional military combat on an open battlefield. As a result, the Bedouin tribes sought to put the Turks under constant pressure. Rather than frontal assaults, the Arabs would engage in several well-planned, scattered attacks (a type of guerilla warfare) that would force the Ottoman Empire to allocate resources and manpower across the Middle Eastern region. With this type of warfare, they would never defeat the Ottomans, but they could frustrate them enough that they would relinquish control and grant the Arab region independence.

The goal became to never engage the Turks. As with the other forces participating in World War I, there seemed to be an inexhaustible supply of manpower available to fight. However, unlike their Western allies, the Ottoman military suffered from a lack of materials. In his 1929 submission to the Encyclopedia Britannica, T.E. Lawrence wrote, "Yet to limit the art to humanity seemed an undue narrowing down. It must apply to materials as much as to organisms. In the Turkish Army materials were scarce and precious, men more plentiful than equipment. Consequently the cue should be to destroy not the army but the materials. The death of a Turkish bridge or rail, machine or gun, or high explosive was more profitable than the death of a Turk."

One of the unconventional strategies used involved firing a shot into the air as the sun set. This forced the Turks to stay alert for the entire night while the Arabs rested peacefully. Another strategy demonstrated in the movie was blowing up railways, especially the Hejaz railway that connected Damascus, Syria to the Arabian city Medina. However, in the movie it appeared as though Lawrence was the only one qualified to place charges and blow the fuse. In reality, by the end of the war almost all of the estimated 5,000 Arab combatants had demolition training and experience.

According to the film, it was after Aquaba that Jackson Bently, an American reporter sent by influential Americans to "[look] for a hero," arrived in the Middle East. In reality his name was Lowell Thomas. Like the movie states, he had gone to the Middle East to find action and a hero to appeal to the United States and, hopefully, bring them into the war on the British side. When he met Lawrence, he realized that he had "a ready made propaganda opportunity." Lawrence may have been a perfect candidate for American propaganda, but he was not one to bask in the spotlight. As a result, Thomas had to "piece together the story…[through] accounts of people around [him]."

Lawrence of Arabia was inaccurate when it showed Bently (Thomas) accompanying Lawrence on a desert raid. During the two weeks that Thomas was in the Middle East, there were no railroad raids, however he did accompany Lawrence and a group of tribesmen on a night raid of a Turkish troop train. With the eventual American entrance into the war, Thomas's original objective proved irrelevant, and Thomas instead created an innovative travelogue that employed the best technology of the day. Thomas supported his narration with music, pictures, and film clips. The travelogue, named *With Allenby in Palestine and Lawrence in Arabia*, took Thomas around the world and it became a stunning success where many people came back for two or three performances. Although even before these theatrical presentations, a French newspaper claimed, "The name of Colonel Lawrence will become historic in Great Britain," the travelogues made "the uncrowned king of Arabia" a household name.

Lawrence became famous after the time span of the movie, and the film implies that because of his massive ego, he craves this newfound spotlight. Earlier scenes likewise emphasize his need for public adoration. After a fictional attack on a train, Lawrence walks along the top of the destroyed train, smiling as his Arab soldiers cheer and chant his name. Later, in the film when he returns to the British headquarters adorned in his Middle Eastern robes, he bathes in their quiet amazement as the entire headquarters stares at him with awe.

However, again the reality differed from the theatrical depiction. Lawrence was not comfortable with the huge amount of publicity. With millions of people, including the Queen, watching Thomas's travelogues, Lawrence began to look for a new life as he became "uncomfortable about being the talk of London" and the rest of the western world. "Lawrence at once loved and hated fame and never forgave Thomas for exploiting his image, calling him a 'vulgar man'."

As a result, in 1922 he tried to secretly enlist in the RAF under the name John Hume Ross, but when his cover was quickly blown, he was forced to enlist in the Tank Corps with a request to be transferred to the RAF. His request was approved and Lawrence, now T.E. Shaw, entered the RAF in 1925 as an airman. Although he avoided the spotlight at every opportunity – refusing awards and promotions – Lawrence's leadership still shined through his façade. When a seaplane crashed at the airbase where he was stationed, Lawrence not only took command from his superior officer, he also personally saved several of the airmen.

But Lawrence did not want to be a hero. In his book *Seven Pillars of Wisdom*, Lawrence says that his ambitions were to present a unified Arab country to a boy that he had become close friends with during one of his earlier trips to the Middle East. Although the boy had since died, Lawrence continued to work to achieve this goal, representing and assisting members of the Arab Revolt at Versailles following World War I.

However, his loyalty was to England and unlike *Lawrence of Arabia* where he was ignorant of the Sykes-Picot Treaty (where the French and British defaulted on their original promise to unite the Arab world and instead created a series of mandates under the control of either France or Britain), Lawrence was fully aware of the agreement and its implications. In fact, Feisal also knew about the treaty. This may have been omitted from the movie because it would have taken away from Lawrence's crusader-like mission to make the Arab Revolt succeed.

Unfortunately, his dream for a united Arab country never blossomed. Following WWI, the French and English divided the Middle

East into two spheres of influence, which "everyone understood at the time…[it] was a thinly disguised new form of colonialism." The new borders in the Middle East – set by British and French politicians – appeared to be arbitrary and they did not fit ethnic, geographic, or language divisions. The resulting conflicts from these divisions continue to affect the world today. Lawrence is partly to blame. He brought the Arabs to the negotiating table with the hope of sovereignty, only to have it torn apart by the Sykes-Picot Treaty. Arab Historian Suleiman Mousa said, "I admire Lawrence as a man. What I don't admire is the 'peace' he and his country imposed on us."

Although some of his exploits were sensationalized, while other less flattering details were omitted, few can argue with Winston Churchill who declared T.E. Lawrence was "one of the greatest beings alive in our time."

Key Quotes

Jackson Bentley: (*following the death of Lawrence*) Yes, it was my privilege to know him and to make him known to the world. He was a poet, a scholar and a mighty warrior.

General Murray: (*discussing the Middle Eastern Campaign*) It's a storm in a tea cup, Mr. Dryden - a sideshow. If you want my own opinion, this whole theater of operations is a sideshow! The real war's not being fought against the Turks, but the Germans. And not here, but on the Western front in the trenches! Your Bedouin Army - or whatever it calls itself - would be a sideshow OF a sideshow!

Prince Feisal: (*characterizing Lawrence*) He is almost an Arab.

T.E. Lawrence: (*before executing an Arab*) Then I will execute the Law. I have no tribe and no one is offended.

T.E. Lawrence: (*discussing how war can be fought in the Middle East*) A thousand Arabs means a thousand knives, delivered anywhere day or night. It means a thousand camels. That means a thousand packs of high explosives and a thousand crack rifles. We can cross Arabia while Johnny Turk is still turning round, and smash his railways. And while he's mending them, I'll smash them somewhere else. In thirteen weeks, I can have Arabia in chaos.

General Allenby: (*predicting Lawrence's legacy*) I believe your name will be a household word when you'll have to go to the War Museum to find who Allenby was. You're the most extraordinary man I've ever met!

Prince Feisal: (*reasoning why victory might be futile*) Young men make wars, and the virtues of war are the virtues of young men: courage, and hope for the future. Then old men make the peace, and the vices of peace are the vices of old men: mistrust and caution.

The Untouchables

1987
Director: Brian De Palma
Starring: Kevin Costner, Sean Connery, Charles Martin Smith
119 minutes – Rated R for violence and language

By Annie Lydens

Synopsis:

Set in Prohibition-era Chicago, Brian De Palma's gangster masterpiece tells the story of how federal agent Eliot Ness and his band of "Untouchables" attempt to bring down Al Capone in a world of corruption and blatant disregard for the law. When Eliot Ness first begins his epic crusade against booze, gangsters, and the man behind it all, he initially fails because he knows no one untouched by the influence of Al Capone. Enter Ness's "Untouchables." Ness handpicks a gang of four men to help him in his fight, and together they work to dethrone Capone on two separate charges - his connection to the bootlegging industry and his blatant tax evasion.

Historically Relevant Scenes

00:16:00>00:19:00	- Ness meets Jimmy Malone
00:29:00>00:37:00	- Formation of the Untouchables
00:37:00>00:39:00	- Capone's Dinner Party
00:47:00>01:01:00	- Canadian Border Raid/Discovering the Ledger
01:35:00>01:37:00	- Reading the Ledger in Court
01:46:00>01:47:00	- Courtroom Scene - Switching the Jury

Ratings:

Entertainment - ★ ★ ★ ★

Historical Accuracy - ★ ★ ★ ☆

Historical Analysis:

The Roaring Twenties was an era of great economic growth. Following WWI and a brief economic slump as the nation struggled to recover from a recession brought about by the end of wartime production, soldiers re-entered the workforce in droves. Soon humming again, factories churned out consumer goods as fast as companies could conceptualize them. Primarily thanks to President Warren Harding, the government during his term deviated from past policies of government activism and instead pledged a "Return to Normalcy." This 'return' included an implementation of laissez-faire policies, which only served to strengthen the mood that business was everything - as later president Calvin Coolidge claimed, "The chief business of the American people is business." The atmosphere of 'anything is possible' fostered during this era came to epitomize the realization of the American Dream.

Often referred to as the Jazz Age, the 1920's was an era stuffed full of self-indulgent, party-hearty, live-young-die-early types. It was an era of big bands, big Broadway, and even bigger boozing. The spirit of the era is most easily associated with a cessation of traditions. This was born from the desire for modernity, which was only amplified by the introduction of new technologies, which brought modern conveniences to the bulk of the nation. With tremendous progress in inventions like the automobile, airplane, ocean liners, and the phonograph, the young and rich were happy throwing money in any direction. Simultaneously, pleasure and hedonism, as if a rebound reaction to the aura of despair fostered during World War I, were emphasized in the culture of jazz and dancing.

Oddly enough, at the exact moment it appeared Americans were most enjoying the party atmosphere of the 1920s was when America was hypothetically in the midst of Prohibition. Following the 18th Amendment which outlawed the manufacturing, transportation, and distribution of alcohol, some predicted the gradual decline in alcohol consumption. They were wrong. This glaring miscalculation of the public's desires and the subsequent 21st Amendment which repealed Prohibition ended once and for all the century long struggle to legislate a key component of social behavior – alcohol consumption.

The initial drive to eliminate alcohol arose before the Civil War, when small groups, mostly church-based, began advocating asceticism. The movement garnered some support, and the heartened prohibitionists began pushing for the banning of alcohol. Nevertheless, the Civil War captivated more attention and the movement dwindled away. When the war ended, however, newly optimistic prohibitionists re-emerged, particularly in the form of a women's movement, which focused on protecting the home and children from the vices of alcohol. These women were also supported by chiefly Protestant churches, and the movement gained velocity.

During this period there was a spattering of state-wide prohibition bans across the nation. In 1846, Maine enacted a liquor consumption ban, which twelve other states quickly replicated. However, the confidence in the importance of these bans dwindled when the involved states realized that prohibition was almost impossible to enforce at a state level. By the time 1868 rolled around, Maine was the only state still banning alcohol, and the temperance movement seemed to have lost all momentum.

However there were organizations popping up during this period that would make a huge difference in the prohibition movement to come - like the Women's Christian Temperance Union, the Prohibition Party, and the Anti-Saloon League. Interestingly enough, the passing of the 18th amendment was actually in a large part due to the pertinacious harassment by the Anti-Saloon League.

Formed initially in 1893 as a state society, the Anti-Saloon League grew to become the most powerful anti-liquor lobbying group in the nation, quickly usurping the supremacy of preceding groups like the Women's Christian Temperance Union. Through strategies such as the lobbying of all levels of government and the usage of "pressure politics," the Anti-Saloon League was successful in intimidating the public and the government into supporting Prohibition. Intriguingly, the potential of the media as a way to manipulate politicians into dealing with the wants of the people is said to have truly been realized during this temperance movement. After a particularly successful attack on Congress, a leader of the Anti-Saloon League at the time was quoted as saying, "We blocked the telegraph wires in Congress for three days. One of our friends sent seventy-five telegrams, each signed differently with the name of one of his subordinates. The campaign was successful. Congress surrendered. The first to bear the white flag was Senator Warren Harding of Ohio. He told us frankly he was opposed to the amendment, but since it was apparent from the telegrams that the business world was demanding it he would submerge his own opinion and vote for submission."

This impetus was mainly fostered by the idea that alcohol was the root of all evils. Specifically, women's groups believed it was linked to wife beating and child abuse; business managers believed it caused a decrease in productivity; and the Anti-Saloon League believed that the implementation of an injunction of some kind would eliminate many societal problems, among which were absenteeism in the workplace and unemployment. Alcoholics, seen as a threat to society's welfare, were branded as dangerous and sleazy. As temperance activist Lyman Beecher so profoundly put it, alcoholics might one day "dig the grave of our liberties and entomb our glory."

And this gets us to where the Untouchables actually come into play. Almost. Officially, Prohibition started in 1920 after the ratification of the 18th Amendment and the implementation of the Volstead Act, which prohibited the sale and consumption of alcohol. However, two years earlier, Congress enacted the 1917 Lever Act, which barred the utilization of grain in alcohol. President Wilson tried to veto the act, but Congress overrode the motion and it was all over for saloons in January of 1920.

Until, of course, the saloons went underground. Hidden saloons called speakeasies were extremely profitable due to the public's continued desire for alcohol. Although U.S. government agents and a few uncorrupted policemen tried their best, speakeasies were so lucrative that it was easy for the owners to pay off anyone that might pose a problem - policemen were infamously bribed to give advance notice of any raid planned. In the higher echelons of society, cocktail parties became a popular (yet still illegal) way to loosen up. Because of the ban, alcohol swiftly had an increase in popularity as the "it" thing to have at parties, predominantly due to the expense associated with it. As it became more difficult to obtain, the black market prices went through the roof. If you could serve champagne in glasses the size of finger-bowls, you were obviously someone to be associated with.

Law enforcement agents at all levels found themselves not only battling the general public's craving for alcohol, but gangsters as well. Once the domain of legitimate (or almost legitimate) businesses, the distribution of alcohol went underground and was taken over by different gangs. These gangs fought for control over the market using such diplomatic tactics as sabotage and mass murder. Of course, this kind of general happy chaos lead to the rise of one very powerful and very smart man - Al Capone.

His cutthroat style made Al the undeclared, unelected "mayor of Chicago." Al Capone, quite frankly, ran the town. During an election in Cook County, Frank Loesch (who at the time was the president of the Chicago Crime Commission) needed a man who would help secure an honest election. At the time, according to him, no uncorrupted elected powers existed, so he turned to the most powerful man he could find. Ironically, with Al Capone's assistance, the county witnessed one of the fairest elections in a long time, with little to no rioting and no background scandals. By 1931, Capone ascended the ranks of celebrity, until everybody in the city knew what he was up to in his spare time - murders, bribery, and running his breweries.

He was so terrible, only one man (with the assistance of a few minor characters) could stop him. That superhero was Eliot Ness (cue dramatic music). In the movie, Eliot Ness does it all. He's a family man with killer aim and a full head of hair. He's everywhere all at once, and doesn't like to fight (although he does once his family, friends, and the 'greater good' are threatened). He has the moral standards of an angel, and doesn't drink - although he does occasionally indulge in a cigarette, channeling his inner Marlboro Man. Is it possible that one man could really be all that and more? Could the real Eliot Ness be as great as the Kevin Costner adaptation?

The short answer is "no," although a lot of the details were based on reality (read: mostly made up with their roots in actual fact). Eliot Ness was not a family man. In the movie, Ness is depicted as being a doting father with a young daughter and a son on the way. This patriarchal role helps motivate Ness to bring down Capone when a young girl is slain just after the opening credits of the movie. In reality, Ness married three different times, and was a bachelor during his dealings with Capone. He only became a father after his career in law enforcement ended, which is ironic seeing how 'family-focused' Costner's Ness appears.

In terms of Ness's character, there seems to be two very different Nesses remembered by the general public. The first is closer to the Costner Ness - a man of high moral standards, committed to cleaning up Chicago's sullied streets and taking down Al Capone. The only difference between this squeaky-clean Ness and the Ness in the film was how appealing he found the shootouts and raids. The real-life Ness was quoted as saying, "Unquestionably, it was going to be highly dangerous. Yet I felt it was quite natural to jump at the task. After all, if you don't like action and excitement, you don't go into police work. And, what the hell, I figured, nobody lives forever!" This depiction contradicts his characterization in the film. Costner's Ness is reluctant to join in the fray, but in real life Ness was eager to test his gung-ho machismo.

With a college degree and a year of graduate study under his belt, it is interesting that Eliot Ness chose an occupation in which he was paid peanuts but risked losing his life. To account for this seemingly selfless lifestyle, some sources claim that Ness was a depraved egomaniac who craved attention in the worst way, and figured that by obliterating Capone's empire he could get the publicity he desired.

In one of the (many) gruesome scenes in the movie, Capone is wining-and-dining with his gangster buddies when he suddenly accuses one of them of disloyalty. Now, Capone may be a benevolent leader, but disloyalty he can't stand. So he solves the problem the old fashioned way: he grabs a Louisville Slugger and bludgeons the poor guy to death. As Hollywood-doctored as this event sounds, not only did it happen in real life but the reality was much more macabre than the film. Capone had invited three Sicilian gangsters over for dinner, and, just as they were tucking into their scallops, he accused them of betrayal. His bodyguards quickly manacled the three offenders to their chairs, while Al took a few practice swings over the butter dish. He then proceeded to pummel each of the gangsters in turn, while everyone else at the table watched. In *CAPONE: The Life and World of Al Capone,* John Koble recounts the horrific event, "Slowly, he walked the length of the table and halted behind the first guest of honor. With both hands, he lifted the bat and slammed it down full force. Slowly, methodically, he struck again and again, breaking bones in the man's shoulders, arms and chest. He moved to the next man and, when he had reduced him to mangled flesh and bone, to the third." In a final grisly flourish to end the luncheon proceedings properly, he summarily shot each of the three Sicilians in the back of the neck - truly proving that his power was as great as his brutality.

Like Capone's tendency to go overboard when it comes to discipline, another aspect that closely mirrors reality was the extent to which the city was corrupted. In the film, almost all the law enforcement agents are corrupted, which is sadly true-to-life.

In a collaborative investigation with Eliot Ness, Clayton Fritchey, a reporter for *The Cleveland Press*, uncovered then-unheard of levels of corruption in the Chicago area police force. He reported that:

> "Out of the wealth of testimony which Director Ness and *The Cleveland Press* accumulated, one salient fact emerges: that the corruption uncovered stems from higher circles than the police department: that the rank and file who have taken money were in many cases the victims of an evil system. In short, the department has been so controlled for the last 20 years that it could not breed or attract men of high character.... young men coming into the department got off to a bad start by having to pay several hundred dollars for the good jobs: anywhere from $500 to $750 for a sergeantcy, more for a lieutenancy and as much as $5000 for a captaincy."

Because they were paying exorbitant sums of money (Ness himself made only $2800 a year) to get the best cases and positions, agents took advantage of any opportunity to make their money back. This desperation most often propelled agents to notify gangsters about upcoming raids (for a small fee) so that the offending evidence could be removed or destroyed. It was through this exchange of small bribes that Capone built up a powerful network of informants.

Additionally, Ness reported in his book that agents who firmly enforced the laws "[were] sent to the woods...received the most unpleasant details...and passed over for promotions." However, if the agent chose to turn the other cheek when it came to the 'misbehaviour' of certain members of society (Capone referred to it as 'playing ball'), they received the best details and were promoted quickly and easily. Because gangs like Capone's quickly learned how to exploit the desperation or desire of these men to receive information about upcoming raids or searches, any attempt to catch them almost always failed miserably.

Another weakness in law enforcement that gangs like Al Capone's took advantage of was understaffing. As one unnamed policeman said, "There are so few of us, we can't make much of an impact." At their peak, law enforcement agents like Ness who were working to enforce Prohibition across the nation numbered a pathetic 2,500 agents. In addition to the gross understaffing, the judicial system was equally useless. Of the 7,000 arrests made during the era, there were only 17 convictions. Originally the work of IRS agents (nicknamed 'Revenues' by their police peers who regarded them as shamefully uncool), the Department of Treasury inaugurated a program in which Treasury agents (like Ness) worked in conjunction with the police, which is what Ness is doing at the beginning of the movie.

This finally brings us to our epic crime fighting posse: the Untouchables. Because the movie *The Untouchables* was based on the book written by Ness himself, the movie is inordinately historically accurate on most accounts except, interestingly enough, the Untouchables themselves. In real life, there were ten Untouchables, but in the movie there were only four. These four were Ness, Jim Malone, George Stone, and Oscar Wallace. Aside from Ness, none of these men actually existed - they are either composite characters loosely based on different attributes of the actual Untouchables, or based on men who weren't 'untouchable' at all.

Oscar Wallace, the accountant who puts together the tax evasion case, is loosely based on two people: an unnamed Prohibition agent and Frank Wilson, head of the criminal investigation unit of the IRS. Because Ness never named the man in his book, the identity of the agent remains unknown. As described by Ness himself, the man was "a mousy little fellow with thick, horn-rimmed glasses" who was an unseasoned Prohibition agent when he went on his first raid with Ness. He was on Ness's team because the head of the Chicago Prohibition Bureau, a man jealous of Ness's immediate success in his brewery raids, mockingly provided the fresh-from-training agent. This agent, shocked by the sheer masculinity and bravado displayed by the fellow men on the raid, did not perform as well as he probably would have liked his first morning on the job. The raid was an unrivalled success; Ness netted well over a hundred barrels and various brewing equipment, and the only setback was the prompt resignation of the timid agent the next day.

Wallace is also based on treasury agent Frank Wilson, who headed the team of IRS investigators that put together the tax evasion case that eventually put Capone behind bars. Wilson was incredibly smart, and later went on to become the head of the Secret Service and almost single-handedly all but eliminated the production of counterfeit money by the time of his retirement in 1947. In the movie, Oscar Wallace has a sudden epiphany that they can charge Capone with 22 separate counts of tax evasion. He then goes on to gather the evidence to make the tax evasion case himself. However, the Untouchables had little to do with assembling the case that put Capone in jail. Although a large part of the physical evidence used against Capone was found by the Untouchables, it was actually the criminal investigations unit of the IRS that constructed the case and this is the unit that Frank Wilson commanded.

Instead of assembling cases, the Untouchables focused their investigative energies mostly on raiding breweries. These represented a large part of the money that gangsters could make off of the sale of alcohol, and by raiding them Ness could both confiscate the equipment and simultaneously gather and destroy the alcohol. Because breweries were expensive to maintain and required significant investments, by closing down breweries the Untouchables could hit the gangsters hard. In *Eliot Ness: The Man Behind the Myth*, Marilyn Bardsley writes, "In [his] first six months [on the job], Ness had closed down some nineteen distilleries and key breweries, worth an estimated $1,000,000." To lose such a massive sum really made gangsters, as Bardsley puts it, "feel the pinch." In the movie *The Untouchables*, the group raids no breweries, which is odd seeing as brewery raids were the basis of Ness's strategy in his war against Capone.

While Ness's strategy was to go for the breweries, Capone preferred to rely on bribes to accomplish his agenda. Al Capone had no qualms about handing out a few extra dollars in order to ensure that police raids would not go as planned, or to receive information. Bardsley writes, "Capone fully believed that every man had his price, so his next move was to have one of his men offer Ness $2,000 a week. A similar offer was made to [other Untouchables], when a man threw an envelope with the cash into their car as he passed them on the road. Ness's agents caught up with Capone's guy and threw the money back at him." The Untouchables were earning $2800 annually, so to turn down such vast sums proves their commitment to their cause and how 'untouchable' they truly were.

Gangs also held political power, and often had ties to members of the highest socioeconomic groups - for example, a raid by the Michigan State police once uncovered a highly embarrassed mayor taking part in a bit of boozing with the sheriff and a local congressman in Detroit in late 1928. Generally speaking, the cities across the nation were a mess of corruption. However, the movie does exaggerate the dishonesty of one notable character: the judge. In the film, the judge in the court scene only switches the juries after Ness threatens to reveal his corruption. The judge is based loosely on Judge Wilkerson, who was known as an upstanding citizen during the era who wanted to eliminate corruption at any cost - a sort of Ness-goes-to-law-school kind of guy.

TIME Magazine, April 11, 1932, reported, "In Chicago, and to a lesser extent throughout the country, James Herbert Wilkerson is something of a judicial hero." Judge Wilkerson was responsible for ultimately putting Capone, and multiple other gangsters, including Terry Druggan and Frankie Lake, behind bars. The TIME article says, "Last summer he capped a long and successful record of imprisoning gangsters when he refused to countenance a 'deal' between Scarface Capone himself, his Federal prosecutor and the U. S. Attorney General's office whereby Capone was to swap a plea of guilty to income tax evasion for a light sentence." Instead of allowing Capone to bargain, Judge Wilkerson quashed the deal and Capone was sentenced to eleven years in jail and a $50,000 fine.

In the film, the judge agrees to switch the juries after it is revealed that Capone has paid off all the jury members. Ness only discovers that the jury has been bribed after finding a list in Nitti's coat pocket, which happens halfway through the testimonies. In reality it was actually Judge Wilkerson's idea to switch the juries, which were switched secretly before the trial began. Additionally, there was never any concrete evidence that the jury members had accepted the bribes, although several of them had been subjected to Al Capone's intimidation tactics before the court date was set. In *Eliot Ness: The Man Behind the Myth*, Marilyn Bardsley wrote, "It was secretly proven to Judge Wilkerson that Capone's gang was bribing and threatening the potential jurors." Al Capone was no rookie at intimidation tactics to get what he wanted - he even used them on Ness. Bardsley wrote, "One day when Ness went from his office to his car, he noticed that the fastener on his briefcase had come open. He put the briefcase on the hood of his car to refasten the snap and happened to notice that the hood was open a little bit. No stranger to assassination attempts, Ness cautiously raised the hood to find a dynamite bomb inside." Because Al Capone had on several previous occasions proven himself willing to take any steps necessary to get people to do what he wanted, it's realistic that he used aggressive intimidation tactics to get the jury to vote his way, even if they may not have accepted.

Generally speaking, the movie is more accurate than your usual shootout blockbuster, though it deviates slightly on the more negligible matters. Brian De Palma's film is truly a masterpiece. It emulates the essence of the era, and it is as close to historically accurate as you can get without losing the quick action and instant gratification of a gory Hollywood feature.

Key Quotes

Reporter: (*commenting on Capone's influence*) An article, which I believe appeared in a newspaper, asked why, since you are, or it would seem that you are, in effect, the mayor of Chicago, you've not simply been appointed to that position.

Al Capone: (*relatively frustrated by the tactics of Ness*) I want this guy dead! I want his family dead! I want his house burned to the ground! I want to go there in the middle of the night and piss on his ashes!

Al Capone: (*discussing his strategy for success*) You can get further with a kind word and a gun than you can with just a kind word.

Jimmy Malone: (*discussing his strategy for success*) He pulls a knife, you pull a gun. He sends one of yours to the hospital, you send one of his to the morgue. That's the Chicago way!

The Aviator

2004

Director: Martin Scorsese
Starring: Leonardo Dicaprio, Cate Blanchett, John C. Reily
170 minutes – Rated PG-13

By Samson Yuwono

Synopsis:

Taking place during the late 1920s through to the 1940s, this Howard Hughes biopic follows Hughes's accomplishments in filmmaking and aviation and then his descent into mental illness and reclusiveness. Hughes uses his money acquired through his Texas oil business to produce the most expensive movie at the time – *Hell's Angels*. After two years of filming and a then record $3.5 billion production cost, the film is released and becomes a financial success. After the movie's release, Hughes pursues his aviation interests by setting the aviation speed record, traveling around the world in four days, buying TWA airlines, and securing a contract with the U.S army to build planes for World War II. From the government contract, Hughes builds a prototype of the XF-11 and develops "The Hercules." Along the way he dates Katharine Hepburn, Ava Gardner, Faith Domergue, and many more Hollywood starlets of the day. Hughes later gets in trouble with the U.S. government for allegedly embezzling government funds. While the criminal investigation and development of the Hercules looms over him, Hughes spirals downwards into a recluse where his obsessive compulsive disorder only compounds his eccentricities.

Historically Relevant Scenes

00:13:30>00:16:04	- Filming of *Hell's Angels*
00:41:03>00:45:10	- Aviation Speed Trial
01:07:32>01:08:10	- Hercules News footage
01:19:13>01:32:00	- Howard Hughes as a recluse
01:43:00>01:53:00	- Hercules/Spruce Goose's Inaugural Flight

Ratings:

Entertainment - ★ ★ ★ ☆

Historical Accuracy - ★ ★ ★ ☆

Historical Analysis

Despite Howard Hughes being a celebrated aviator, movie producer, and tycoon, he has been more characterized for his reclusiveness. In 2004, Martin Scorsese attempted to bring Hughes's lesser-known accomplishments to the big screen by creating the film *The Aviator*, a biopic of Howard Hughes that follows his life from the late 1920s through to the 1940s. Although it is hard to do justice to the life of Howard Hughes in a three-hour movie, Scorsese manages to paint a clear picture of Hughes in that amount of time.

The film starts off with a young Howard Hughes being bathed by his mother who is teaching him about disease. The film then immediately cuts to the epic production of the most expensive movie of the time, *Hell's Angels*, and introduces Leonardo Dicaprio's Howard Hughes as the director of the movie. There is a significant chunk of Hughes's life missing between the two scenes and the film never explains Hughes's family background and childhood.

Hughes was born on Christmas Eve of 1905 to father Howard Hughes Sr. and mother Allene Hughes. Throughout Howard's childhood he had no interest in school, but did have an interest in engineering. He even built a wireless broadcast system at eleven and a motorized bicycle at twelve after his mother forbade him from having a motorcycle. Through his father's influence, Hughes attended math and engineering classes at Cal Tech. He also received flying lessons at fourteen. These skills and early childhood experiences paved the way for his later success as an aviator.

Howard Hughes's Sr., the father of Howard Hughes Jr., made a fortune by inventing a revolutionary tri-cone oil drill bit that included 166 cutting edges. His new drill bit replaced the old fishtail-shaped drill. This innovation then led to the creation of the Hughes Tool Company in 1909. At the age of sixteen, Hughes lost his mother to ectopic pregnancy and two years later his father also passed away from a heart attack. Hughes received 75% of his father's estate, with 25% of the rest given to his relatives. When Hughes turned 19 he became emancipated, giving him full control of his father's company, and he also married Ella Rice during that time.

With his inheritance and a new wife, young Hughes moved to Hollywood in 1925 to spend time with his uncle, Rupert Hughes, who was a screenwriter and director. Howard became so interested with movie making that he made his first movie, *Swell Hogan*, the same year he moved. Hughes thought his movie was so bad he never released it. He later made another movie, *Everybody's Acting*, in 1927, and this movie succeeded at the box office recuperating the costs for his previous movie failure. A year later Hughes produced another successful movie called *Two Arabian Nights* which earned him an Academy Award for Best Director of a comedy picture.

Scorsese chose to leave out Hughes's earliest accomplishments before *Hell's Angels*. Scorsese also makes it seem like Hughes's acquired his fortune by digging oil in Texas, but in real life Hughes got all his money through his inheritance. He also leaves out his early filmmaking experience, his Academy Award winning movie and his first wife. Instead, Scorsese chose to pick up with Hughes's life with the filming of *Hell's Angels*.

Some critics thought that the first hour of the movie should not have dealt exclusively with the production of *Hell's Angels*, but instead with the critical events of his young life. Stephen Hunter of the Washington Post thought that Scorsese was so "fascinated with *Hell's Angels* [because] he may see in it a parallel to his own embattled *Gangs of New York*..." Although Hunter thought Scorsese's decision stemmed from his own empathy for Hughes's production difficulties, the reality is that *Hell's Angels* was truly a landmark film in the history of Hollywood. It had 137 pilots and about 150 planes - enough to make it the biggest private air force in history. The movie used 35 cameramen and 2000 extras. The film was also shot twice for sound with the final budget approaching $4 million. At the time (especially since it was filmed on the eve of the Great Depression), four million dollars was an unimaginable sum. Two financial factors left out of the film was Hughes's 1929 divorce settlement to Ella Rice for $1.25 million and, more importantly to the nation, the Stock Market Crash and eventual Great Depression. Scorsese might have chosen to ignore the financial crisis, because during this era, Hughes continued to profit from his father's oil drilling company and his wealth subsequently went relatively unaffected.

Scorsese does emphasize the many complications Hughes survives while filming – from the eight month postponement due to a lack of clouds to Hughes's decision to reshoot the film to make it a "talkie." Like in reality, the film shows Hughes inspired after watching a talkie (probably *The Jazz Singer*), and decides to reshoot and recast the film.   Because of the inclusion of sound in *Hell's Angels*, Jean Harlow replaced Greta Nissen (because of her Norwegian accent).

After the movie was done re-shooting, it premiered at the Grauman's Chinese Theatre on May 24, 1930 with many of Hollywood's biggest stars attending the premiere. At the time, the film was a commercial success and a moderate critical success. Most critics criticized Harlow's acting at the time, but ironically today it is seen as the best performance in the movie. This is because she didn't act in the energetic, flamboyant manner common to silent actors of that era.

As Hughes's fame in Hollywood rose from the success of his movies, he became a playboy who dated the era's "Who's Who" of Hollywood beauties: Katharine Hepburn, Ava Gardner, Rita Hayworth, Lana Turner, Bette Davis, Faith Domergue, and many more. One woman that Scorsese chose to emphasize in his movie was Katharine Hepburn who was portrayed by Cate Blanchett. Scorsese showed that Hepburn was a very important figure in Hughes's life and suggested the emotional depth of their relationship. A. Scott Berg, a friend and a Pulitzer Prize winner who wrote the best selling memoir *Kate Remembered* thought that "whenever [Hepburn] would talk about Hughes there was always this kind of glint in her eye that suggested that of all the relationships in her life it might have been the lustiest in fact."

During the scene in the movie where Hughes visits Hepburn's family in Connecticut, Hepburn's ex-husband is shown filming the couple. In the movie Hepburn tells Hughes that her ex-husband "is here all the time."   This actually was true in real life. Hepburn actually supported her ex-husband Ludlow Ogden Smith financially after their divorce. The "other man" that Hepburn found in the movie and started a new relationship with after the breakup with Hughes was Spencer Tracy. Scorsese made it seem like the break up and subsequent union with Spencer Tracy happened in a very short time, but in actuality Hughes and Hepburn broke up long before Tracy and Hepburn became an item. In the movie, after the breakup, it is implied that Hughes was so distraught that he burned all of his clothes. This is not true. In real life, Hughes ordered every piece of clothing and bed linens to be destroyed because he caught syphilis, not due to the ending of the relationship.

Perhaps what Hughes is best known for is his obsessive-compulsive disorder.   According to the movie, his OCD started in early childhood.   During the bathing scene early in the movie, Hughes's mother lectures him about germs. The scene suggests that his overprotective mother, Allene Hughes, was to blame for his later emotional and mental neuroses. Most psychologists agreed his mother's actions did play a significant role. Another possible cause of Hughes's illness was an episode where he caught the aforementioned syphilis. Hughes was warned by his doctors not to shake hands for a period of time, but Hughes ended up avoiding handshakes the rest of his life. In the movie, Hughes is also shown to be deaf. Scorsese never explains the reason why Hughes had a hard time hearing. In real life, this was probably caused by his childhood bout of tinnitus, a disease that affects the ear and later caused him much frustration. It was only when Hughes was flying in a plane's cockpit the ringing stopped. This could partially explain Hughes's joy of flying.

Before this movie, Hughes's most forgotten achievements were in in the field of aviation. Scorsese attempted to resurrect this part of Hughes's life by showcasing his accomplishments in breaking the speed record, his around the world flight, and his technological achievements in the field of aviation. Amazingly, the film just scratches the surface of his aviation accomplishments. In 1933, Hughes started in the aviation industry as a co-pilot for American Airways under the name of Charles W. Howard, but eventually his cover was blown. A year later, Hughes built the H-1 racer, and with this plane he won a race in Miami and set the world speed record at 352 mph. A year and a half later, he improved the H-1 and set a new transcontinental airspeed record by flying non-stop from Burbank, California to Newark, New Jersey in 7 hours, 28 minutes. In the movie, Scorsese recreates Hughes's record-setting speed, but leaves out his race in Miami and the transcontinental flight.

As shown in the movie, Hughes does fly around the world from New York to New York in three days, nineteen hours and eight minutes outdoing "Jules Verne's wildest dreams." He flies in a Lockheed 14-N Super Electra with a crew of four and during the journey he breaks Lindbergh's New York to Paris record in half. But the movie exaggerates Hughes's purchase of TWA during his trip. In reality, he bought into TWA during 1937 and took full control of the company in 1939 a year after his around the world trip. Although not mentioned in the movie, that same year Hughes was awarded the Congressional Gold Medal for his achievements "in advancing the science of aviation and thus bringing credit to his country around the world."

In 1942, Hughes obtained $18 million through a U.S. government contract to construct flying boats. From this contract Hughes managed to build and design the XF-11 and the H-4 Hercules. The contract never produced any planes that saw action in the war because Hughes only completed the planes after the war was over. Hughes first flew the XF-11 on July 7, 1946. In the movie, due to an oil leak, Hughes wanted to land the XF-11 at the Wilshire Country Club, but ended up at a nearby Beverly Hills neighborhood and was saved by a soldier – Master Sergeant

William L. Durkin. Although most of this is true, one minor change Scorsese makes was that the plane was supposed to land at the Los Angeles Country Club. According to the movie, Hughes suffers burns to 78% of his body, a collapsed lung that shifted his heart completely to the right side of his chest cavity, nine broken ribs, a broken cheek and a shattered knee. In real life, Hughes actually suffered a crushed collar bone, six broken ribs, a collapsed lung that didn't affect his heart, a fractured skull, and third degree burns.

Finally in 1947, the Hercules, also known as the "Spruce Goose" by its critics, made its first flight. Built for transport, this plane was made from laminated wood and when finished became the largest plane in aviation history. Like in the movie, its maiden voyage was successful (although only reaching an altitude of 70 feet), but this did little to dissuade those that believed Hughes misused government funds to produce a beast that would never see wartime action. After its only flight, Hughes maintained it at an annual cost of one million dollars. Today, it is stored at the Evergreen Aviation Museum in McMinnvile, Oregon.

By the 1950s, Hughes's escaped into relative isolation, living out his days in a darkened room, usually under the influence of prescription medication. Many gossip columnists attributed a variety of behaviors, real and fictional, to Howard Hughes, though few know how he actually behaved. One story has him only cutting his hair and nails annually and even forcing his business managers (of whom most were Mormon) to purchase hundreds of gallons of his favorite Baskin-Robbins ice cream. By the 1960s, he had moved to Las Vegas and purchased the Desert Inn, living on the 8th floor for years and fighting the government to discontinue the underground nuclear bomb testing that was being done in Nevada. Eventually, he moved to Nicaragua, and in 1976 he died while, ironically, on an airplane. By this point, he was almost unrecognizable, weighing in at less than 90 pounds and having uncut hair and nails that made him look almost beastly.

Scorsese chose to ignore this final phase of his life, instead focusing on his many accomplishments. Although in today's world, his eccentricities would overshadow his achievements (see Michael Jackson), thanks to Martin Scorsese's *The Aviator*, the world can see Howard Hughes for what he was – a billionaire, an aviation innovator, a daredevil, a movie mogul, and an overall brilliant man.

Key Quotes

Howard Hughes: (*on the set of Hell's Angels during the eight months with no clouds*) You see that it has cost me $5,271 a day to keep those planes on the ground. You find me some goddamn clouds.

Katharine Hepburn: (*breaking up with Howard Hughes*) Let's be honest. It's been a grand adventure but it wouldn't possibly last.

Howard Hughes: (*as a young man being lectured by his mother*) Quarantine. Q-u-a-r-a-n-t-i-n-e. Quarantine.

Enemy at the Gates

2001
Director: Jean-Jacques Annaud
Starring: Jude Law, Ed Harris, Rachel Weisz, Joseph Fiennes
131 minutes – Rated R

By Jose Acevedo

Synopsis:

In the film *Enemy at the Gates*, the German 6th Army's advancement into the Soviet Union during World War II was stopped by the Soviet Red Army at the Battle of Stalingrad. Unable to fight a conventional war on the plains outside Stalingrad, the battle for the city enters the streets where the Soviets resort to guerilla warfare and sniper activity. As his number of enemy officer kills rises, Vassili Zaitsev becomes a popular national war hero who gives hope to his people in a time of great suffering. Eventually, the Germans realize they must neutralize this topic of hopeful propaganda, so they subsequently send Major Konig to kill Zaitsev. In the climactic scene, these two men square off amongst the destroyed city's buildings, and only one man will leave this deadly duel alive.

Historically Relevant Scenes

00:03:00>00:14:15	- Deployment of Soviet soldiers to battle
00:21:20>00:22:08	- Danilov reading the army newspaper to Vassili

---

Ratings:

Entertainment - ★ ★ ★ ☆

Historical Accuracy - ★ ★ ☆ ☆

Historical Analysis:

In the decade that followed World War I, Germany struggled to escape the crippling effects of the Treaty of Versailles. This agreement to end World War I placed all blame on Germany's soldiers and forced the nation to dissolve their military, surrender territory, and pay ridiculous war reparations that left their economy in ruins. The only way Germany was able to survive was through American loans that helped them satisfy their reparation requirements. However, this cycle of debt proved inescapable when America entered its Great Depression, plunging Germany into a hole where money was worthless and the nation's political structure descended into chaos.

This is where Adolph Hitler stepped in. Promising to return Germany to its previous glory by ignoring the terms of the Versailles Treaty, Hitler gained a steady following for his Nazi party. With his flaming vitriol that placed blame on Jews and capitalists, Hitler and the Nazi Party's popularity grew, eventually forcing then President Paul von Hindenburg to appoint him Chancellor of Germany. In the coming year, Hitler used a fire at the Reichstag to do away with individual rights and gave himself absolute power to arrest and punish anyone who threatened his party's ascension – primarily the Communists. When Hindenburg died later that next year, Hitler assumed the duties of the President and made himself the unchallenged leader of Germany – the *Führer*.

Once in power, Hitler came through on his promises – ending unemployment through a massive rearmament campaign and regaining land lost following World War I, including Austria and Czechoslovakia. As Hitler gradually ignored each tenet of the Versailles Treaty, Great Britain and France stood by and made idle threats, each hoping to avoid another catastrophic world war. However, this policy of appeasement proved a failure and in 1939, Hitler, with support from the Soviet Union, invaded Poland, and war in Europe erupted.

Hitler's invasion of Poland only came after the 1939 Nazi-Soviet Non-Aggression Pact which promised that Germany and the Soviet Union would settle all problems without force. Hitler needed the Soviet Union to stay out of any future war because he realized Germany's defeat in World War I came primarily due to its inability to fight a two front war. Likewise, the Soviet Union did not want to have to fight Germany to the West because they feared an offensive from Japan to the East. In addition to the non-aggression agreement, the two sides also agreed to divide up Central Europe, especially Poland. This would give the Soviet Union a "buffer zone" if in fact Germany later decided to invade. This agreement was to last ten years. It lasted two.

In 1940, the same year that Italy declared war against the Allies, Germany used its stunningly successful lightning fast attacks (*blitzkrieg*) to capture Norway, Denmark, France, and the Netherlands. The Germans then set their sights on Great Britain and planned for a sea-land invasion. The invasion never occurred, but German attacks, mainly from the air, continued to terrorize the British mainland throughout the war. At this point, things were looking pretty good for the Axis Powers, as Japan was having success of its own in Asia.

In June 1941, however, Hitler made what would become his largest tactical error of the war – the invasion of the Soviet Union – codenamed Operation Barbarossa. Hitler had long believed that the German Empire would be fed and supplied by the agricultural region of the Ukraine and the oil fields of Baku. Simultaneously, Germany would enslave the Slavic peoples living in these regions that would later provide "living space" (*lebensraum*) for the German people.

Initially, the surprise attack was a success. By the end of 1941, Hitler's troops held St. Petersburg in siege and reached the suburbs of Moscow, the capital, until they were stopped in the Battle of Moscow in December. As winter came, fighting died down, and preparations for the summer were being made. The Germans believed that once the winter was over, they could easily stomp over the Soviet Red Army and gain complete control of the Soviet Union. They planned to achieve this by taking Stalingrad which is located on the banks of the Volga River. The capture of Stalingrad would secure a path to the Soviet's oil reserves, give them control of the Volga River, and give them a major propaganda victory because the city was named after Soviet leader Josef Stalin. The result was the bloody Battle of Stalingrad, where Germany's advance into the Soviet Union was stopped.

This is the setting for *Enemy at the Gates*. Facing one of the most successful military forces in human history, the Soviet Union's survival is dependent on, according to the movie, hope. Commisar Danilov, a journalist for the army newspaper, comments, "We must make them believe in a victory. We must give them hope, pride, a desire to fight. Yes. We need to make examples but examples to follow. What we need are heroes."

One of these heroes became Soviet sharpshooter, Vassili Zaitsev, who provides this needed hope by killing many (maybe even hundreds of) German officers. In reality, a Soviet sniper named Vasilli Zaitsev did exist, but he was not the best sharpshooter in the Soviet Union (Ivan Sidorenko and Fyodor Okhlopkov were far more prolific WWII snipers), albeit a successful one with 242 verified kills. Also, to believe that the Soviet victory came from the actions of one sharpshooter is ridiculous. In real life, the Soviet Red Army's victory at Stalingrad was due to 1) the combined efforts of millions of Soviet soldiers that outnumbered the Germans, 2) the harsh winter of 1942, and 3) the successful techniques of Soviet leaders, such as the massive counter-offensive launched in 1942 that encircled the German 6th army preventing the German bases from resupplying. It is a shame that in the film, the victory is solely credited to the effect that Vasilli Zaitsev had on his people and on the battle. This was just not accurate.

Another aspect of Soviet battle techniques depicted in *Enemy at the Gates* is the Soviet's brutality towards their own men. In the film, when the Soviet soldiers retreat, their superiors shoot them on the spot. The film also has soldiers jumping off the boat transport to evade enemy fire, only to be murdered within seconds by their officers. Unfortunately, this was also true in real life. The Soviets fired at retreating soldiers they called "traitors" to set examples for the others so they wouldn't even contemplate turning back themselves. In addition, Josef Stalin Order No. 270 mandated that officers who retreated would immediately be shot and "all enlisted men [were] threatened with total annihilation as well as possible reprisals against their families."

An interesting topic that comes to play in the film is that Vassili meets and falls in love with a beautiful woman, Tanya Chernova, who decides to join the sniper division after being inspired by Vassili. In the film, the military allows women to join the sniper division and fight in front line combat for the Soviet Red Army. In reality this was also true. In the Red Army during World War Two, there were Soviet women serving in the military and paramilitary units in virtually every position. In addition, Tanya Chernova is a real historical figure, a former ballerina turned sniper who had no problem killing "sticks" – Germans who are only good for breaking. She eventually trained at Vasilli Zaitsev's sniper school and went on to terrorize Germans until she herself was wounded. So yes, the two Stalingrad snipers knew each other, but there is no record of romance.

In the film, Vassili's successful killing of German officers forces the Germans to bring in their own marksmen – Major Konig. This duel becomes the major conflict for the film with the boyhood hunter turned sniper Vassili squaring off against the evil antagonist Konig. The final section of the film sees these two employing any means necessary to draw out their nemesis with the hopes of earning a key kill. In the end, Vassili is victorious, but only after losing what he holds dear.

Although this storyline follows the legend surrounding Vassili Zaitsev, there is no historical proof that this duel existed. Different stories do mention a Major Konig being enlisted to end the sniper menace, while others point to an SS officer – Heinz Thorwald. In both renditions, Vassili downs the German foe with one shot between his eyes. However, history tells us these Germans and this duel never happened. No German record (and the Germans were known for keeping meticulous records) mentioned sending an officer named Konig or Thorwald to the Eastern front, and knowing the extent to which Soviets manufactured tales for propaganda purposes, it is more than likely that the entire story was created for sentimental purposes.

However, one version seen today on the Voice of Russia website recounts how Vassili, after that famous duel, recounted:

> "This fight lasted for three days, but it ended in one second. The fascist started the duel already aware of what I could do. Besides he had shot two snipers the day before. However I managed to slay him with the help of my fellow-snipers. I knew that he was a very skillful and important figure. When we dragged him out of the trench, and examined his documents, we understood that he had been the head of the Berlin sniper "school". Altogether I destroyed 242 fascists in the battle of Stalingrad. Many enemy soldiers and officers died by my apprentices' bullets. I managed to train 30 snipers who then destroyed 1126 fascists."

Although this account and much of the plot surrounding Vassili Zaitsev might be disputed, the bottom line is that at Stalingrad the Soviet Union did stop Hitler's invading force, a force that conquered almost all of Europe in a matter of months. Whether or not Vassili actually downed a German marksman sent to Stalingrad to kill him is irrelevant. What really matters is that at a time when other cities, other citizens might have quit, the residents of Stalingrad refused to yield and the hope (albeit manufactured hope through state-sponsored propaganda) generated by a few native heroes, combined with a resistance unwilling to break, led to the destruction of the German army and the eventual downfall of Hitler and his Third Reich. Although Vassili's sniper days eventually ended after a landmine left him blinded, his impact will continue to live on as a stirring example of how a man who spent a lifetime perfecting a skill and who loved his country above all else, could bring an end to the reign of one of history's most despised characters.

Key Quotes

Vassili: (*narrating at beginning of film*) Autumn, 1942. Europe lies crushed beneath the Nazi jackboot. The German Third Reich is at the height of its power. Hitler's Armies are charging through the heart of the Soviet Union towards the oil fields of Asia. One last obstacle remains, a city on the Volga, where the fate of the world is being decided - Stalingrad.

Danilov: (*talking to his supervisor*) We must make them believe in a victory. We must give them hope, pride, a desire to fight. Yes. We need to make examples but examples to follow. What we need are heroes.

Danilov (*writing for the army newspaper*) Armed only with a rifle, he [Vassili] quickly made the Fascist invader realize that from now on he would be punished for every step he took in the motherland, that from here on the only way was back.

Vassili: (*while talking to Danilov*) It's not like firing at a distant shape. It's not just a uniform. It's a man's face. Those faces don't go away. They come back and they get replaced by more faces.

Patton

1970
Director: Franklin J. Schaffner
Starring: George C. Scott, Karl Malden
171 minutes – Rated PG

By Zachary Moilanen

Synopsis:

Patton takes us back to World War II and the experiences of General George S. Patton, one of the most controversial and revered generals of all time. In Africa, we see him shape up a fighting force that eventually pushes the Germans out of Tunisia. Then, on the Sicily campaign, Patton and British Field Marshall Bernard Montgomery compete to see who will be the first to take Italy. In Italy, Patton's career takes a nosedive after he slaps a young soldier, but then after missing out on D-Day, he eventually regains the respect of his superiors and leads the Third Army across Germany and, ultimately, into Berlin.

Historically Relevant Scenes	
00:17:00>00:27:30	- Problems in discipline before Patton arrives
00:31:10>00:32:30	- German perception of Allied command
00:44:00>00:52:00	- Battle of El Guettar
00:53:55>00:54:36	- "MovieTone" news coverage of Tunisia
01:14:55>01:18:25	- Conflict in Sicily
02:18:40>02:19:40	- Allied victories in Europe
02:20:00>02:35:33	- Battle of Bastogne

Ratings:

Entertainment -   ★ ★ ★ ☆

Historical Accuracy -   ★ ★ ★ ☆

Historical Analysis:

It received seven Oscars, was a hit with critics and movie-goers alike, and even inspired the President of the United States to bomb Cambodia. But can a movie like Franklin Schaffner's *Patton* be all this and stay true to history? Amazingly enough, Schaffner deserves kudos for not only accurately portraying the story of one of the most revered generals of all time, but also by making it entertaining. Few biographies have shown the good, the bad, and the ugly and still have you loving the character by the end of the movie. Yes, yes… some things are omitted and a few details are smudged, but for the most part, World War II never seemed so real.

To start off, the Hollywood Patton and the actual Patton were almost physically identical. However, the soldier depicted by George C. Scott had, in reality, a much higher-pitched voice than Scott's. Although they were both equally tough, demanded perfect discipline and slapped soldiers for being "too tired to fight," Hollywood altered the voice in order to keep the perception that all military generals are gruff and battle-hardened.

Although his voice wasn't quite right, Patton would be proud to see that Schaffner's version still exhibited his most important quality — knowledge. Patton was a military genius. He had read all the 500 books in his personal library, some even in French, a language he practically taught himself. These books were about troop formations, tank warfare (as shown in the movie) and even the history of weapons. The general also believed he was the reincarnation of all the famous generals and commanders in history. Throughout his life, he envisioned himself actually leading troops over historical battlefields. This belief is touched on in the Hollywood version when Patton orders his jeep jockey to take him to the battleground where Carthage fell to the Romans.

Although Schaffner explored Patton's military knowledge and eccentricities, he shied away from his racist views. In reality he held many beliefs that today would be deemed racist. In addition to praising the Nazi treatment of the Jews, he also demeaned blacks and Russians. For example, while serving with the Ninth Army, Patton wrote down his views in an undated chapter of his journal:

> "The difficulty in understanding the Russian is that we do not take cognizance of the fact that he is not a European, but an Asiatic, and therefore thinks deviously. We can no more understand a Russian than a Chinese or a Japanese, and from what I have seen of them, I have no particular desire to understand them except to ascertain how much lead or iron it takes to kill them. In addition to his other amiable characteristics, the Russian has no regard for human life and they are all out sons-of-bitches, barbarians, and chronic drunks.

Wow. Now that's a bit… offensive. And that's what he thought about his allies. I'm sure other people in the world had racist views of Russians,

Slavs, and Asians (especially due to the need to dehumanize the enemy during wartime), but the general takes the cake. Some might point to his usage of the first black tank regiment – the 761st Black Panthers – as an example of his progressive, almost liberal views toward race relations. However, in his memoirs, Patton later revealed, "Individually [blacks] were good soldiers, but I expressed my belief at the time, and have never found the necessity of changing it, that a colored soldier cannot think fast enough to fight in armor." Although many of the black soldiers that served under Patton knew he was a bigot, they still felt honored to serve under such an esteemed, brilliant military commander.

Now, if you were to ignore that last bit and focus on Patton's military achievements, the film hits it spot on. Before Patton took control of the Allied forces, Germany had dominated the North African battlefield culminating in the Battle of Kasserine Pass, a huge victory for the German Afrika Corps. This was before Patton was in command of the US forces, but once he was firmly in charge, the next head-to-head battle would be in America's favor. At El Guettar, Rommel was met by Allied tanks, artillery and infantry. One inaccuracy in the film can be seen in the actual fight. It does a good job of getting the point across—Germans attack, Americans attack, Germans retreat—but it was far longer. The American's suffered heavy casualties as the "Germans quickly overran [the] front line infantry and artillery positions" before Patton's troops pushed them back. However, this battle that took eight minutes in the film actually spanned over fifteen days in reality.

Schaffner also does a good job illustrating the rivalry between the American and British forces. According to the film, during the Sicily campaign, otherwise known as "Operation Husky," Patton and Montgomery race their armies across the island in an attempt to be the first to capture Messina. In reality, although competition and glory did motivate these generals to some extent, another priority was trying to keep the 60,000 Germans from escaping to the mainland. Initially the two armies, Montgomery's Eighth Army and Patton's Seventh, were to take two separate routes, but because the Allied landing went off so successfully, the British army was ahead of schedule and Montgomery petitioned General Sir Harold Alexander to use the main highway previously assigned to Patton. Alexander agreed, forcing Patton to take a circuitous route, that, in the long run, allowed him to reach Messina first.

After reviewing historian Carlo D'Este's interpretation of the greatest amphibious landing in history to that point, book critic Walter Lord noted:

"Fans of the movie *Patton* think they know what happened next. Montgomery marched into Messina at the head of his triumphant troops - to find a smirking Patton waiting for him. Mr. D'Este assures us it didn't happen that way. Patton was indeed trying to beat Montgomery to Messina, but Montgomery would not make a race of it. He wanted only to keep the Germans from escaping and realized Patton was in the best position to accomplish that. In fact he urged Patton to use roads assigned to the Eighth Army."

One omitted event, however, occurred much later in Patton's military career while he was leading forces in Europe. Known as Operation Hammelburg, the general ordered a small unit of 314 soldiers, led by Captain Abraham Baum, to free a German P.O.W. camp. Now, this camp, located in Hammelburg, Germany, actually held Patton's son-in-law. Nobody on the raid knew that there was a personal reason to liberate the camp, and even Patton later said that "his goals were to [liberate] American POWs and to bluff the Germans about the Third Army's direction of attack." This would have been fine, even if it was a bit selfish of him, if it had been a success. Unfortunately, by the end of the operation, 26 men had died, few were able to return to base and the rest of the soldiers, as well as the equipment, ammo and vehicles were captured.

Another inaccuracy in the film was the weapons and equipment used. The American military, let alone any military at this time in history, did not use the M-47 Patton tanks. Not only were these tanks created a decade later, but in the movie they were used by both the American and German military. In reality, the Allied choice of tank was the M4 Sherman while the Germans used a variety of Panzers and Tigers. However, the halftracks and mobile artillery used were accurate. The M7 Priest, seen from artillery positions behind Patton during the battle at El Guetter, is one of the most well-known mobile artillery and was used by both the British and Americans. In addition to the vehicles, the German Maschinenpistole 40 and Karabiner 98k as well as the American M1 Garand Rifle were all correctly used in the film. However, the American troops were shown carrying the less common Navy-issue Thompson Sub-machine guns when in reality, the main infantry force used the M1A1 variant. But hey, if the director can get his hands on three out of the four guns that were actually used in World War II, I'm fine with that.

Another slightly modified section of the movie was the infamous "slapping incident." In real life, Patton was known for visiting wounded soldiers, and as seen in the film, "ol Blood 'n Guts" actually had feelings. In the film, Patton is shown awarding soldiers Purple Hearts, until he comes to one who says that he can't take the shelling any longer. Ultimately, he slaps the soldier, calls him a coward and sends him to the front. In reality, Patton actually "slapped and verbally abused two privates who he thought were exhibiting cowardly behavior" while he was visiting a number of field hospitals during the war. Because of that, he was demoted and forced to apologize. As another punishment, for the historically pivotal D-Day invasion, he was merely given command of a faux army in another region of England in a brilliantly planned effort to convince the Germans that the actual invasion was not coming at Normandy.

After his probation, Patton was appointed commander of the Third Army in Europe. After surviving a lack of supplies, harsh weather and heavy casualties, Patton continues on toward Bastogne, one of the last major bottlenecks of Europe. Needless to say, the Third Army crushes the Germans and, as Patton's last major military achievement in the movie, he finally links up with the surrounded American 101st Airborne.

With the help of military officials such as Gen. Omar Bradley and actual letters and journal entries from Patton, as well as actual props, stuntmen and vehicles, Schaffner did a superb job bringing World War II and General Patton to life. With so many movies using CGI, it's a nice change to see and hear actual planes fly over battlefields, tanks fire and artillery rounds explode. Sure, there are a few of these "props" that are out of place, but it's amazing how much of it is historically accurate. Also, Schaffner introduces and builds on Patton's character so well throughout the movie that by the end, after all the good and bad you've seen of him, you can still enjoy the cheesy Hollywood ending of the general walking into the sunset.

Key Quotes

Patton: (*in his speech to the soldiers*) "No bastard ever won a war by dying for his country. He won it by making the other poor, dumb bastard die for his country."

Patton: (*after describing the battle of Carthage*) "The battlefield was here…2000 years ago. I was here."

Steiger: (*describing Patton to a fellow officer*) "Patton is a romantic warrior lost in contemporary times. The secret of Patton is the past."

German General: (*while watching Patton's Sicily landing*) "Obviously they have two prima donnas in Sicily… Montgomery and Patton!"

Patton: (*in response to "How do your troops feel about you?"*) "Damnit, I don't want these men to love me. I want them to fight for me!"

Bradley: (*discussing Messina with Patton*) "There's one big difference between you and me, George. I do this job because I was trained to do it. You do it because you love it."

Walker: (*talking about Patton*) "Colonel, there are 50,000 men on this island who would like to shoot that son-of-a-bitch."

Los Diarios de Motocicleta (Motorcycle Diaries)

2004
Director: Walter Salles
Starring: Gael García Bernal, Rodrigo de la Serna
127 minutes – Rated R

By Tiffany Varinata

Synopsis:

In the 2004 biopic, *Motorcycle Diaries*, Ernesto Guevara, a medical student, and best friend Alberto Granado, a biochemist, take a road trip in 1952 to discover and improve health conditions in their home land, South America. Starting in Buenos Aires as a light hearted journey, their voyage takes them through Argentina, Chile, the Andes, Peru, and the San Pablo leper colony, where Guevara experiences a poignant moment of self-discovery. More important than the places, however, are the people they meet and how their stories teach and mold the boys' beliefs. Yet the magnitude of the impact this adventure has on the two does not become apparent until the boys separate and Guevara becomes notoriously known as Che Guevara, author, Marxist, political figure, guerilla warrior and Argentinean leader of the Cuban Revolution.

Historically Relevant Scenes	
00:54:18> 00:56:37	- Communist couples in Valparaíso
01:09:00>01:09:21	- Meeting Dr. Pesce
01:43:38>01:48:02	- Crossing the river barrier at San Pablo

Ratings:

Entertainment - ★ ★ ☆ ☆

Historical Accuracy - ★ ★ ★ ☆

Historical Analysis:

Friends and family knew him as Ernesto Guevara de la Serna, a footballer, "occasional asthmatic," and medical student who loved to read. The world knows him as Che Guevara, the legendary, communist leader of the Cuban Revolution who used brutality and violence to overthrow the government, while attempting to improve the living conditions of Cubans.

Rewind all back to 1928. The setting was Rosario, Argentina, where Celia de la Serna gave birth to Ernesto Guevara de la Serna, the first of five children. Celia de la Serna and her husband, Ernesto Guevara Lynch, a construction engineer, lived comfortably as middle class citizens. At four years old, a doctor diagnosed Ernesto with asthma, which forced the family to move to Alta Gracia, Córdoba in 1932. By 1942, fourteen year old Guevara met his soon-to-be best friend, Alberto Granado, who also lived in Córdoba, but belonged to a poorer class. When 1951 came around, Guevara, now twenty three, and Granado, a biochemist at age twenty nine, planned a trip around South America. However, their spirit and will to travel required them to abandon comfort and routine. One semester away from a medical degree, Guevara postponed his education for the trip. Granado risked a long-term relationship with his girlfriend whom neighbors were certain he would marry. Their journey, documented by both Granado and Guevara, later created the basis for the cinematic production called *The Motorcycle Diaries*, directed by Walter Salles.

In this movie, the boys first stop at Miramar, Argentina, to visit Guevara's girlfriend, Maria del Carmen "Chichina" Ferreyra. Here, Guevara presents Chichina with a dog named Comeback, symbolic of his promise to "come back" to Chichina after the trip. In return, Chichina asks Guevara to buy her a swimsuit in the United States and provides him with US$15 just in case he reaches America. Although Guevara *did* present Chichina with a dog, there is no evidence to support that he received US$15 from Chichina. In reality, Guevara asked for Chichina's bracelet to guide and remind him of her.

After their elongated stay at Miramar, Salles accurately demonstrated the slow deterioration of *La Poderosa*, the boys' motorcycle and only mode of transportation. In truth, its senile body, mended with bits of wire, Granado's favorite fixing tool, lost its tire en route to San Martín but lacked the spirit to admit defeat. La Poderosa brought the boys to San Martín de Los Andes, where, in the movie, the boys immediately meet Von Puttkamer, a cold man who, after Guevara diagnosed him with a tumor, turned the boys down when Alberto pleaded for hospitality. However, in Guevara's real diary, Von

Puttkamer's name is spelled Von Putnamer, and instead of the unwelcoming vibe he gives off in the movie, in reality, Sir Von Putnamer and his wife allowed the friends to lodge with them.

Though the movie accurately depicts their next event, crossing Lagos Frias, Guevara did not document, in his real diary, their wish to set up a clinic there. Perhaps Granado, who Salles kept on standby to prevent historical inaccuracies, could verify this notion. In the film, as the boys enter Temuco, Chile, Guevara walks into the office of a newspaper company and gives them a story to write about: two prestigious leprosy specialists, Guevara and Granado, and their brave journey through South America. The newspaper article gained the friends respect from locals and, most importantly, food and shelter during their journey. Historically, the doctors in Temuco, unfamiliar with Leprosy, were gullible and easily impressed by the friends' dreams and deeds, which allowed them to accomplish their clever newspaper coup. *El Diario Austral*, the newspaper company who publishes their glowing article misspells Granado's name both in the movie and in reality (the newspaper writes Granados instead of Granado). Fifty years later, *El Diario Austral* released another news article on the making of this movie and purposely misspelled Granado's name once more.

Still at Temuco, Salles inserted a scene which exemplifies family values. He introduced a mechanic who, after reading the boys' article in the newspaper, agrees to fix La Poderosa only after he finishes playing a card game with his wife. Afterwards, the boys attend a local dance party where the mechanic's wife invites Guevara to dance, flirting with him and pushing the situation so far that eventually, Guevara accidentally pushes her over. In truth, Salles accurately depicted the eventful dance, but omitted the fact that the mechanic, too drunk to dance, asked Guevara to dance with his wife instead. The rest of the scene, stopping the party with a dramatic quarrel between Guevara and the mechanic's wife and then being chased out of town by the crowd, was spot on according to Guevara's real-life diary.

The movie accurately depicted them continuing towards their next destination, Los Angeles, Chile, but as they tackle a sharp bend, La Poderosa's breaks fail and the two face a cattle nightmare which results in their motorcycle hitting a cow's leg. To get to Los Angeles, the boys hitch a ride on a lorry, but lug around La Poderosa's carcass, too attached to let go. At Los Angeles, in the movie, the boys follow two Chilean ladies, whose father is the chief of the fire station, into a bar and trick them into buying the duo food and drinks. In actuality, the boys concocted a formula to garner a bit of free food. First, they'd say something stereotypically Argentinean to allow the victim to identify them as foreigners. Once the victim and the boys start talking, Guevara asks what the date is. Automatically after someone responds, Alberto "sighs and says: 'What a coincidence, it was exactly a year ago,'" which prompts the question, "What was a year ago?" The boys tell the victim they commenced their trip exactly one year ago, and immediately afterwards, Alberto "heaves a tremendous sigh and says, 'Shame we're in such dire straits, we won't be able to celebrate.'" To this, the victim usually offers to buy them a drink. They first refuse the kind offer but then accept it afterwards, and once the first drink is consumed, Guevara politely and profusely refuses a second drink while Granado teases him to consume more. As the victims watch on in frustration, wondering why Guevara won't drink, they ask Guevara his reason for abstaining, to which Guevara "[confesses], rather shamefacedly, that in Argentina, it's the custom to eat when [they] drink." Jackpot – free cuisine.

Although Salles truthfully depicted the boys' clever tactic, Guevara's diary notes the duo were attracted by *three*, not two, Chilean ladies whose father was the caretaker, *not* chief, of the fire station. Guevara and Granado joined the fire brigade as Little Che and Big Che (*Che*, in Argentina, means 'pal'). According to Guevara, their two day stay at Los Angeles "simply flew by" as other volunteer firemen, along with the caretaker's daughters, showered the two with attention. On their last day at the fire station, cut out from the movie, the friends engaged themselves in a mission to rescue a burning, wooden house, but as they sprayed water onto the flaming abode, they heard a meow where the fire hadn't reached. Spotting a cat, Alberto leaped through twenty centimeters of flames and saved the little life – what a hero!

Unlike the movie, none of the firemen approached the doctors to cure anybody; nor did the travelers relinquish their trusty motorcycle in Los Angeles. In truth, the boys traveled to Santiago, where they finally abandoned La Poderosa's corpse. Afterwards, historically, the boys departed north by boat, where they hid in tons of melons and "[stuffed themselves] silly." As skins of melons trailed the waters behind the boat, a sailor discovered and forced them off, which resulted in the duo visiting the famous copper mine, Chuquicamata.

In the movie, before the two enter Chuquicamata, they visit a hotel where Guevara receives a letter from Chichina which ends their relationship. However, truthfully, Guevara received this note earlier on in the journey at San Carlos de Bariloche on February 11th, as opposed to March 7th, as depicted in the movie. After Guevara reads the letter, Salles correctly depicted the boys' meeting with a Communist mining couple who invite Granado and Guevara to eat with them. Historically, from 1948, militants of the Chilean Communist Party were persecuted under the Law for the Defense of Democracy. Because of this, the exiled couple traveled through the desert alone in search of work, their friends dead at the bottom of the sea. In the movie and in actuality, the man of this relationship, just freed from jail after three months, and his starving, loyal wife share their story with the traveling duo. This couple had such a profound impact on Guevara in real life that he remembered their faces even as he continued the journey, and the thought of the government oppressing the poor, simply because they fought for their right to a better life, angered him. In addition to that, Guevara felt guilty because he and his best friend traveled for the sake of traveling, while this poor mining couple traveled because their lives depended on it.

At Chuquicamata, as the boys are slowly walking by, Salles added in details of people carrying a coffin and a cross. Truthfully, although the boys did encounter a funeral before entering Cuzco (their next destination), the procession described in Guevara's real diary differs slightly from Salles' simple depiction. In fact, Guevara noted in his diary a crowd of black-suited villagers, who carried a coffin, "led by a dozen monks in colorful habits," whereas Salles only showed ten people, those in black carrying a coffin, and a few colorfully clothed people carrying a cross.

When the boys arrive at Cuzco, Peru, in the movie, Don Néstor, their official guide, gives them a tour of the small town. Here, they pass an old church with two bell towers, a clock and plain, glass windows and two differing walls: one made with only four rather large stones, and one consisting of smaller stones. Don Néstor then explains to the boys that the wall built from four large stones was known as the Incan wall, while the other wall represented the civilization introduced by the Spanish, whom they regarded as the "incapables." In actuality, this depiction is true, as Guevara documents Cuzco's churches and the history he learned while at Cuzco, "whose plaintive voice is heard in the fortress destroyed by the stupidity of illiterate Spanish *conquistadores*, in the violated, ruined temples, in the looted palaces, in the brutalized Indians." Salles then depicted a historically accurate scene (still in Peru) where Salles exposes the audience to Guevara's thoughts of how he regards the Incans as a much more intelligent race than the Spanish. Through this scene, the audience begins to sense the formation of Guevara's anti-Western political stance and ideology.

After their stay in Cuzco, not shown in the movie but recorded in Guevara's real diary, the boys traveled to Machu Picchu by a train in a carriage filled with local Indians. To emphasize the lack of education and civilization amongst the Indians, Guevara noted their unhygienic lifestyle. Men, women, and children would take a dump by the side of the road, but seldom wiped themselves. When they did, their clothes would become "veritable warehouses of excrement," as women wiped themselves with their skirts and wiped their children with their petticoats. The men did not wipe at all. Then, in his diary, Guevara mentioned Cuzco's archaeological museum curator of Indian descent. He recorded the curator's desire to educate Indians and to ameliorate their lives in order to create an ideal society, where Indians would not be ashamed of who they are. This man surrounded by inanimate, historical objects made Guevara realize the curator "was a living museum, proof of a race still fighting for its own identity."

Historically, left without a motor, the two became lorry parasites, which seasoned their journey with various personalities not depicted in the film. One of them, an Indian-blooded schoolteacher from Puno, told the boys of the Spaniards' attempt to wipe out Indian culture four centuries ago. He spoke of modern civilization's efforts to suppress the Indians and of the need to build schools that inspire its students to value their world – this garnered two pages of notes in Guevara's diary.

In actuality, on April 14, 1952, Guevara and Granado visited a small, grossly unsanitary leper colony where "thirty one hopeless cases…wait for death with indifference." Shortly afterwards, they visited another leper colony, a newer version of the old but without much improvement. Both lacked surgical facilities and a laboratory, but at least the new building had more rooms and better sanitation. After days of traveling, accurately depicted in the movie, the boys reach Lima and meet the famous leprologist, Dr. Pesce. By day, they visited the Archaeological and Anthropological Museum and a leper hospital, but by night, they ate dinner at Dr. Pesce's house. Although they did not spend a full month in Lima, both in the movie and in reality, the two self-proclaimed doctors had such a connection with the lepers that before they left, some of their patients cried and thanked them for bridging the gap between the healthy and the diseased. Their affection, noted Guevara in his actual diary, provoked the boys to specialize in leprosy.

The voyage out of Lima to San Pablo required the boys to board a ship called *La Cenepa*. In the movie, Salles fabricated a small scene to clarify how Guevara feels about the poor. The director showed a small boat behind *La Cenepa* packed with a number of dark skinned migrant workers. The screen then flashes to Guevara's sad expression. In actuality, Guevara did not record this in his diary, so this scene might not have occurred as Guevara recorded almost everything that later influenced his political views.

On the boat, as depicted in the film, Guevara suffers from asthma attacks while Granado works on buying Luz, a prostitute working on the boat, by gambling and winning an astounding ninety *soles* after starting with only one *sol*. Although Salles accurately portrayed the gambling incident, he incorrectly portrayed Granado's intentions to produce a nonexistent romance between Granado and Luz to make the movie more exciting. In actuality, their days, as Guevara describes it, passed by uneventfully – the only activities included eating, gambling and being bitten by mosquitoes.

In the movie, Salles depicted the San Pablo leper colony as a place which lacks necessary facilities. His portrayal proves historically accurate, as Guevara noted in his diary the condition of a leper colony without "daily electric light, a refrigerator, a laboratory, [and] … a [professional] surgeon to operate on nerves, eyes, etc." However, Salles emphasized not the inferior state of the colony but the connection between the two doctors, their patients, and the nuns who did not get along too well with the boys. Almost everything is historically accurate – even the speech Guevara gives at his birthday party is taken word by word from Guevara's diary – until the most climactic scene, where Salles shows Guevara, on the night of his birthday, crossing the river which separates the doctors from the lepers, the healthy from the ill. According to Glen David Short, an author and Che Guevara enthusiast, Guevara completed this feat during daylight on a different day rather than on the night of his party. In addition to that, the real Alberto Granado recalled that, scared of the piranha-infested water, he followed Guevara behind on a raft with a torch light. The rest of the movie, and its ending, where the boys depart on their Mambo Tango raft, Salles depicted accurately.

For this semi-documentary, Gael García Bernal, who plays Che, adopted an Argentinean accent and learned how to ride an ancient motorbike with his costar, Rodrigo de la Serna, coincidentally Che Guevara's second cousin. To create depth in his film, Salles used local extras and even included lepers from the actual San Pablo leper colony to shoot his scenes. He accurately traced Guevara and Granado's steps, and in the end produced a movie short of historical inaccuracies.

However, because there are so many adventures that constitute this journey, the movie would have played on longer than two hours and seven minutes had Salles not excluded a few stories. Just as memories often fade, details of this trip, documented by Guevara a few years after the actual events, contain slight inaccuracies. Yet, one thing remains certain. Granado broke a promise he made to Guevara's family fifty years ago – to bring their son home safely. Instead, Granado opened up a medical research facility in Cuba, where the duo reunited. Guevara, on the other hand, well… you might recognize him - his notorious face decorates shirts, key chains, posters, and coffee mugs today.

His true fame would come from his revolutionary involvement throughout the 1950s and into the 1960s. After his motorcycle escapade across South America, he eventually finished his medical degree in 1953 and then journeyed to Guatemala where he witnessed the CIA-led coup that overthrew what Guevera saw as the only true democratic government in South America. It was here that Guevera dedicated his life to overthrowing the imperial control of Western capitalism and from here he would act to fulfill his belief that the only way to gain equality for South Americans was through armed revolution. After Guatemala, he moved to Mexico where he met Fidel Castro, and the two men plotted the course for capturing and reforming Cuba. It was these years in Mexico that he gained the nickname "Che" because he constantly used the colloquialism (which means "hey"or "pal").

Once in Cuba, Guevera became the revolutionary leader known for the brutal implementation of his military and political actions. Che readily executed any who stood in his way, punishing both the opposition and those within his own camp. After leading Cuba through the transition period to Communism, Che travelled to the United States where he made numerous public and private appearances to a liberal-leaning American intelligentsia who struggled with the conservative, seemingly imperialistic nature of American foreign policy. After leaving the U.S., Che set off to foment revolution in Africa (his failed attempt to liberate the Congo) and in Bolivia, where he was eventually captured and executed by the CIA-assisted Bolivian Special Forces.

However, although he died a revolutionary, he will forever live on as the spirit of rebellion and the embodiment of those willing to put their words into action.

Key Quotes

Ernesto Guevara: (*reflecting on the trip*) Wandering around our America has changed me more than I thought. I am not me any more. At least I'm not the same me I was.

Ernesto Guevara: (*replying to Granado's Indo-American Revolution plan*) A revolution without guns? It would never work, Mial.

Alberto Granado: (*referring to the rule book after being denied food*) I think if I find it, I'll eat it.

Quiz Show

1994

Director: Robert Redford

Starring: John Turturro, Rob Morrow, Ralph Fiennes, David Paymer, and Paul Scofield

133 minutes – Rated PG-13

By Jack Pitfield

Synopsis:

The movie *Quiz Show* begins with university professor Charles Van Doren defeating Herbert Stempel, resident champion on the popular game show *Twenty-One*. Stempel is upset that Van Doren stole his fame and feels betrayed by the producers. His complaints incite a New York Grand Jury to look into the possibility of game show fraud. However, when the case gets sealed, lawyer Richard Godwin senses a cover-up. Using old fashioned detective skills, he goes after the television giants who allegedly prevented a scandal. The climax of the movie comes when Van Doren testifies before a Congressional Committee. Although Stempel and Godwin feel reassured that Van Doren will tell the truth, Van Doren is torn between his conscience and his loyalty to NBC.

Historically Relevant Scenes

00:00:00>00:03:00	- Sputnik's impact on the United States
00:06:00>00:10:30	- Introduction of *Twenty-One*
01:58:00>02:05:00	- Congressional Committee Hearing

Ratings:

Entertainment - ★ ★ ★ ☆

Historical Accuracy - ★ ★ ★ ★

Historical Analysis:

In the decade following World War II, America entered into an economic explosion. Relatively free from the catastrophic impact of World War II that left most of Europe and Asia in ruins, the United States entered an era of unprecedented expansion. Returning soldiers took advantage of the G.I. Bill, purchased homes and started fueling the economy. As the other nations of the world struggled to recover from the destruction of their infrastructure, the U.S. stepped in and became the suppliers of goods to the world. With a seemingly inexhaustible domestic and global market, it seemed that nothing could stop the American juggernaut, and everyone maneuvered to get a piece of the economic pie.

At this exact same time, a new invention, the television, entered homes across the nation. Because of mass production and the increase in disposable income and leisure time, Americans jumped on the TV bandwagon. In 1946, less than 1% of all US households had a TV, but by 1960, that number had skyrocketed to over 90%. With so many households staring at the tube, an entire generation was molded by the images on the silver screen. Commercial marketing soon dominated television programs, creating an idealized world for all viewers to emulate.

One of the first types of shows that gained a national following was game shows. It all started with *The $64,000 Question*, a quiz show in which contestants would eventually be asked a question that – if answered correctly – would mean they would win $64,000. The show was an instant success and immediately a host of other quiz shows followed. At its peak in 1958 there were 24 other game shows and over 50 million viewers. These shows were the American Dream, "[reflecting] the promise of hope, excitement, and potential sought by middle class America."

Twenty-One is one of the shows that followed *The $64,000 Question*. In 1958 it became the center of a scandal that captured the nation's attention. Charles Van Doren, a university professor and noted academic, had captivated Americans with his genius. However, a Congressional inquiry brought Van Doren to Washington so that he would testify about alleged corruption in the quiz show industry. This is the plot for the 1994 Robert Reford movie, *Quiz Show*.

The movie opens with crowds of people rushing home to watch defending champion Herbert Stempel, played by John Turturro, defend his winning streak against a variety of contestants. Stemple is portrayed on *Quiz Show* as a greedy, struggling, egotistical Jewish man who would do anything to support his family. At one point when he is asked whether he is nervous, he replies "It's only money." Later he says to his wife, "That box is the biggest thing since Guttenberg invented the press and I'm the biggest thing on it."

His ego "bubble" is burst by Charles Van Doren, played by Ralph Fiennes. A university instructor of English, he came from a well known academic family – his father was a Pulitzer Prize winner and his other relatives were also well known academics. Jack Barry, one of the producers of *Twenty-One*, described him as "just right for our show. No freak with a sponge memory but a genuinely charming young guy."

In the movie, Van Doren was waiting during one of his father's book signings, when his interest in quiz shows was peeked. He was watching Herbert Stempel answer questions about Paul Revere's horse. Van Doren answers about half the questions, but is puzzled at Stempel's range and depth of knowledge, and asks "How did he know that?" Later, Van Doren applies for *Tic-Tac-Dough*, another game show under producer NBC's umbrella. However, instead of being invited to play on that show, one of the producers for *Twenty-One* discovers him taking the preliminary questionnaire for *Tic-Tac-Dough* and invites him for an interview. They then immediately ask him to become a *Twenty-One* contestant.

In the movie, he takes the bait and reluctantly agrees to go on the show only after the producers casually mention that it will benefit education promising that "kids would run to do their homework" to be like Van Doren. The reality is slightly different. Although he "believed that he could become a role model for school children," he might have been trying to establish himself in the academic world, while getting out from under his father's daunting shadow.

Van Doren became an instant celebrity after defeating Herbert Stemple in an intense game of 21 that lasted two shows. He offered a "seductive performance" that quickly had all the "all the trappings of modern publicity." His university classes were full, he received proposals on a regular basis, and he had an enormous amount of fan mail. In addition, he was constantly guaranteed a set amount of money in a secret agreement with his producers that ensured his allegiance.

Producers were desperately looking for ways to boost their ratings. *Twenty-One*, as the name implies, was based on the card game Blackjack. Contestants were given categories from which they would have to choose questions worth 1-11 points. In the spirit of the card game, neither competitor knows his opponent's score. To emphasize that, *Twenty-One*'s producers placed the contestants in soundproof booths, ensuring that they couldn't hear anything. All of this was accurately described in the beginning of *Quiz Show*.

But the soundproof booths also acted as a way for the producers to control the climate. By turning off the air conditioning in the booth, the contestants sweat, making them appear extremely nervous.

Unfortunately for all involved, the producers were not afraid to go beyond making the players sweat. They played off their initial success by inducing the players to cheat. They had quickly discovered that by increasing a player's time on the game and subsequently raising the money at stake, the shows would get more publicity and more viewers. Once the producers of the shows started to give answers to the contestants, they became elaborately choreographed.

Producer Daniel Enright was Stempel's contact at NBC. One night before Stempel's debut on *Twenty-One*, he arranged to meet Stempel at his home. After arriving, Enright asked whether Stempel was interested in making $25,000. Stempel's reply was "Who wouldn't?" Enright, after saying "play ball with me kid and you will," then proceeded to prepare Stempel for the show.

Enright "selected a blue double breasted ill-fitting suit [for Stempel] which had belonged to [Stempel's] deceased father-in-law." Attempting to create a pathetic, underdog image for Stempel, he then proceeded to pick worn and low quality items from Stempel's wardrobe. Along the same line Stempel was told to address Jack Barry, the host of *Twenty-One* as "Mr. Barry."

Stempel was far from the perfect champion, which may explain his underdog appeal. He was described as having a "face for radio." The producers dressed him up to look like an ex-GI struggling to make it through college. In the movie, Stempel makes a big point of thanking Geritol for letting him get through college (in reality he was on the GI bill).

Later, Enright told Stempel to take notes such as "take 5 seconds pause, stutter, say nine points." Then he "showed [Stempel] how to ... show extreme tension." Then in a similar manner used to coach other contestants, Enright explained how to bite his lip, pat his brow (like in the movie), stutter, and breathe into the microphone. During the hearing Stempel said "this [acting] was the hardest part of the show." The *Quiz Show* powers-that-be wanted to create an ironic scenario where the supposed "genius" wouldn't know a simple, well-known fact, believing this situation would boost the show's ratings. After weeks on the show, during his final lesson, Stempel was told to answer an extremely easy question wrong.

Even the nation's sweetheart, Van Doren, was not above these less-than-moral practices. He had many "secret" meetings with his producer Albert Freedman that took place not in their offices like the movie suggests, but rather at their homes. In the film, the conflict Van Doren felt in the very beginning was reflected in his later Congressional testimony where he talked about "the intense moral struggle that went on inside me."

It is tragic that these two honest men were turned into cheaters before the eyes of their nation. Even though they were both extremely qualified, Stempel was in university on the G.I. Bill and Van Doren was a professor's assistant, they changed from game show participants to well-paid actors. Blessed with a photographic memory Stempel did well on *Twenty-One*, especially as he was receiving answers from Enright. However, like all actors, contracts expire, and Stempel was "ordered to take a plunge" after his ratings had reached a plateau. The movie brings up a conspiracy theory when it shows the sponsor ordering the producers and the president of NBC to let Stempel go.

Nevertheless, the producers did not appear to be unhappy when they were told to drop Stempel. Although they liked his underdog characteristics, they understood that the producer "[wanted] a guy on *Twenty One* that could get a table at 21." Later, when they are convincing Van Doren to join the show, they describe Stempel as the "annoying Jewish guy with a sidewall haircut."

After he was forced to end his stint on *Quiz Show*, Stempel created a huge ruckus. Under the illusion that he was an extremely popular figure, he demanded that the producers give him other positions on TV. In reality, Stempel went straight to a reporter. He felt he had been betrayed by NBC and was not afraid to blow the whistle on the game show fraud. Stempel told the story to David Gehman, a reporter for the *New York Post*. However, the Post decided not to publish the story because they were afraid of a libel lawsuit. His complaints and allegations about the rigging of *Twenty One* went unheeded until a Grand Jury case in New York. Although the Grand Jury listened to lengthy testimony, the verdict was sealed and never revealed to the public.

Quiz Show's third main character, Dick Goodwin, played by Rob Morrow, notices the sealed verdict and convinces his superiors – members of a Congressional oversight committee – that something is going on. Goodwin's first scene is in a crowded room with fellow lawyers. There he is depicted as the committee's "go to" lawyer, who not only is persistent but is also extremely talented. Goodwin is one of the few composite characters in *Quiz Show*. The writer, Paul Attanasio explained that "we wanted a detective story." Throughout the movie he was shown searching through phonebooks, watching endless reruns of various quiz shows, and interviewing multiple participants.

The reality is a little different. Dick Goodwin was a member of the "meritocratic elite," who, just like in the movie, really did finish first in his class at Harvard. However, the rest of his film portrayal is false. He didn't do any detective work and he definitely didn't reveal the scandal. Instead, he was one of the two Congressional consuls, along with Robert Lishman, who conducted the Congressional Inquiry.

The real credit for revealing the fraud must go to Joseph Stone, the Assistant New York District Attorney and the prosecutor for the Grand Jury Case in New York. Unfortunately, he received no credit in *Quiz Show* – one of the few, but very significant oversights made by director Robert Redford.

When the verdict was sealed with the findings never reaching the public, politicians in a Congressional oversight committee smelled a cover-up and they started a Congressional inquiry. Interestingly, there wasn't a legal issue in the beginning. There were no laws about fixing a game show, but it was an extremely popular subject and one that had the nation's attention. However, once the companies, participants, and producers began denying that they were given answers, it was perjury – an illegal and punishable offense.

Van Doren was asked multiple times about cheating on game shows, especially after the Grand Jury trial, but he stuck to his $50,000 annual paycheck and denied the allegations of fraud. He was under severe pressure from NBC, who had hired him for another job when he lost *Twenty-One*. However, it was only during the Congressional hearings that Van Doren finally confessed to cheating on the game shows.

James Snodgrass, an artist, was another contestant on *Twenty-One*. Just like in *Quiz Show*, Snodgrass provided the smoking gun. After a session with producer Albert Freedman, Snodgrass would type up a script of his answers and "put them in a sealed envelope...and address them to [himself] at [his] home address in a registered mail envelope." This became the proof needed to demonstrate the sketchy practice of prematurely revealing answers.

Twenty-One's three producers – Daniel Enright, Albert Freedman, and Jack Barry – all accepted responsibility for rigging the show. However, just like the movie implies, they justified their actions. "Our purpose was entertainment" and that "you cannot ask random questions of people and have a show," especially a popular one. However, the members of the hearing were not forgiving. They accused the three producers of "[conspiring] to bamboozle a trusting audience."

Unfortunately, because the producers of *Twenty-One* and other quiz shows had not committed any illegal transgressions under oath (they could lie all they wanted to the media), the Congressional Committee was unable to take any action other than to rewrite the laws governing television quiz shows.

After finding out that their hero had not only cheated but lied, the nation was outraged. Van Doren resigned from Columbia and disappeared to work on the Encyclopedia Britannica. He published under a pseudonym but his work did not receive near the acclaim of his father's. Sadly, the game show scandal ruined a promising career.

Both Van Doren and Stempel were tainted by *Twenty-One's* scandal. Stone called the scandal a "mass perjury that took place on the part of scores of well-educated people who had no trouble understanding what was at stake." Ironically, the producers managed to get away almost unscathed. After living in Canada for seventeen years to escape the media, they returned to the United States. Jack Berry and Daniel Enright produced *The Joker's Wild* – a popular show that made them millionaires. Goodwin became a speech writer for Robert Kennedy and Lyndon Johnson and happily retired in Concord, Massachusetts.

And today a new generation of game shows dominates the television airwaves, and even though many of these operate under the heading of "Reality Shows," many of their producers manipulate the characters and the outcomes in much the same way as the NBC producers did years ago. Maybe one day we'll learn that the TV provides entertainment and the only true reality is that which is in front of our face every day.

Key Quotes

Stempel: (*reflecting on his success*) That box is the biggest thing since Gutenberg invented the press and I'm the biggest thing on it.

Enright: (*reminding Stempel of the power structure*) You lose when I tell you to lose!

Van Doren: (*responding to allegations of fraud*) Then everyone lied.

Freedman: (*during the Congressional hearing*) It's entertainment!

Mark Van Doren: (*commenting on the ridiculousness of the situation*) Cheating on a quiz show? That's sort of like plagiarizing a comic strip.

Capote

2005

Director: Bennett Miller

Starring: Phillip Seymour Hoffman, Chris Cooper, Catherine Keener,
Clifton Collins Jr.

114 minutes – Rated R

By Alex Casella

Synopsis:

When a family of four is found dead in Kansas on November 14, 1959, *New Yorker* editor Truman Capote goes out to write a column on the crime; upon arriving he finds himself intrigued by the crime and the criminals as well. When he first arrives in the small town of Holcomb, Kansas, Capote doesn't seem interested in whether they catch the killers or not; he is just determined to write his article and return to his social life in New York City. Once he meets Perry Smith, one of the convicted killers, his attitude towards the crime changes and Capote decides he will write the first "non-fiction novel." As he writes, he finds himself more involved with the killers' lives and soon helps them in their appeal for justice. The novel begins to take over Truman's life and he realizes that there must be an ending for the murderers for there to be an end for his book, and he must sit and wait for the fate of his main characters to be decided.

Historically Relevant Scenes

00:13:00>00:14:10	- Clutter bodies in funeral home
00:21:55>00:22:30	- Detective Dewey's pictures of cadavers
00:35:25>00:36:52	- Famous pictures of killers
01:23:50>01:28:05	- Perry Smith's description of murders
01:44:00>01:46:45	- "Necktie party"- hanging executions

Ratings:

Entertainment -

Historical Accuracy -

Historical Analysis:

Today, the town of Holcomb, Kansas isn't well-known. Holcomb is "a lonesome area that other Kansans call 'out there.'" In fact, the only thing that the town is truly known for is the savage murders that took place there decades ago. On November 14, 1959 a family of four was gruesomely murdered for what seemed to be no reason at all. The murders and the events that followed became the basis for Bennett Miller's 2005 biopic *Capote*.

The Clutter family had been fairly popular in the community. Each family member had been known throughout the town. Herb, the father, was a strict Methodist and leader of the community. He was a widely respected self-made farmer, who gave jobs to farmhands whenever they needed one and often employed over a dozen at a time, paying each a fair salary. Nancy, the daughter, was a sixteen year-old high school student who had been very popular among classmates as well as the town folk. Herb's fifteen year-old son Kenyon was not as popular as Nancy. He often stayed home, putting things together and taking them apart to observe how they worked. Herb's wife Bonnie was almost the complete opposite of him. She couldn't keep up with his role in the community and suffered from depression. Bonnie had had anxiety problems since the birth of her children and spent a good deal of time in her own private room, in bed. On November 13, the family all went to bed, not knowing that they would not see the sunrise of the next day.

In the film, the family is not depicted at all; they are merely killed, photographed and put into caskets. The bodies are found by one of Nancy's friends, when in reality, the family had been found by two of the young girl's classmates. Less than a mile from the house was the farm hand, Mr. Helms, who claimed not to hear anything suspicious from the night of the murders. The background of these murders plays an important part that is not mentioned in the film. Truman wrote about the detailed history of the family in the entire first third of his novel, *In Cold Blood*, but in the movie it barely shows him researching the families after he first read about the killings.

When *New Yorker* editor Truman Capote read about the murders of a prominent family of four in the November 16th issue of *The New York Times*, he immediately jumped at the chance to do a story. The film *Capote* accurately portrays Truman's journey out west for the first time, with long time friend Nelle Harper Lee. The two set out for Kansas shortly after the article came out. Another historical accuracy that's portrayed is the fact that Truman set out to do an article, but after learning about the crime he decided to turn it into the first "non-fiction novel." Although the term seems somewhat contradictory, it was the first of its kind and created a new type of writing. The non-fiction novelist takes true events and narrates them as if the subject matter was fiction.

His creation of a new genre of books only added to Truman's larger than life persona. Truman had always been openly gay, but the writer also loved to be the center of attention. The man was known for his "high-pitched voice and odd vocal mannerisms, his offbeat manner of dress and his fabrications." Phillip Seymour Hoffman received praise for his "uncanny performance" portraying the five-foot-four writer, earning him an Academy Award. Being one of New York City's high-society members, Capote's obnoxious attitude and new age values were all questioned in the small, conservative town of Holcomb.

Capote had an open relationship with fellow author and playwright Jack Dunphy. During this time, the relationship was only something accepted in the art/writer/beatnik-scene of New York City. Truman always had been a controversial person. His photograph in the jacket of his 1948 novel, *Other Voices, Other Rooms* had caused a stir in the literary world as well as among the general public because it depicted Truman, reclining in a chair, staring into the camera with a somewhat "suggestive" look. Different interpretations of the photo have been discussed over the years, but Capote never cared, since the controversy only contributed to his fame and book sales. Before writing *In Cold Blood* the author had been well-known for his novella, *Breakfast at Tiffany's,* which inspired the film of the same name. The story was about a young socialite who moves to Hollywood to begin a film career.

Truman's childhood was not as positive as his adult life. His abusive childhood at the hands of his mother led him to drink, a point that is seen clearly throughout the film. In *Capote,* the author is seen with a drink occasionally in the beginning, but as the stress of writing the book weighs on him, his drinking increases. Much like in his real life, the drinking played a prominent role, leading to severed relationships and ultimately his death in 1984.

One of Truman's oldest and dearest friends was fellow writer, Nelle Harper Lee. The two had been neighbors as children in Alabama and remained friends in later life. Accurately depicted in the film, Harper Lee accompanied Truman to Kansas, as a research assistant and to help gain the trust of locals. Truman's new-age values and flamboyant attitude were seen as something questionable to the conservative locals and his friend was there to bridge the gap. Lee was portrayed by Katherine Keener in *Capote* as a strong female character, which in reality, she was. Harper Lee was a self-made author. In 1960 Harper Lee published *To Kill a Mockingbird*, a book that would go on to become one of the most famous novels of the twentieth century, if not all time. Although Lee claimed that the book was not autobiographical, she did take aspects of her life and put it into the book, including basing one of the characters off her good friend and fellow writer. Dill Harris, one of the female protagonist's friends who has an abusive and absent mother, was based on Truman Capote and his own troubled childhood. In turn, Capote used Lee as the basis for one of his characters in *Other Voices, Other Rooms*.

Harper Lee's novel was the focus of a few key scenes in *Capote* involving Jack Dunphy and Truman. The two attend the film release of her novel, showing how she has become a true literary celebrity. The film *To Kill a Mockingbird* was released in late 1962 and received immediate praise. The film was nominated for eight Oscars and won three, as well as three Golden Globes, securing *To Kill a Mockingbird* a place in movie, as well as literary, history.

Although Harper Lee had a bestselling novel, it never stopped her from supporting Truman when he needed it most - during his writing of *In Cold Blood*. At first, when Capote decided to turn his article into a book, his interest in the subject was not fully developed, but as the case grew, so did his interest. When he and Nelle first arrived in the small town, Truman was somewhat of an outcast and found it hard to get interviews. The only way that he gained enough trust from the people to conduct interviews was because of Lee's easygoing, kind southern nature.

In the film, Capote is seen interviewing the Clutter's main farm hand, Mr. Helms, as well as one of Nancy's good friends. These interviews did actually happen, as well as many others with the town folk that were left out of the movie. By conducting interviews with people like Kansas Bureau of Investigations officer Alvin Dewey, Capote was able to get police reports and the important information that provided the backbone to his book. Alvin Dewey and Truman Capote became close in real life, much like in the film. One of the many disputed aspects of this friendship was that when Capote immortalized Dewey in his book, he gave Dewey most of the credit for catching the killers. In actuality, there had been agents working around the clock in several other cities besides Garden City.

Truman's masterpiece has been criticized ever since it first hit stands. Although crime analysts and critics don't deny the facts, it is the portrayals of the murderers that cause the greatest consternation. Truman portrayed Perry Edward Smith as a gentle man, a portrayal many see less a reflection of reality and more a reflection of Truman's "close" relationship with Smith. Another fact that has been disputed was the killers' flight from the law. Aside from what was told to Capote by the killers, there is no evidence for what the two men did after committing the heinous crime. Another contentious part of the book surrounds the allegedly sexual relationship between Richard Eugene Hickock and Perry Edward.

Once the killers had been caught and brought to Kansas, Capote's interviews centered on the suspects' backgrounds. The two were incarcerated at Lansing Prison in Kansas, and Capote made frequent trips to see them. In the film, he bribes the warden to let him interview them whenever he likes. The only support for this claim comes from former Kansas Bureau of Investigations assistant director, Harold Nye, who worked on the case. The prison set in *Capote* was based off the writer's own personal notes, but making it as authentic as possible was a major task for the production crew. Capote interviewed Hickock and Smith in these cells, taking their stories and using them as his primary research for his non-fiction novel.

During the interviewing sessions, Truman brought in a fashion photographer to take pictures of the killers. The scene was in fact accurate, but in reality Truman's publisher, Mr. Shawn, did not allow these pictures to surface, for reasons unknown, until after his departure from *The New Yorker*.

When one compares the fashion pictures taken of Hickock to actor Mark Pellegrino, the likeness is uncanny. The real-life version was also equally morally bankrupt. Unlike his partner in crime, Richard Hickock had no worries whatsoever about the crime that the two would commit. A few years before the crime actually happened, Hickock spent time in jail with a cellmate who had worked for Mr. Clutter. This cellmate said that he had heard that the farmer kept $10,000 at all times in an office safe. After hearing this, Hickock began hatching a plan; little did he know that it was that cellmate who would turn him in years later. He met a new cellmate, Perry Smith, and the two began to talk about a "perfect score." The duo's plan was to flee to Mexico after securing the money. Hickock came from a middle class family who cared for him very much, and unlike Perry's, this family stayed together. One main point of Hickock that was only briefly mentioned in *Capote* was his sexual deviancy. In the movie, it is mentioned that he wanted to rape 16-year old Nancy, but Perry wouldn't allow it. In Capote's masterpiece, Perry remembers a time when he and Dick had been in Florida and Hickock tried to lure a young girl to come with him. His pedophilia was not mentioned at all in the film.

Of the two murderers, Perry Edward Smith was portrayed in both the film and the book as a soft, gentle man. It has been debated whether Truman had a romantic or physical relationship with the prisoner. The general consensus is that the two men shared so much common ground with their childhood experiences that they felt as though they had always known each other – which is incidentally how Truman describes their relationship in the film. Perry Smith was half Native-American, half- Irish and he grew up in a broken home. Two of his siblings had killed themselves, his mother had drunk herself to death and his father had been absent during most of his life. Perry had been in a motorcycle crash when he was a late teen and spent six months in a hospital recovering. As a result of the crash Smith's legs were permanently disabled. *Capote* director Bennett Miller never made a point of telling the viewer the reason why his character had a limp. Perry's legs had always been described as short and stubby, causing to him to walk with a limp. But in the film his legs appear normal and he only limps occasionally.

After years of trying to get the reason for the murders out of Perry Smith, Truman finally succeeded with only two weeks to go before their execution. In the film, Perry recounts the murder. He and Dick had gone in not expecting to kill anyone. The pair had just wanted to enter the office, grab the money from the safe and get out. When no safe was found, they began to worry. As a precaution, they took Herb Clutter down from his bed into the basement and chained him to the radiator. After realizing that there was no money in the house (Clutter did business by checks) the two became frustrated. Smith once said about Mr. Clutter, "I didn't want to harm the man. I thought he was a very nice gentleman. Soft spoken. And I thought so right up until the moment I cut his throat." After slitting the man's throat, Perry shot him in the head with a shotgun. He then went through the house, first shooting Kenyon on the couch in the face, then Nancy in her bedroom and finally Mrs. Clutter in her room. An interesting aspect of the murders is that they made the bodies "comfortable," tucking them in and putting their heads on pillows before shooting them.

There is no direct evidence as to whether Smith did the shootings alone or if both had. Smith confessed that he was the only one who committed the murders. Bennett Miller's depiction of these murders closely follows the novel, even down to the Jesus painting on Bonnie Clutter's wall and the goose engravings on the shotgun pump. After fleeing the house, the two murderers drove across several states to make sure they weren't caught. The next morning two of Nancy's friends, not one as the film portrayed, walked into the house after their ride for church was late. They then discovered the gruesome scene. The two men were caught a few weeks later in Las Vegas and brought back to Kansas where they received the death penalty.

About six years after the murders first occurred, Perry Edward Smith and Richard Eugene Hickock were executed by hanging at Lansing

Prison. Capote was present to witness the execution of the two men he had spent an incredible amount of time with over the previous few years. Capote wrote several short stories after the murders. His last book, *Unanswered Prayers,* was never completely finished due to drugs, alcohol and social events that Capote regarded as more important. *In Cold Blood* took over six years of his life, and turned out to be his most famous book. The sheer brutality of the murders and the impact it had on the literary world, make this one of the most famous murders in American history. The non-fiction novel, *In Cold Blood* and its author, Truman Capote remain two of the most memorable icons of the twentieth century.

Key Quotes

Truman Capote: (*talking to reporter*) Two Worlds exist in this country. The life of the quiet conservative life and the life of those two men. The underbelly. The criminally violent. And these worlds converged that bloody night.

William Shawn: (*talking to Capote on the phone*) It's going to change the way people see your writing… I think it's going to change the way people write.

Truman Capote: (*looking at pictures of Clutter family dead*) Why would they put a pillow under the boy's head just to shoot him? Why would they tuck Nancy in?

Perry Edward Smith: (*recounting the murders to Truman*) I thought he was a nice gentleman, and I thought so up until I slit his throat.

Perry Edward Smith: (*when asked if he has last words with noose around his neck*) Well…tell them, I can't remember what I was going to say for the life of me.

Full Metal Jacket

1987
Director: Stanley Kubrick
Starring: Matthew Modine, Adam Baldwin, Vincent D'Onofrio
116 minutes – Rated R

By Chris Theisen

Synopsis:

Taking place during the Vietnam War, this film follows the military career of Private Joker, from where he first learns to fight on Parris Island, a Marine Corps boot camp, all the way to the battlefield in Vietnam. Split up into two parts, the film initially depicts life in boot camp and how some Marines crumble in the face of intense mental and physical abuse from their taskmasters. After boot camp graduation, the film follows Private Joker to Vietnam where he becomes a reporter for the United States Military newspaper, "Stars and Stripes." While on assignment, Joker meets up with an old friend from boot camp, Cowboy, and follows his platoon around the battlefield and assists him in confrontations with the Vietcong. After Cowboy is fatally wounded and the members of his platoon thirst for revenge, Private Joker must decide whether to follow his morals and put the female sniper out of her misery or band with the other members of the platoon and let her suffer.

Historically Relevant Scenes

00:01:35>00:45:25	- Marine Corps Training
00:09:00>00:09:57	- Abuse by Sergeant on Trainees
00:51:00>00:51:45	- Exaggerations of "Stars and Stripes"
00:54:35>00:56:31	- Tet Offensive
00:59:00>01:01:10	- Killing civilians believed to be Vietcong

---

Ratings:

Entertainment - ★ ★ ★ ☆

Historical Accuracy - ★ ★ ★ ☆

Historical Analysis:

Stanley Kubrick's 1987 action film *Full Metal Jacket* shows viewers what life was like for a soldier during the Vietnam War, starting from treatment at the training facilities and going all the way to the battlefields of Vietnam. Although the characters in the movie *Full Metal Jacket* were completely fictional, Kubrick's depiction of the training, the treatment by superior officers, and the battlefield conditions made the movie one of the most accurate Vietnam War films ever made.

So how did the Vietnam War start? In 1941, a Communist party known as the "League for the Independence of Vietnam" or the "Viet Minh" was formed. Ho Chi Minh returned to Vietnam and led the Vietminh after years of experience as a member of the Comintern, an international Communist organization formed in Moscow in 1919. This organization founding purpose was created "by all available means, including armed force, for the overthrow of the international bourgeoisie and for the creation of an international Soviet republic as a transition stage to the complete abolition of the State." During World War II, the United States funded and trained Ho Chi Minh's troops in exchange for Japanese troop movement information. After the Japanese surrendered, they handed over ruling power to the "Viet Minh," who declared Vietnam's independence from France. This independence did not last long, for at the Potsdam Conference, "the allies decided that Vietnam would be occupied jointly by China and Great Britain, who would supervise the disarmament and repatriation of Japanese forces."

After the British left Vietnam in May 1946 (they had finished supervising the disarmament of the Japanese), the French pressured them to return Vietnam to their authority. After negotiations between the French and the "Viet Minh" failed, the French began bombing Vietnamese cities and taking over the country by force. Ho Chi Minh called upon America for help (seeing as Vietnam and the United States were once allies during World War II), but the United States government prioritized appeasing France, a nation it needed to prevent the spread of Communism across Europe. In addition, some government advisors warned that if Vietnam went the Communist route, other Asian nations might follow, an ideology eventually labeled "The Domino Theory." Therefore, even though the United States had pledged to end European imperial rule across the globe, in this instance, they ignored Vietnam's pleas for assistance, and, in fact, funded almost the entire French effort to quell the Vietnamese independence resistance.

However, even with U.S. assistance, the Vietnamese proved too much for the French forces. After the French were defeated by the Vietnamese at the battle of Dien Bien Phu, the country of Vietnam was split into Communist North Vietnam and Democratic South Vietnam, but "as dictated by the Geneva Conference of 1954, the partition of Vietnam was meant to be only temporary, pending national elections on July 20, 1956. Much like Korea, the agreement stipulated that the two military zones were to be separated by a temporary demarcation line." Backed by the United States, the President of South Vietnam, Ngo Dinh Diem, refused to hold public elections (knowing he would lose to the popular Ho Chi Minh) and therefore maintained control in South Vietnam. Instead, "beginning in the summer of 1955, he launched the 'Denounce the Communists' campaign, during which communists and other anti-government elements were arrested, imprisoned, tortured or executed." Groups such as the Cao Dai followers and Buddhists were accused of being communist, and since the majority of Vietnam was Buddhist (Ngo Dinh Diem was Roman Catholic), "his attack on the Buddhist community served only to deepen mistrust."

In 1956, Ho Chi Minh ordered "Viet Minh" members in South Vietnam to start a small insurgency to gain control of South Vietnam. This insurgency targeted government officials, and in 1957, over 400 government officials were assassinated. "While the terror was originally aimed at local government officials, it soon broadened to include other symbols of the *status quo,* such as school teachers, health workers, agricultural officials, etc." In 1959, Ho Chi Minh authorized an "armed struggle" where the "Viet Minh" fought to gain control of South Vietnam.

As stated before, the United States supported South Vietnamese President Ngo Dinh Diem because of his strict anti-communist beliefs. However, as Ngo Dinh Diem became more and more out of control, the CIA and Vietnamese generals agreed on his removal. On November 2, 1963 Diem was overthrown and executed. Due to the lack of leadership in South Vietnam, the "Viet Minh" used this advantage to promote their cause, and South Vietnam suffered a period of extreme political instability. As the situation in Vietnam grew more intense, "Kennedy increased the number of U.S. military advisers from 800 to 16,300 to cope with rising guerrilla activity." On August 2, 1964, the USS Maddox was on a recon mission along North Vietnam's coast when it was "allegedly" attacked by Vietnamese torpedoes. In the same area two days later, the USS Turner Joy was attacked. The two attacks influenced Congress to give the President the power (Gulf of Tonkin Resolution) to start military operations in Vietnam to oppose the North Vietnamese, and the Americans began bombing Vietnam. Over the next nine years, over 600,000 American men would serve in Vietnam, with 58,000 of these giving their lives to stop the spread of Communism.

Full Metal Jacket follows the lives of a few of these American soldiers. The film begins with the marines shaving their heads (required for boot camp) and immediately begins showing the harassment many of the troops suffered from their Gunnery Sergeants while at training. The training was broken down into two parts - physical and psychological. The physical training (taking place at Parris Island, an actual Marine Corps training facility) is what people expect to see at a Marine Corps boot camp - marching, martial arts training, weapons training, and physical fitness (ropes courses, running, monkey bars). Not shown in the movie, but during the thirteen week Marine Corps training, soldiers were also taught about STDs, Marine Corps history, and good hygiene. In fact, hygiene (fingernails trimmed, facial hair shaved, uniforms pressed) is still a big deal today, and as shown in the movie, the Gunnery Sergeants used to go around the barracks inspecting the trainees to make sure they took care of their bodies and looked respectable.

The psychological part of the Marine Corps training was what most soldiers found most difficult. Many instances of abuse from the Sergeants have been recorded by soldiers, and that is because many Sergeants believed that abuse was a significant part of military training. "Their [trainee's] aggression had to be heightened, their obedience had to be secured, and their senses had to be honed in order for them to wreak the most havoc on the enemy and still return home alive. In many cases, military trainers felt that violence and abuse directed at recruits would create compliant soldiers, ready for military education. Basic training thus became instrumental to military instruction and survival in Vietnam." Some examples of abuse besides name calling included making the men feel like women, making the soldiers eat garbage, or making the soldiers stick their heads in dirty urinals.

In *Full Metal Jacket,* although all the soldiers suffer abuse from Sergeant Hartman (played by R. Lee Ermey, an actual former Vietnam Gunnery Sergeant) in one way or another, nobody suffers as much as Private Pyle. Coming into boot camp as a chubby, cheerful young man, Private Pyle tries to become a talented soldier, but due to his weight and lack of intelligence he often fails, making Sergeant Hartman upset, leading to more abuse and insults. Sergeant Hartman finally starts punishing the entire group of trainees for Pyle's mistakes, and after Pyle is given a blanket party (a common form of punishment from a group of trainees to another trainee, where the trainee is held down to his bunk with a blanket and beaten with objects by the other soldiers) he starts talking to his gun, develops glazed over eyes, and finally kills Sergeant Hartman and himself.

People who experienced what Private Pyle went through were not uncommon during the 1960s and 1970s. John Ketwig, a soldier in the war, recounted how his sergeant consistently hurled a slew of insults at his troops, one of which was a recruit nicknamed "Fatso." He commented:

> "I know your problem. You're fat! Fat! FAT! You're a fat, filthy, fucking pig, aren't you boy?' [became] common refrains employed to break Fatso's spirit. At the end of one particularly striking episode of abuse, Sergeant Anderson forced Fatso to defecate on a cigarette and carry the mess off the parade field before allowing the cold recruit to dress and return to the barracks. It is no wonder that Fatso finally broke under the psychological abuse and committed suicide."

Private Pyle suffered from psychosis, a condition induced by stress where the person loses touch with reality, has impaired judgment, and suffers from hallucinations. In real life, this condition was so serious that Fort Dix, a military academy in New Jersey, averaged over 200 suicides each year.

The second part of *Full Metal Jacket* takes place in Vietnam and starts off with the event known as the Tet Offensive which occurred in January 1968. Tet is the Vietnamese Lunar New Year Holiday, and the Vietcong decided to attack US bases during this holiday. The particular base Private Joker was stationed at seemed to be able to defend the base pretty easily from the Vietnamese, but in reality, a lot of damage was done to the allied powers (United States, Korea, New Zealand, and Australia). In fact, during the three phases of the Tet Offensive, about 6,300 soldiers were killed and over 20,000 soldiers were wounded. Although eventually the American-led forces pushed back the Vietnamese offensive, the public relations fallout had already been done. Because this battle came at the same time that government and military leaders had been promising that the war had turned in the U.S.'s favor, many became even more frustrated with the establishment. After this event, the anti-war movement that had been in its infancy evolved into a nationwide phenomenon that severely handicapped the government's ability to wage a successful war.

While stationed at this base, Private Joker becomes a reporter for the military newspaper known as "Stars and Stripes." This is an actual newspaper that still exists today. This newspaper has been criticized for its pro-war stance that oftentimes embellishes the truth. In the film, this form of patriotic propaganda was touched on when Joker's editor asks him to make up a death of a Vietnamese colonel, hoping to boost the morale of the soldiers and gain support of the people back home. In a war whose success was based more on body counts than territory lost or won, the American military was criticized for exaggerating "kills by 100 percent."

The movie *Full Metal Jacket* also demonstrated how the United States soldiers interacted with both the Vietnamese locals and the Vietcong. The very first scene in the second part of the movie depicts a Vietnamese woman as a cheap hooker and a local Vietnamese man as a thief. In reality, "many Vietnamese women were forced to become prostitutes to make a living because they were dirt poor." The American GIs played into this reality by creating a system where goods were exchanged for favors. "Richard Marlotas, a Vietnam veteran, described what happened when he gave small gifts, such as a bar of soap, to his favorite prostitutes 'They loved them! In that country they don't have things like that. Small things like that they look at as great - a bar of soap! That's how poor those people are!'" Also in the movie, Joker and his friend Rafter Man try to drive down the price for the hooker. To many viewers, this would seem cruel to pay a hooker only 10 dollars for sex. However, United States Marines were extremely underpaid during the Vietnam War. "Low ranking soldiers were paid between $150 and $200 a month for their service and an additional $50 to $65 for hazardous duty a month." The average yearly salary for Americans was $4,700 in the 1960s. If the Marine made $200 a month, it would be just over half the average American's income.

Although it was shown a few times in the film, one major thing left out of the movie was the brutal ways many American soldiers treated the Vietnamese civilians. Although it was by no means a common occurrence, U.S. soldiers did kill and rape innocent civilians. Although it was rarely shown in the film, the truth of the matter is that there were more civilian casualties then there were North Vietnamese soldier casualties. Due to the difficulty in identifying the enemy and also the indiscriminate nature of the bombings, although over one million North Vietnamese soldiers were killed during the war, anywhere between 2 million and 5 million civilians died. The Vietcong also disguised soldiers as civilians to attack American soldiers, so many Americans came to wonder if all civilians were members of the Vietcong. An example of this was shown in the movie, where Joker and Rafter Man are in a chopper, and a soldier is shooting out of the chopper at random civilians. He says, "Anyone that runs is a VC. Anyone that stands still is a well-disciplined VC!" Massacres even happened during the Vietnam War, most famously, the My Lai Massacre where hundreds of women and children were slaughtered.

Although not explored in depth, the Vietcong (coming from the word Vietnamese Communist) were mentioned on a few occasions. In addition to illustrating their role in the Tet Offensive, the film also depicts how the United States soldiers felt about them. The Vietcong was also known as the National Front for the Liberation of South Vietnam, and they were funded mainly by the People's Party of Vietnam and communist sympathizers. The United States Army usually referred to the Vietcong as VC. Soldiers referred to them by other derogatory names, such as "gooks," "grunts," "zipperheads," and "dogpatches." Less offensive names included "Charlie" and "Victor," coming from the NATO phonetic alphabet.

The Vietcong were also shown to have women fight for them during the war. Like the majority of historical events portrayed in this movie, this did happen. Generally, it was the wives, daughters, and sisters of men who went off to war, but some women volunteered just to fight. Some women learned to fire weapons on their own and were used for battle. It may have surprised many viewers that a female sniper killed three Americans, but women did fight throughout the Vietnam War.

Full Metal Jacket, although following a fictional storyline, was able to put key events in order and accurately portray the lives of American soldiers who fought in the Vietnam War. Both the physical and psychological aspects of boot camp were accurately portrayed, showing how the trainees were constantly pushed physically and trained through abuse, leading to cases of psychosis. Going into Vietnam, Kubrick also shows viewers the poverty in Vietnam and why many of the civilians supported communism. Overall, this highly entertaining film *Full Metal Jacket* does an excellent job focusing on the life of an average soldier, and the enemies he encountered during the Vietnam War.

Key Quotes

Gunnery Sergeant Hartman: (*talking to trainees*) Today you people are no longer maggots. Today, you are Marines. You're part of a brotherhood. From now on until the day you die, wherever you are, every Marine is your brother. Most of you will go to Vietnam. Some of you will not come back. But always remember this: Marines die. That's what we're here for. But the Marine Corp lives forever. And that means YOU live forever.

Recruits: (*reciting Sergeant Hartman's creed*) This is my rifle. There are many like it but this one is mine. My rifle is my best friend. It is my life. I must master it as I must master my life. Without me, my rifle is useless. Without my rifle I am useless. I must fire my rifle true. I must shoot straighter than my enemy, who is trying to kill me. I must shoot him before he shoots me. I will. Before God I swear this creed: my rifle and myself are defenders of my country, we are the masters of my enemy, we are the saviors of my life. So be it, until there is no enemy, but peace.

Door Gunner: (*shooting at civilians*) Git some! Git some! Git some, yeah, yeah, yeah! Anyone that runs, is a VC. Anyone that stands still, is a well-disciplined VC! You guys oughta do a story about me sometime!

Gunnery Sergeant Hartman: (*to Private Cowboy*) Holy dog shit. Texas? Only steers and queers come from Texas, Private Cowboy. And you don't look much like a steer to me so that kinda narrows it down.

Apollo 13

1995
Director: Ron Howard
Starring: Tom Hanks, Kevin Bacon, Bill Paxton, Gary Sinise, Ed Harris
139 minutes – Rated PG

By Shannon Middleton

Synopsis:

Taking place during NASA's 1970 Apollo 13 mission to the moon, *Apollo 13* explores the series of technical failures that threatened the safety of the crew. Jim Lovell (Tom Hanks), Fred Haise (Bill Paxton), and Jack Swigert (Kevin Bacon) make up the three-man crew sent into space to recover information about the moon. A routine mission takes a life-threatening turn when an explosion cripples their spacecraft, "Odyssey," making landing on the moon impossible and getting safely back to earth a huge endeavor. The uncertain fate of the crew triggered unilateral sympathy around the world, and for a few days, the malaise that had surrounded America's space program since America's first MOON landing was replaced with universal interest and concern.

Historically Relevant Scenes

00:34:20>00:35:35	- Launch of Apollo 13
00:49:38>00:53:42	- "Houston, we have a problem"
02:05:10>02:13:53	- Re-entry

Ratings:

Entertainment - ★ ★ ★ ☆

Historical Accuracy - ★ ★ ★ ☆

Historical Analysis:

In the decades following World War II, tension gradually rose between the two remaining superpowers – the Union of Soviet Socialist Republics and the United States of America – leading to a struggle that would become known as the Cold War. As much of the world recovered from the catastrophic war, one by one, nations began aligning themselves with either the communist USSR or the capitalist, democratic USA. In addition to this bipolarization of the world, the nations also competed in an arms race (stockpiling both their nuclear arsenal while enhancing their military forces) that eventually moved into outer space as both sides needed to improve their missile delivery technology and satellite capability.

On October 4, 1957, the USSR launched the first manmade satellite (Sputnik) into outer space, setting in motion a space race that would dominate headlines and the governments' priorities for nearly two decades. Fearing they were falling behind technologically, this "Sputnik Crisis" urged U.S. President Dwight D. Eisenhower to produce a new federal agency that would oversee all non-military space exploration - DARPA (Defense Advanced Research Projects Agency). Many of DARPA's earlier missions were soon transferred over to NASA.

The successful launch of the American satellite Explorer I propelled United States President Dwight D. Eisenhower to establish NASA (the National Aeronautics and Space Administration) on July 29, 1958. NASA officially began in October of that year and consisted of four laboratories and 80 employees. NASA's first agenda was human spaceflight and the possibility of safely sending a man into space and bringing him back to earth. Although the Mercury program, initiated in 1958, faced numerous initial setbacks, eventually it became a very successful program that tested the possibility of human space travel. Once it was proven that humans could survive space travel, the next step was to get a man to the moon. This is when the Apollo program began.

Urged on a by a pledge from President John F. Kennedy that the United States would put a man on the moon by the end of the decade, on July 20, 1969 the space program finally achieved their ultimate goal as Neil Armstrong and Buzz Aldrin took the first steps on the moon. The footage of this first landing was seen by over 600 million worldwide, but in the subsequent years, interest in the space program started to wane. Once America had proven they were technologically superior, many Americans questioned the need to maintain the space program. In the midst of the Vietnam War and Civil Rights tension, many people in America saw the space program as a waste of time and money. Budget cuts threatened the future of space exploration.

The film *Apollo 13* does an excellent job representing the threat of budget cuts and the lagging public interest. In the film, when Jim Lovell (Tom Hanks) gives a tour of the Kennedy Space Museum a politician inquires, "Jim, people in my state are asking why we're continuing to fund this program now that we've beaten the Russians to the moon" to which Lovell responds, "Imagine if Christopher Columbus came back from the New World, and nobody returned in his foot steps." This lagging interest by politicians was echoed by the public's diminishing curiosity. Whereas 600 million people tuned in to see Neil Armstrong walk on the moon, just a year later, Apollo 13's space broadcast wasn't even televised. However, as portrayed in the film, the near tragedy of Apollo 13 revived interest in space exploration.

As for the movie's historical accuracy, *Apollo 13* director Ron Howard explained, "I wanted the movie to be as exciting as it could be with out compromising the authenticity." This dedication resulted in perhaps one of the most historically accurate Hollywood movies of all time. Whereas most Hollywood blockbusters' only goal is making money, even if that means sacrificing accuracy, *Apollo 13* is accurate in almost every single detail, including not only what happens in space but also at mission control and with the families living through it. Howard spent extensive time studying the actual NASA footage and transcripts from the doomed mission. Howard, and cast members, also took the time to meet and talk with personnel involved in the Apollo 13 mission. Howard brought Dave Scott, Apollo 15 commander, to the movie set to ensure accuracy. Scott recalled how impressive accuracy of the set and script stating, "They were so interested in getting this accurate and precise, down to not only the words, but the inflection of the words and the meaning behind the words." Even though it is a testament to historical authenticity, *Apollo 13* still has some minor inaccuracies.

One scene, in particular, that never occurred according to Jim Lovell and Fred Haise, is when the crew is up in the space ship after there is a quadruple failure and Fred Haise accuses Jack Swigert of not paying attention to the oxygen levels. In reality, there was a quadruple failure, but the men did not blame each other. However, this scene creates drama, and makes the characters' scapegoating more relatable to the audience. However, in reality, this never transpired, and the men were so busy trying to stay alive that whose fault it was didn't matter.

Like the friction between the crew, re-entry footage was enhanced for the film. NASA footage did not provide any details pertaining to re-entry (ion storm), which left visual effects supervisor, Robert Lebato, to rely solely on testimony from astronauts. Lebato explained in an interview, "We thought when you're hit with friction it would just glow red and then go on fire, I guess." However, following investigation into the science of re-entry, Lebato realized, "It doesn't really happen that way. It's a particular kind of heat shield where the gas is being formed by its friction with the atmosphere. It creates basically a white shield, which is protecting the ship from re-entry. And later it starts to burn away." In order to film re-entry accurately in the film, Labato had to portray the space ship with an almost liquid white flame surrounding it, as it careens toward earth. In order to create this illusion, fire had to be shot at four seconds per frame instead of 24 frames per second. The result, in Lebato's own words, "…it gets really blurry and smeary and creates this kind of…well it looked like and ion storm to me." In the film, this re-entry is a climatic scene that not only appeared realistic, but also added suspense.

Another visually spectacular scene in the film is the launch sequence, which, like the re-entry scene is not completely accurate. In the film, the launch of Apollo 13 not only follows NASA footage of the launch, but also adds some additional camera angles that were not possible then and are still not possible today. In the film there are close-up camera shots of the rocket when it breaks away from the tower, and as it leaves the earth's atmosphere. These close-up shots of take-off are not possible due to the incredible heat of the rocket's engine as it hurdles toward space. The camera shot from above the rocket is also not possible because there would have to be a helicopter flying above the rocket, which, to say the least, violates some serious air traffic control laws. However, these over-the-top camera angles create great visual effects, which mirror the actual launch video, and lend dramatic effect to the film. Howard was especially proud of the launch footage, stating "That's a sequence that I'm very proud of. I think as a film maker that might be the most cinematic matching I've ever been involved with."

In addition to the slight improvisation with camera shots, there were also scenes in the film that were accurate, but were questioned by critics of the film. In American culture, "13" is a dubious number and the film accurately portrays the belief that Apollo 13 was an ill-fated mission from the start. In the film, before the launch, the reporters are questioning the crew by asking how they feel about their mission being number 13 and their response is simply, "Well it comes after 12." True to reality, both the crew and NASA officials appeared to be unconcerned about the number 13. However, Marilyn Lovell, Jim Lovell's wife, recalled that it just didn't sit right with her. She did not understand why it had to be 13. Marilyn Lovell was correct in her assumption that bad luck was to follow her husband's mission. However, there is one scene in the film that seems "hokey," but it is actually true. In response to the scene where Marilyn Lovell's wedding ring slips and falls down the drain while taking a shower, Kenneth Turan of the Los Angeles Times criticized Apollo 13 for including that ridiculous scene; however it actually happened. In reality Marilyn's rings did fall off her finger, as she explained in an interview, "Of all the years we had been married, at that point, anytime I'd ever taken a shower my rings didn't fall off and this ring slipped off, and to me it was an omen." Despite, this scene appearing "hokey," Howard made sure that it was accurate. Although initially NASA was not concerned with the mission being numbered 13, after the near tragedy of Apollo 13, Jim Lovell pointed out, in an interview, "After that no space ship was numbered 13." In fact, Lovell, in his novel, *Apollo 13: Lost Moon,* explained that there were actually several bad omens that he should have noticed, such as, mission command module pilot Ken Mattingly being replaced by back up crew member, Jack Swigert.

In the film, it is determined that an injured coil inside the oxygen tank sparked while the cryo tanks were stirring, which caused the explosion that damaged the Odyssey. This defect supposedly occurs two years before Jim Lovell is even named flight commander of the Odyssey. In reality, this is a simple way of explaining what actually went wrong with Apollo 13. It was not just the oxygen tank that caused problems for the mission; there was also a problem five minutes into the launch. The center engine shut down two minutes before it was supposed to, which in turn caused the other engines to burn longer than they were supposed to. This normally would not be that big of a problem; however, because the oxygen tank had exploded, and the oxygen tanks were relied on to generate electricity, every bit of power mattered.

Later in the mission, there is a period of grave suspense, as people around the world wait for Apollo 13 to regain radio contact after reentry. A space ship, according to the film, never takes more than three minutes to regain radio contact after reentry. However, Apollo 13 takes longer to reenter the earth's atmosphere and regain radio contact with NASA. In reality, Apollo 13 did take longer to regain transmission, because the space ship was coming in shallow (instead of coming in straight which would have taken less time). The normal time to come out of re-entry or ionization period was three minutes. Therefore, this is not a ploy by the film crew to make a more dramatic ending by prolonging the outcome. Apollo 13 actually took longer than expected. Jim Lovell recounted, "I think we came in shallow, which meant that we stayed in this ionization phase longer than the normal three minutes, which added to the suspense of everything. We didn't know anything about that, we were just waiting for…being able to hear the transmission and also to transmit back again."

There are very few inconsistencies in *Apollo 13* because this film was a personal project for cast and crew. They wanted to tell the story of what the three men on the Apollo 13 mission went through, and they wanted to tell it accurately. Director Ron Howard wanted to ensure the film was as authentic as possible and that the cast cared as passionately for the story, as he did. Howard recalls how important the film was to everyone, "Nobody wanted to let this story down, not the actors, not the crew members, no one." As a result, *Apollo 13* was a beautifully told story of the "successful failure" of a mission. *Apollo 13* even impressed NASA astronaut Dave Scott, Apollo 15 commander, who stated, "In addition to being a very entertaining film it'll go into the records as being a source of accurate data in the future." It succeeded in reminding the audience of the dangers of space travel and the incredible determination of the human spirit.

Key Quotes

Jim Lovell: (*upon hearing an explosion*) Houston, we have a problem.

Jim Lovell: (*watching Neil Armstrong land on the moon*) From now on we live in a world where man has walked on the moon.

Gene Kranz: (*responding to re-entry obstacles*) I don't care what it was designed to do. I want to know what it can do.

Gene Kranz: (*considering crew's safe return*) We have never lost an American in space, and we sure as hell aren't going to loose one on my watch.

Marylyn Lovell: (*finding out there are problems with her husband's space ship*) Don't give me that NASA bullshit. I want to know what's happening to my husband!

The Day After

1983

Director: Nicholas Meyer
Starring: Jason Robards, Steve Guttenberg, John Lithgow
127 minutes – Unrated

By Ellie Stanton

Synopsis:

Set in a peaceful town in Kansas in 1983, *The Day After* tells the story of several average Americans as they struggle to recover from a nuclear attack. Although the events that culminated in war are explained, the real focus of the film is on the devastating consequences of war for its victims in the heartland of America. Russell Oakes is living a comfortable life as a doctor when he suddenly finds himself caught in traffic at the time of the nuclear blast. He heads to the local hospital, where he spends the rest of the film treating the wounded along with Dr. Sam Hachiya and Nurse Bauer. Meanwhile, farmer Jim Dahlberg and his family, who live in a rural area close to a missile launch site, must seek shelter from the fallout in the basement of their home. They slowly develop symptoms of radiation sickness while they try to cope with the chaos that has followed the attack. The movie's concentration on the destruction of individual lives, social order and the environment leaves the viewer with a strong sense of the hopelessness we would face in the aftermath of nuclear war.

Historically Relevant Scenes	
00:15:00>00:16:00	- Depiction of missile launch site
00:58:00>01:01:00	- Explosion of nuclear bomb
01:06:00>01:22:00	- Impact on environment
01:32:00>01:48:00	- Deteriorating health of survivors

Ratings:

Entertainment - ★ ★ ★ ☆

Historical Accuracy - ★ ★ ☆ ☆

Historical Analysis:

The TV movie *The Day After* portrays a scenario in which forty years of Cold War tensions have led to a nuclear war. While this war did not in fact happen, a nuclear attack felt like a real possibility in 1983 after decades of ideological confrontation and a continuing arms race. The real significance of the film lies in its visualization of the horrors of "the day after" a nuclear strike, as well as the American public's reaction to the film within the context of the fear of nuclear war prevalent in the early 1980s.

At its most basic level, the Cold War was a war over ideas. The United States operated as a democracy with a capitalist economy based on free enterprise, while the Soviet Union was a one-party state in which the Communist Party controlled the government, the economy, and the lives of its people. The leading ideologies of the Soviet Union conflicted with those of the United States, which refused to recognize it until 1933. As Nazi Germany became more aggressive with the onset of World War II, the United States and the Soviet Union entered an alliance of convenience. Though underlying tensions between the two nations remained, they worked together to defeat Nazi Germany from 1941 to 1945.

By the end of World War II in 1945, the United States and the Soviet Union emerged as superpowers, nations with the strongest military forces in the world. Meanwhile, the war had left many of the countries in Europe in economic ruin and political chaos. The stark contrast in the economic and political policies of the two superpowers meant that they had very different ideas for how to handle post-war reconstruction. The United States wanted to ensure the return or establishment of democracy in post-war Europe, fearing that the Soviet Union would exploit the instability in order to spread communism and Soviet control, as it ultimately did.

From the perspective of the Soviet Union, their nation had endured enormous suffering during World War I and II, including horrific casualties. Over three million of their people died in World War I and over 23 million died in World War II, more than any other participating nation. The Soviet Union sought above all protection from future losses, and therefore moved in to Eastern Europe to secure its borders. To contain this threatening advance, the United States enacted the Truman Doctrine in 1947, which supported vulnerable Greece and Turkey with economic and military aid. It proclaimed that "it must be the policy of the United States to support free peoples who are resisting attempted subjugation by armed minorities or outside pressures." The Marshall Plan followed shortly after. It pledged to aid allies in Europe with reconstruction while countering communist threats at the same time. These actions represented the policy of containment, which grew out of the desire to stop the spread of communism. This idea would become a cornerstone of American foreign policy for the remainder of the Cold War. In fact, one scene in *The Day After* shows a young man suggesting that "maybe [we] can contain it," in reference to the "containment" of a possible Soviet nuclear attack.

The growing Soviet threat caused the Western democracies to establish the North Atlantic Treaty Organization, or NATO, in April 1949. The organization committed all members to agree that "an armed attack against one...shall be considered an attack against them all." The Soviet Union perceived this alliance as a threat, and in turn organized the Warsaw Pact of all the nations under its control. British Prime Minister Winston Churchill coined the phrase "iron curtain" to describe the division that had descended upon Europe. It was a symbolic barrier that marked the physical and ideological divide between the democratic West and the communist East.

The tensions between the superpowers grew with the onset of the Arms Race, in which both sides competed for supremacy in the number and technological sophistication of nuclear weapons. The United States had dropped two atomic bombs on Japan (one on Hiroshima and the other on Nagasaki) to "hasten the end of war [and it had] the 'bonus effect' of pressuring the Soviet Union." Once the military potential of nuclear weapons had been demonstrated, the governments of the United States and the Soviet Union poured billions of dollars into the development of more powerful weapons. At its peak number of nuclear weapons in 1965 the United States possessed around 30,000 nuclear warheads, and the Soviet Union at its peak in 1986 had over 45,000 warheads. The most important of the new technological developments, the intercontinental ballistic missile (ICBM), could deliver the weapons at targets thousands of miles away. The new long-range weapons could hit any target in the world, and the threat of complete annihilation led to the mounting fear of a nuclear holocaust.

Both the Soviet Union and the United States, however, were aware of the total destruction that an exchange of ICBMs would cause. Both nations therefore adopted the so-called doctrine of Mutual Assured Destruction (MAD), the policy of avoiding a nuclear war because neither country could survive a nuclear exchange. An integral component of this was the "Launch on Warning" strategy, whereby, if the United States received indications that the Soviet Union planned to attack, it would launch a full-scale attack on the Soviet Union before U.S. missiles could be destroyed. *The Day After* illustrates what happens when deterrence fails and this strategy is implemented.

Mutual Assured Destruction arose out of the fear of the other side's capacity to retaliate. This was evident during the Cuban Missile Crisis, a brief period in 1962 when tensions peaked to the point that a nuclear war between the United States and the Soviet Union appeared inevitable. The Soviet Union thought their nuclear weapons were inferior to those of the United States, so Khrushchev decided that placing missiles in Cuba would increase his "strategic arsenal" and deter an American attack on the Soviet Union. U.S. reconnaissance aircraft spotted the missile sites, and the crisis began when the Soviet Union shot down an American U-2 spy plane over Cuba. The two week-long confrontation ended with the United States agreeing not to invade Cuba if the Soviet Union removed its missiles. For many Americans, the Cuban Missile Crisis was a period of "imprisonment in fear, expectation, and/or denial." It became the single moment in which the Cold War came closest to escalating into nuclear war. *The Day After* shows what might have happened if the Cuban Missile Crisis had not been resolved peacefully.

Although the 1970s were a decade marked by a gradual increase in arms control measures, the election of Ronald Reagan in 1980 signaled a shift in U.S.-Soviet relations. Reagan ran on a campaign platform that opposed détente (peaceful coexistence with an enemy) and the concessions associated with it. The early 1980s became what is known as the "Second Cold War," as hostility escalated once again. Reagan authorized the spending of $2.2 trillion on the military. He installed cruise missiles in Europe, and he launched the Strategic Defense Initiative, or SDI. Based on the idea of shooting down enemy missiles while they were in mid-flight, the SDI strategy, nicknamed "Star Wars," inspired a great deal of resentment in the Soviet Union. Arms control talks and bans on nuclear testing had completely halted by the time *The Day After* aired, in the midst of growing nuclear tensions.

By the summer of 1983, President Reagan and Soviet leader Yuri Andropov's relationship grew openly hostile. Andropov lashed out in response to SDI, claiming Reagan was "inventing new plans on how to unleash a nuclear war in the best way, with the hope of winning it." Reagan saw SDI as a defensive measure, while Andropov interpreted it as an aggressive action. Andropov accused Reagan of "deliberately lying" to justify the program. In response Reagan denounced the Soviet Union as the "Evil Empire." This was a far cry from the relative détente of the previous decade.

The diplomatic tension coupled with the breakdown in arms control talks instilled a widespread fear of attack. For the first time since the Cuban Missile Crisis, nuclear war seemed like a very real possibility. This peak in Cold War fear inspired "nuclear realism" as film and television attempted to graphically depict nuclear war scenarios.

Nuclear war films such as *War Games*, *Threads*, and *On the Beach* all posed scenarios that ended in the detonation of a nuclear weapon. *The Day After* was no exception. The movie follows the lives of the citizens of a Kansas town while numerous television and radio news reports discuss an escalating international conflict. The media reports that there has been a rebellion in the East German army, causing the Soviet Union to impose a blockade of West Berlin. Such an event actually happened in 1948 when the Soviet Union blockaded all railroad and road access to the Western-occupied areas of West Berlin (control of the city had previously been divided between the Soviet Union, the United States, France, and Great Britain). In that instance, the massive Berlin airlift, which ensured the survival of West Berlin, averted the crisis. No such solution occurs in the plot of *The Day After*.

The United States responds by issuing an ultimatum that the Soviet Union end the blockade by the next day or it will be regarded as an act of war. The Soviets flatly refuse. The President then places the U.S. armed forces on DEFCON 2 alert (the same precautionary measure enacted by Kennedy during the Cuban Missile Crisis). There is an initial nuclear exchange in Belgium, but the filmmakers are deliberately vague about which superpower attacks first. Regardless of who started it, because of Mutual Assured Destruction, both sides face annihilation. The overall emphasis of the movie is not the events leading to nuclear war, but rather the stories of ordinary Americans who survive the initial blast and face a horrific aftermath.

Even so, the catalyst for war in the film, although fictional, may be compared to what could have happened had the Cuban Missile Crisis not been resolved diplomatically. In fact, the character Dr. Russell Oakes declares that "it's 1962 all over again," to which his wife replies "it didn't happen then…it's not going to happen."

Unlike 1962, when Kennedy and Khrushchev made choices that averted the potential use of nuclear weapons, in this fictional scenario the "crisis" is realized. In an instant a mushroom cloud flashes over a highway in the countryside. The high-altitude of the explosion means that it is not instantly lethal, but its radiation creates an Electromagnetic Pulse that burns out the entire supply of electricity, in cars as well as homes and businesses. The air burst is immediately followed by a ground burst that vaporizes anyone in its vicinity and devastates the surrounding area. The survivors are left without electricity or any means of communication. The infrastructure of modern life is destroyed and the soil is rendered infertile. In the months that follow, with their livestock dead and with no engines to drive machinery, farmers are at a loss as to how to produce food. Even wood, contaminated by radiation, cannot be burned as fuel.

There is no exaggeration in this depiction if we compare it to the aftermath of the atomic bomb's detonation in Hiroshima. That bomb detonated at 1,900 feet above the ground and struck the city with an explosive force of 12,500 tons of TNT. A college student described the extreme force of the explosion:

> "I felt as though I had been struck on the back with something like a big hammer, and thrown into boiling oil... The vicinity was in pitch darkness; from the depths of the gloom, bright red flames rise crackling, and spread moment by moment. The faces of my friends who just before were working energetically are now burned and blistered, their clothes torn to rags."

280,000 citizens lived in Hiroshima. 100,000 died instantly, while the blast obliterated much of the city. As a witness described it, "the wave knocked down buildings, burned trees and people, and started the thousands of fires that finished off much of the city's structures." The bomb completely destroyed 48,000 of Hiroshima's 76,000 buildings. Even so, one of the doctors in *The Day After* cries that they "are not talking about Hiroshima anymore! Hiroshima was... was peanuts!" Here the filmmakers allude to the fact that in the decades since Hiroshima, nuclear technology had surpassed the earlier atomic weapons technology. The audience is thereby reminded that the devastation caused by the more powerful bombs of the 1980s would be much more horrific.

Aside from the environmental impact of nuclear attack, *The Day After* vividly portrays the hopelessness of post-war governance and social order. The President comes over the radio and delivers a less than inspiring speech, speaking of "no retreat from the principles of freedom and democracy" while violence and mob rule spread through the small town. Firing squads shoot people for looting, rape, and murder, while neighbors kill each other over shelter. The aftermath is grim, with no hint of a better future. Unlike *The Day After* and other disaster films that predict a world of utter chaos, the Japanese reacted quite differently to the only nuclear attacks in history. In the aftermath of Hiroshima, a peaceful festival "gave people, crushed by privation, a glimmer of hope which heightened their desire for restoration of the city." Reborn under the principle of democracy, the city elected Shinzo Hamai as mayor in the first post-war Elected by Popular Vote election. Yet a key difference between the real and the fictional post-nuclear strike societies lies in the scope of the attack. *The Day After* presupposes an entire nation under attack, while the bombs in Hiroshima and Nagasaki were singular events, making it much easier to regain control in chaos. As the credits roll in *The Day After*, it is difficult to imagine the ravaged town "rising from the ashes as a Mecca of world peace."

This is especially true for the survivors of the bomb who face long and painful deaths from radiation sickness. The film depicts a single hospital that is crowded to the point of anarchy as panicked people seek treatment for their fatigue, weakness, and bleeding. In the days following the explosion the characters' faces grow increasingly grotesque from radiation sickness. This change in the physical appearance of the victims appears to be accurate, as make-up designer Michael Westmore studied footage of the aftermath of the bomb in Hiroshima when creating his depiction of the sick. If anything, the physical horrors suffered by the victims are downplayed and some of the more gruesome effects of a nuclear blast were omitted from the film. For example, in one scene a child looks into the mushroom cloud and is instantly blinded. In reality, his eyeballs would have literally melted out of his head. The film also does not fully portray the gruesome symptoms of radiation poisoning. For example, a grocer in Hiroshima described the people around her as having "skin blackened by burns... They had no hair because their hair was burned, and at a glance you couldn't tell whether you were looking at them from in front or in back.... Their skin not only on their arms, but on their faces and bodies too hung down." To some extent the minimization of the physical horrors of a nuclear blast can be attributed to the film's brief time horizon because many of the more severe side-effects such as cancer and the collapse of the immune system take longer than a few days to set in. *The Day After* was a made-for-TV movie, and for a TV audience in the early 1980s especially, regulations for broadcasts muted reality. At the end of the film the audience is therefore left with the jarring disclaimer that "the catastrophic events you have just witnessed are, in all likelihood, less severe than the destruction that would actually occur in the event of a full nuclear strike against the United States." The fact that the side-effects of radiation were not depicted with complete accuracy is partly because the truth was simply too horrific.

ABC preyed on public fears and anxieties about a nuclear war in the attention they gave to the broadcast of *The Day After*. The network spent $7 million on advertising -- a huge sum then. Teachers assigned students to watch the film, and parents were encouraged to watch it with their children. As a result, half of the U.S. adult population (100 million people) watched it, a record for a TV movie.

It was no surprise therefore that the film generated such an enormous reaction from the American public. It created widespread psychological distress over the grim hopelessness and horrific aftermath of nuclear war. ABC set up toll-free phone lines and distributed half a million viewer's guides "as a way to help the Cold War-paranoid audience psychologically deal with the subject matter." Even Mr. Rogers, the host of America's most popular television show for children, made an effort to prepare children; he ran five shows about children's anxieties over nuclear war in the days preceding the broadcast. Many nonetheless viewed it as an extremely important educational film depicting a future which Americans should try to avert. Dr. Kenneth Porter, co-chairman of the New York chapter of Physicians for Social Responsibility at the time, said that if "families sit down and talk together about the dangers depicted in this television show, we'll be able to make it into the 21st century."

The Day After had an impact on more than the perceptions of ordinary Americans. More significantly perhaps, it affected the thinking and policies of one of the world's most important leaders at the time. President Ronald Reagan, the former film actor and a man who often spoke of movies as if they were real, had a private screening and said the film influenced him more than any military briefings did; in his diary he wrote, "It left me greatly depressed. We have to do all we can to see there is never a nuclear war." Reagan began to change his course, and would soon visit Moscow in an effort to ease tensions. Three years later, Director Nicholas Meyer received a telegram from Reagan after the President signed the Intermediate Range Weapons Agreement at Reykjavik with Soviet leader Mikhail Gorbachev that said, "Don't think your movie didn't have any part of this, because it did."

The Treaty marked the beginning of a gradual decrease in tensions and the beginning of the end of the Cold War, which came with the collapse of the Soviet Union in 1991. The Soviet Union and its state-controlled economy were ridden with corruption, inefficiency, and low growth rates, and its technology was falling behind that of the West. Selected to be the new Soviet Communist Party leader in 1985, Mikhail Gorbachev proposed economic reforms and more meetings on arms control initiatives. While Soviet society started to open up in the face of economic stagnation, countries in Eastern Europe began to hold free elections to oust Communist leaders. From 1989 to 1991, the Communist party dictatorship in Eastern Europe collapsed, the Berlin Wall came down, and the Soviet Union disintegrated. The iron curtain had been lifted, and the Cold War ended without the nuclear apocalypse portrayed in *The Day After*. The movie stands as a reminder and a warning that history doesn't necessarily always produce happy endings.

Key Quotes

Stephen Klein: (*discussing the dangers of exposure to radiation*) You can't see it... you can't feel it... and you can't taste it. But it's here, right now, all around us. It's going through you like an X-ray. Right into your cells. What do you think killed all these animals?

Alison Ransom: (*explaining her loss of hope preceding the birth of her baby*) We knew the score. We knew all about bombs. We knew all about fallout. We knew this could happen for 40 years, but nobody was interested.

Joe Huxley: (*discussing the future of war in the aftermath of nuclear war*) You know what Einstein said about World War III? He said he didn't know how they were gonna fight World War III, but he knew how they would fight World War IV. With sticks and stones.

Dr. Russell Oakes (*in a state of shock after witnessing the air burst over the highway*) I was on the freeway, about thirty miles away. I'm not sure...it was high in the air, directly above downtown. Like the sun...exploding.

Lord of War

2005

Director: Andrew Niccol

Starring: Nicolas Cage, Bridget Moynahan, Jared Leto, Ethan Hawke

122 minutes – Rated R

By Breno Cavalheiro

Synopsis:

Taking place during the late 80s and early 90s, this crime drama tracks the story of an opportunistic businessman who got rich quick off the instability of the Third World. After the end of the Cold War and the demise of the Soviet Union, billions of dollars of Soviet military technology began to disappear, mainly into the hands of gunrunners such as Yuri Orlov (Nicolas Cage). Yuri's main buyers include leaders of African nations who pay cash and don't ask unnecessary questions. In the movie, the primary buyer Andre Baptist, based on Liberia's Charles Taylor, watches his nation fall into chaos as he uses conflict diamonds to finance his weapon acquisitions. Orlov soon finds himself in the scopes of Interpol agent Jack Valentine (Ethan Hawke) who is eager to put him away, but when he finally succeeds, Orlov proves he has friends in high places.

Historically Relevant Scenes	
00: 38:00>00:41:00	- Post-Cold War Ukraine
00:44:30>00:45:20	- Explanation of AK reliability
0 1:41:00>01:47:40	- RUF and using diamonds as currency

Ratings:

Entertainment - ★ ★ ★ ★

Historical Accuracy - ★ ☆ ☆ ☆

Historical Analysis:

There are over 600 million small arms and light weapons in circulation around the world. Nearly 40% of all of these are in the US - enough for every man, woman, and child. Europe has around 84 million.

Contrary to popular belief, places like sub-Saharan Africa have a meager 30 million, however, the 30 million light arms in Africa cause devastation to a much higher degree than the 250 million in the US. The 30 million small arms in sub-Saharan Africa are mostly brought in illegally and are, for the greater part, from the warehouses of former Soviet nations, such as the Ukraine. Andrew Niccol used this situation as a basis for his film *Lord of War*.

The Cold War (1940-1990) was a period of competition and fear that saw the two emergent superpowers after the Second World War clash over the ideal form of government and economy. The capitalist and democratic United States heavily conflicted with the communist and socialist USSR (Union of Socialist Soviet Republics). The term Cold War, popularized by writer Walter Lippman in the 1940s, described the era where contact between the nations often occurred through espionage or through their support of factions in proxy wars, such as the Vietnam War and the Korean War. One reason it never became a 'hot war' was the premise of mutually assured destruction (appropriately labeled M.A.D.), which guaranteed that if one nation deployed its nuclear weapons, the other possessed the capability to completely annihilate the other. Because of the nuclear arms race that followed the Soviet's successful testing of an atomic bomb in 1949, by 1985 the two nations together had an arsenal of over 70,000 warheads able to destroy every chunk of land on the earth several times over. The Cold War was so much more than a mere clash of ideals. The two superpowers raced for nuclear and space capabilities. Both the Soviet Union and the United States were spending crazy amounts of money on both defense and arms development. Eventually the arms race paralyzed the Soviet economy, which eventually forced them to adjust their economic and governmental structure, forcing them to relinquish their control of their satellite nations. This Soviet collapse left newly independent nations like the Ukraine with nothing but a devastated economy, weak regulations and a vast stockpile of military goods - primarily AK-47s.

Mikhail Timofeyavich Kalashnikov, the creator of the AK, fought in WWII and noticed the advantage the Germans had because of their automatic weapons. While recovering in a military hospital, Mikhail decided to develop an automatic weapon to defend the "Mother Land." While he was healing his arm, Mikhail studied every firearm book he could get his hands on, and finally in 1946, the Main Artillery Commission approved his sketches and gave Kalashnikov permission to begin developing prototypes. In 1949, the Soviet army finally accepted one of the prototypes and the AK-47 (Automat Kalashnikova Obrazes 1947) was born. Little did Kalashnikov know, his weapon, which was intended to defend Russia would become the most widespread weapon in the world and almost synonymous with modern warfare. The AK-47 is said to be the most reliable ever, and "so simple a child could use it." The AK-47 is Russia's best export, mostly due to its effectiveness and ease of use. The AK was even put on the Mozambique flag and coat of arms to always remind its citizens of the struggle and hardships the country went through to acquire independence. The AK-47 is so common that in the film it was cheaper to acquire real AK's than use studio props. Aside from the prevalence of AK-47s, another interesting acquisition for the production of the film proved the availability of arms from non-military sources. In the scene where Yuri makes his first buy from his uncle in the Ukraine, the tanks shown were not props, but actually tanks borrowed from an arms dealer who lent them to Niccol before reacquiring them for delivery to a scheduled buyer. If it wasn't already obvious to the world before, merely the ease in which Niccol acquired weapons for this film proves the abundance of black market weaponry in the world today.

In the film, Yuri Orlov is an immigrant from Odessa, Ukraine. His family pretended to be Jewish in order to facilitate their exit from the Eastern Bloc. It is said that Andrew Niccol's creation, Yuri Orlov, is very closely based on a famed gun runner, Viktor Bout, however there are several discrepancies between the two. Viktor Bout was Russian and a former decorated soldier, more specifically, a Major, where Orlov is an immigrant from Ukraine with no military background. Another difference between the two is their beginnings. Orlov obtained his first deal through an acquaintance of his father. Bout became an international arms dealer in 1993 shortly after his retirement and the collapse of the USSR. Similar to Orlov, Bout is well known for supplying areas in Africa (like Liberia), especially places in which the U.S. has placed embargoes. Also, like Orlov, international agencies like Interpol also sought his capture.

However, after evading arrest for years, Bout finally stuck "his neck out for new business" and played right into the hands of a U.S. Drug Enforcement Agency's sting operation. After living in exile for years and having $6 billion of his transactions frozen, Bout fell into the DEA trap where American agents played the role of representatives for a Colombian rebel group. Once Bout agreed to deliver surface-to-air missiles and armor-piercing rocket launchers, DEA agents stepped in and arrested him in Bangkok, Thailand on March 7, 2008, where he currently sits awaiting extradition to America, Russia, Belgium, South Africa or the United Arab Emigrates. If Russia ends up bringing him home, "it is unlikely he would face any charges at all. But, for Viktor Bout, it doesn't look like he gets to write his own ending."

Although their fates might differ, one specific connection between the fictional Orlov and Viktor Bout revolves around the relationship with a Liberian president. The film's Andre Baptiste closely resembles Charles G. Taylor, Liberia's president from 1997 to 2003. Taylor, after attending college in the United States, rose to power after gaining 75% of the votes in a democratic election. His "popularity" was due in large part to his threat to plunge the nation back into a violent civil war should he not be elected. In *Lord of War,* transactions are made using diamonds as the main currency. In reality, Taylor did engage in diamonds for weapons transactions, especially with the neighboring country of Sierra Leone. Willy Kingombe Idi, an African diamond broker who buys his diamonds directly from the diggers in the Congo, stated, "You can't wage war without money, and diamonds are money."

These "conflict diamonds" refer to diamonds which were mined in a war zone and used to finance an insurgency. Conflict diamonds are a hot commodity because they are hard to trace and incredibly easy to transport. This exchange in fact really did happen, as Charles Taylor did help Sierra Leone by supplying them with military goods, however it's unknown if Taylor did his dealings through Bout or not. With these weapons and thousands of others, the RUF launched an attack in 1991 against the government, and this devastating conflict ravaged Sierra Leone for over a decade.

The RUF employed up to 23,000 child soldiers, many of whom were drugged to maintain allegiance. The film touches on this issue in a scene where Orlov, facing his conscience after killing an opposing arms dealer, sits in a bar and prepares to drink his sorrows away. The bartender urges Orlov to try "brown brown," a mixture of cocaine and gunpowder often given to child soldiers in West Africa. It encourages the children to do whatever they are told without even thinking about the consequences, and the bowel irritation the gunpowder causes promotes aggression. Aside from brown brown, child soldiers are also given amulets that supposedly protect them from bullets. This drug-induced anger and talisman-created courage transformed a generation of children into ruthless fighting machines who rarely thought of their actions and even more rarely were in charge of their own activities.

One other alteration involves the film's setting. In the movie, the capital of Liberia, Monrovia, is depicted as an incredibly run-down, underdeveloped city. Although because of years of civil war, Monrovia is not by any means an African New York or Los Angeles, Niccol grossly exaggerated the worn down state of the city. *Lord of War* represents Monrovia as essentially a war-torn ghost town, having only a couple cars, dirt roads, and only one filthy, dilapidated three-story hotel. In reality,

Monrovia has an 8-lane highway, many skyscrapers and even has traffic jams.

Each day that the arms trade business survives, child soldiers will fight and die. Andrew Niccol opens our eyes to the atrocities of child soldiers through the faceless industry of illegal arms dealing, even implying that American participation actually fuels wars in Africa. Dr. Sylvester Rowe, Sierra Leone's ambassador to the United States, warned, "For every child that is killed, you are destroying, a future of that country, so it goes on and on, the consequences of small arms and light weapons, illicit weapons, is intolerable, we cannot allow this to go on, it must be stopped." One can only hope *Lord of War* has encouraged someone to push stop.

Key Quotes

Yuri Orlov: (*opening credits, voiceover*) There are over 550 million firearms in worldwide circulation. That's one firearm for every twelve people on the planet. The only question is: How do we arm the other 11?

Yuri Orlov: (*challenging the motives of his consumers*) Every faction in Africa calls themselves by these noble names - Liberation this, Patriotic that, Democratic Republic of something-or-other... I guess they can't own up to what they usually are: a federation of worse oppressors than the last bunch of oppressors. Often, the most barbaric atrocities occur when both combatants proclaim themselves freedom-fighters.

Yuri Orlov: (*in custody, prior to being freed*) Enjoy it.
Jack Valentine: What?
Yuri Orlov: This. Tell me I'm everything you despise. That I'm the personification of evil. That I'm what- responsible for the breakdown of the fabric of society and world order. I'm a one-man genocide. Say everything you want to say to me now. Because you don't have long.

American History X

1998
Director: Tony Kaye
Starring: Edward Norton, Edward Furlong
119 minutes – Rated R

By Stevie Day

Synopsis:

The film revolves around ex neo-Nazi Derek Vinyard, a former gang leader of the prominent Venice beach gang D.O.C (Disciples of Christ), and his younger brother Danny. After brutally murdering an African-American would-be burglar, Derek lands in jail where he begins to reconsider the roots of his racism. In Derek's absence, his brother has fallen into Derek's world of white supremacist gangs, and once the reformed Derek returns home he must fight to save his brother from a life filled with violence and hatred.

Historically Relevant Scenes

00:16:02>00:22:30	- Venice beach and gang interactions
00:33:40>00:40:10	- Nazi gang racial attacks
00:40:41>00:50:50	- Racial argument
00:56:45>00:58:16	- Neo-Nazi culture
01:27:09>01:29:59	- Dr. Sweeny's speech to Derek in prison
01:53:57-01:54:53	- Danny's final words

Ratings:

Entertainment - ★ ★ ★ ★

Historical Accuracy - ★ ★ ★ ☆

Historical Analysis:

When the final shots of World War II were heard in 1945 it was believed that the diabolical subculture Hitler had spent two decades creating would fade silently into the night. Many hoped the death of its radical zealot leader, Adolph Hitler, would symbolize the death of the German Nazi Party that fostered an ideology of racial dominance and a culture of intolerance that led to the sadistic murder of millions of undesirable across Europe. However, this was not the case as the Nazi subculture merely went into hiding, only to once again re-emerge in the 1960's where instead of it being the platform of a national party, it became the uniting factor for a generation of ultra-conservatives willing to openly promote their intolerant beliefs.

Offering a modern look at the real life evolution of the Nazi subculture into what it has become today is Tony Kane's *American History X*, set in 1990's Venice Beach, California. As the evil subculture gradually sucks in the film's protagonists Derek and Danny, the audience comes to understand the extent of racism in America and the racist message of scapegoating that continues to attract thousands of adherents. The movie not only explores extreme racism in society, but also the extent to which the neo-Nazi, Skinhead, and white supremacy movement continues to influence young people and popular culture.

The roots of the neo-Nazi movement trace back to the Nazi Party's founding of the Hitler Youth during the Second World War. Adolf Hitler's totalitarian political movement sought to rid the world of impurities that could possibly infect the Aryan race. Unlike the historic Aryans who were a group of nomads who moved throughout Asia and settled in India, Hitler's "Aryans" were blonde-haired, blue-eyed Nordic people who he saw as the preeminent race. Hitler's idea built on the notion of eugenics, an ideology that gained popularity in the 1920s in Western countries and that promoted the selective reproduction of certain races to improve the human species and prevent genetic flaws from spreading. Hitler took this idea to the extreme, eventually supporting and implementing his Final Solution that managed to exterminate 6 million Jews during his racist reign over Europe.

One of the elements of Hitler's Nazism was the indoctrination of German's children. Starting in 1922 and ending in 1945, the Hitler Youth was a paramilitary unit which focused not on recruiting adults, but children. The units attempted to brainwash young children, ideally between the ages of fourteen to eighteen, in an attempt to forge life long members. Mimicking the actual ranks and structure of the Third Reich, it offered a stepping stone for the children to graduate into full blown soldiers and party members after adolescence. Focusing on physical rather than academic training, the Nazi party saw those in the Hitler Youth as future "Aryan supermen."They learned weapons training and military strategy, in addition to skills normally attributed to the Boy Scouts. Symbolically linked to Hitler's private military force, the SS (from the German Schutzstaffel which meant "protective force"), the Hitler Youth adopted the same s-shaped lightning bolt emblem, the Sig Rune.

However, whereas the SS used the double Sig Rune the Hitler Youth only used one.

As the Hitler Youth program became the pool from which later military officers and soldiers were pulled, its numbers increased in line with the rise of Nazism and Germany's eventual military incursions across Europe. Whereas in 1923, less than one thousand boys participated in the Hitler Youth programs, by 1940 membership had swelled to over 8 million recruits. Whereas prior to World War II, the Hitler Youth primarily trained for military participation, during the war, they actually took on an active role, helping the fire brigades, aiding in the rebuilding of bombed German cities, and assisting with anti-aircraft defense squads. With the German defeat in 1945, the Allies broke up the Hitler Youth. Because membership was essentially compulsory for any male born in the 1920s and 1930s, participating boys were not punished as men for their role. By the 1950s, essentially every male leader in German society held a link to the Hitler Youth.

Although 1945 represented the official death of the Hitler Youth, its racist ideology lived on throughout the Cold War decades. In the 1960s, the sons of former Hitler Youth members revived the tenets of the fascist movement, prescribing to a doctrine known as "neo-Nazism." With the aspirations of reviving Nazi ideology, neo-Nazism seeks to replicate the anti-Semitic (anti-Jewish), nationalist, Aryan supremacy military movement of World War II. It is crucial to take into consideration that neo-Nazism should not be confused with other Skinhead or white supremacy movements. All three act separately with differing beliefs, but overlap on many key areas and characteristics. One of the many key characteristics of neo-Nazism is that adherents deny the Holocaust or claim the actual severity or numbers killed are grossly exaggerated. Others simply attempt to justify the Holocaust citing it was retaliation for "sabotage, terrorism and subversion" against the party, claiming more or less that the Jews had it coming to them. The neo-Nazis wish to remove the Nazi association with genocide and mass murder, instead focusing on the positives of the initial Nazi ideology.

Similar to the neo-Nazi movement is that of the Skinheads. The original Skinhead movement began in England in the late 1960's as a fashion statement. With a growing disposable income, the younger generation hoped to "cultivate the right look," creating a fashion of clean short cropped hair, dressing in suits and smart clothing. This initial "mod" appearance later led to shorter hair and the replacement of suits with jeans, military jackets and boots. In addition to their fashion emphasis, the involved youth also became synonymous with a new form of music. After a decade of listening to music combining Jamaican reggae beats and Skinhead beliefs, the movement started to die off until the reggae influence was replaced with punk music of the 1980s, thus signaling a rebirth of the Skinheads.

Skinheads can be racist, anti-Semitic, anti-Islamic, white supremacist, anti-gay and neo-Nazi. Other offshoots have been created, and even a surprising amount of gay Skinhead groups exist and some more recent groups actually reject Nazi ideology. In recent years splits have begun to form in the culture with Skinheads disagreeing over musical taste, political alignment, Nazi ideology and the actual fashion and aesthetic quality of what makes a Skinhead. Due to these arguments many groups have broken off from the main movement creating sub-genres of Skinheads, most of which are traditionalist groups stressing the value of the "original look," referring to those who no longer follow the old dress codes and beliefs as simply "bald punks."

This mixture of racist movements makes up the foundation of the *American History X* world. Derek falls into the typical stereotype of a neo-Nazi Skinhead and engulfs himself in the culture. Director Tony Kaye's depiction accurately reflects the contemporary world of neo-Nazis, from the shaven heads and neo-Nazi uniforms, to their slang and habits, to their music and key attitudes and beliefs. Joining local neo-Nazi gangs, Derek adopts this way of life, branding himself with the numerous tattoos and insignias blatantly displaying all his new beliefs. In one key scene, he rips off his shirt in front of his former teacher, who is Jewish, revealing his giant Swastika tattoo across his chest shouting "this means, Not Welcome!" Throughout the film, such tattoos, clothing symbols and icons are worn and displayed by the gang members.

More often than not, both the neo-Nazi and Skinhead movements utilize key visual features from WWII Nazi culture. The two groups use tattoos, graphics, slogans, mottos and chants all taken from the original posters, propaganda and military regalia used by the Nazi Party, in some cases exactly replicating symbols as worn by members of the SS or Nazi soldiers. Some of the most common symbols the movements use are ones such as the number 88 which refers to the 8th letter of the alphabet H making up the acronym HH, short for "Heil Hitler." Perhaps the most recognizable would be the Swastika, the inverted Hindu religious symbol that adorned the Nazi flag and pretty much all other Nazi paraphernalia. Two others that are very recognizable would be the Iron Cross and the Nazi eagle. The use of symbols is extremely rampant in Nazi culture and has been passed onto the neo-Nazis and Skinheads. The use of runes (ancient alphabets believed to have special powers) goes back to the Nazi fixation on Norse mythology and Germanic history. More recently, the number 14 has become more prevalent, as it represents the teachings (*The*

14 Words) of David Lane, an infamous white supremacist, former Ku Klux Klan member and founding member of white supremacist group The Order. This number has come to represent Lane's belief that "We must secure the existence of our people and a future for white children."

Aside from merely depicting the dress and ornamentation of adherents of this philosophy, the film also attempts to document the rising influence of White Supremacist factions, many of which are becoming powerful organizations reaching out and infecting thousands of people, young and old, with their racist propaganda of hatred. Three of the largest and most influential White Supremacist groups are the White Aryan Resistance (also known as WAR), the National Alliance and the Aryan Brotherhood.

The White Aryan Resistance is a neo-Nazi white supremacist group founded by ex-California Ku Klux Klan leader Tom Metzger. As described by their website, "WAR is dedicated to the White working people..." adhering to the old notions of Nazi Aryan supremacy and advocating racist beliefs. Their main goal is to increase the population of pure white people, rooting out in their eyes any genetic and racial impurities, in turn condemning all mixed-race marriages and homosexuals of either gender (due to the fact they do not reproduce). WAR achieved its goals of spreading propaganda on many fronts, the largest being its operation, printing and distribution of its own newspaper – *The Insurgent*. They also made and released online racist videos via their website. Adopting the eugenics beliefs prominent in the first two decades of the 20th century, WAR believed in "biological determinism," the idea that white people are genetically superior, and that social and economic accomplishments of each person should depend solely on their ethnicity. Also unlike many white supremacist groups, WAR is anti-Christian, claiming it is a form of "Jew nationalism." In addition, in perhaps a legally-motivated move to prevent connection to any illegal activities of its members, WAR promotes "leaderless resistance" meaning that members should operate on their own without having to be led by actual given orders by the group. Surprisingly, they also offer equal rights to both men and woman – a radical position in the White Supremacist community. Once extremely active (although numbers are hard to calculate due to its "lone wolf" policy of leaderless resistance), the group was recently put out of business after a law suit regarding some of its followers' racial attacks destroyed their financial standing and forced most of the group's activities to end.

Another group, the National Alliance was founded in late 1967 by Dr. William Pierce and is a white nationalist or white supremacist organization. The NA holds revolutionary right wing political beliefs infused with Christian ethics. The key political idea of the National Alliance revolves around "White survival," the concept of creating a white living space in North America free of any trace of other races. Similar to WAR, they promote pure white births, preventing the blending with the genetic impurities of other races. The NA also makes up one of the most anti-Semitic groups in the United States today, claiming that "Jews exert a negative influence at nearly every level" of modern society and most importantly they own and control every level of entertainment and media throughout the country. As well as publishing pamphlets and magazine articles via the NA, Pierce owned Resistance Records using it as a white power music producing company, creating and selling white power and neo-Nazi music successfully marketing and distributing "neo-Nazi paraphernalia" to young people worldwide. Branching off from the record company was also an internet-based radio broadcast show named Resistance Radio, airing white power rock 24 hours a day, 7 days a week. Resistance Records almost single-handedly funds the NA, bringing in more than one million US dollars in profit from sales a year. Fortunately, the National Alliance has been in a state of internal confusion and chaos since Pierce's death in 2002. He left no clear successor, causing the members to fight over who should take his place and how the organizational ladder should be arranged. Over the next few years, a stable leader would not be found, causing operations and membership to fall drastically. Originally consisting of almost three thousand official members, in recent years their numbers have dropped to less than a hundred, showing how the NA has lost almost all of its influence, now able to only spread their propaganda with minimal impact.

The Aryan Brotherhood is a notorious US based extreme neo-Nazi prison gang, containing over fifteen thousand members both in and out of prison. It is the same gang Derek joins while in prison during *American History X*. Aryan Brotherhood membership is incredibly exclusive, including only white males judged as worthy, males who have passed the "requirements" of membership. Entrance to the gang is based on a "blood in, blood out" system where in you have to either kill, or grievously assault, another prisoner to prove your worth. Membership is also for life; once you join you can never leave. Those that attempt to leave or change their minds are often killed or their lives become a living hell as they must suffer through constant beatings, verbal and physical abuse, and even rape. Brotherhood activities typically include drug trafficking, hired muscle, contract killing, extortion and some degree of involvement at all levels of organized crime. The FBI claims the Aryan Brotherhood is responsible for 20% of all murders and the majority of crime in the entire prison system.

Because of groups such as these, racial tension, crime and gang related violence are on the rise causing numerous social problems, not just in America but worldwide. According to USA TODAY "figures show an alarming increase of hate crimes in this country (America). The groups have changed in that they've turned from what was the Klan into groups like the Skinheads and neo-Nazi's." The rise of these groups is causing both legal and social problems, as more young people buy into the widespread propaganda and conform to the cultural image of the groups, transitioning away from popular fashion taken from music influences found on MTV, radio and other sources. Law enforcement is running into even more problems trying to prevent the activity of such groups as they cannot stop the existence of them purely because they exist. Because of American freedom of speech provisions, these groups operate just outside the law. On the bright side, some progress has been made in the courts using civil suits against the groups distributing the neo-Nazi media. One case involved an Ethiopian student killed in Portland, Oregon, beaten to death with a baseball bat by three Skinheads. It was found they were motivated to do the crime by members of the White Aryan Resistance, and so a law suit was filed against Metzger and WAR. The jury decided in favor of the student demanding reparation of $12.5 million dollars to the student's family by WAR. For many people it is not the issue of hate that is the problem as there has and always will be hatred towards one group or another, but it is the violence and physical manifestation of this hate which is the problem. As Morris Dees, writer for USA TODAY, wrote, "In this country you have the right to hate, but you don't have the right to hurt."

In the film this violence is horrifically displayed. In one disturbing scene, Derek's gang attacks a local supermarket run by foreign workers. Using baseball bats, they attack the employees then proceeding to trash the store in order to "teach them a lesson." In addition to physically harming the male employees, they horribly abuse the one female employee (who like the others is Mexican), attacking her with food and pouring milk and other items on her while they verbally molest her. While the milk runs down her face, they mock her, "Now you can get a white woman's job!" These outbursts of violence and taunting towards foreigners and minorities are carried on throughout the film, reflecting the terrifying real problem of racial violence. These events may be fictional but are based on real attacks and events still taking place today.

Not confined to the United States, Germany is also having similar problems with the recent New Hitler Youth forming and gaining members rapidly around the country causing trouble in "frightening dimensions." Providing a ghostly similarity to the old Hitler Youth, the new version is recruiting young children mostly around the age of fifteen, all shaving their heads and shouting Nazi slogans while terrorizing the general public. Its gang leaders are in their twenties and are attempting to recruit and influence those in their teens, catching them while they are young and easy to impress with the Nazi ideology. The police are running into the same problems as those in the States. In selected areas of Germany, street violence caused by gangs has shot up by almost 50%.

These gangs use many methods to capture its members, but the most prominent tool they seem to thrive upon is the Skinhead and neo-Nazi music and pop culture surrounding it. This is prominently shown in the film with Danny and his friends all being drawn into the world via the music and concerts played by the local Skinhead bands, the concerts and racist music operating as a gateway for the neo-Nazi beliefs to infect them. This form of music really began back in the 1970's as punk exploded worldwide, the Skinhead being reborn under its flag. Music was quickly identified as the ultimate way to spread neo-Nazi ideas and within no time bands were being formed creating their own genres of music which would come to be known primarily as "Nazi-rock," "Oi!" or "hatecore."

Bands use racist music as a "marketing tool" to promote their messages of hatred, manipulating kids via the music and the fashion surrounding the music scenes. Bands such as Skrewdriver are a prime example of artists using their music to promote their views. Not only do their lyrics contain blatantly racist material and neo-Nazi elements, but their actual gigs resemble World War II Nazi rallies with chants of "Sieg Heil" with Nazi slogans found throughout. In *American History X,* we can see an example of such a gig during the party at the Cameron house where Nazi bands perform while Skinheads and neo-Nazis surrounding the stage shout Nazi chants while singing along with the band's racist lyrics.

Skrewdriver front man Ian Donaldson, in addition to running his band, also set up the label "White Noise Club" to release and mange political right wing bands. Through this label, he made ties with white power bands world wide and with the help of the German neo-Nazi record label "Rock-O-Rama," he founded the magazine *Blood and Honor* which promoted and acted as an "umbrella corporation" for other right wing Skinhead bands. As mentioned before, companies such as Resistance Records and Donaldson's White Noise Club record, promote and distribute racist music as well as organize concerts for the bands targeting youth culture, drawing kids into the excitement of the rock music scene using it as a vehicle to spread propaganda and gain more followers. Resistance Records also has links to racist games and media on its website, one such game being called "Ethnic Cleansing" in which you enter a "cyber ghetto" and attempt to kill Jews, Blacks and Hispanics. This use of the Internet is an ever increasing way for these groups to expand their racist reach.

In many ways *American History X* stands as a counter measure to these companies' advances into media, becoming a tool that presents an extremely accurate view of the racist neo-Nazi culture in North American by exposing its evil roots. Although the actual events in the film are completely fictional, the background and portrayal of these gangs and the subculture mirror the real life world of White Supremacy.

The film's racist activities all revolve around one man, Cameron Alexander. Cameron is the leader of the Venice beach neo-Nazi gangs, controlling all aspects of their legal and illegal activity. Distributing Nazi, White Power, and right wing political literature, promoting White Power bands, hosting/organizing concerts and funding and selling racist videos, Cameron is a composite of almost all of the key figures in the neo-Nazi White Supremacist world, most resembling Tom Metzger, William Pierce and to some degree David Lane. His first name, Cameron, is a reference to the Cameron family in the D.W Griffith film – *Birth of a Nation*. Griffith's epic film is set around the American Civil War and follows the actions of the Ku Klux Klan as they attempt to rid the south of Africans brought there as slaves and recently freed by President Lincoln. *Birth of a Nation* is now used as a KKK promotional tool as it promotes white supremacy and violence against non-white races.

Dr. Sweeny is another character that is highly symbolic. Sweeny represents the ideas of affirmative action and anti-racism that arose at the end of the sixties to counter the ever growing racist climate in the United States. His character reflects the personality of Martin Luther King who promoted civil rights and a peaceful resolution to racial conflict. During the film he acts as the voice of reason for both Danny and Derek, helping them escape their world of hatred. In an attempt to open Derek's eyes while visiting Derek in prison, Dr. Sweeny challenges, "Has anything you've done made your life any better?"

The next character with significance is the stereotypical dumb, white, fat redneck - Seth. He is a composite of all the stereotypes of those who blindly follow neo-Nazi and Skinhead beliefs and propaganda. Seth is a composite of our idea of the heavily tattooed, violent, unintelligent Skinhead who shares his beliefs by blasting racist music from his shoddy beat down truck. The song you comically see Seth singing along to during the film is an actual real song by Johnny Rebel, a white supremacist artist, sung to the theme of the "Battle Hymn of the Republic."

Perhaps the most important characters to understand are Derek and Danny Vinyard, the films protagonists. Both represent misguided youths that due to their lower class social standing and the racist gang influence around them have bought into the racist ideology of hatred. Derek in the film is the leader of the D.O.C. (Disciples of Christ), and with the help of Cameron is led into the world of the neo-Nazis after his father is shot by a black gang. Eventually he kills two black men who attempt to steal his car and is sent to prison for three years for manslaughter. While in prison, his younger brother Danny follows in his brother's footsteps, getting involved with Cameron and the same gang Derek once led. Both of the brothers show the qualities of misguided youth who buy into the false safety, brotherhood and unity of the gangs believing they are helping a higher cause by blaming their problems on minorities and people of other races rather than attempting to actually make their society better. Danny even goes as far as to write an essay arguing that Hitler was a civil rights hero.

In prison, Derek sees the hypocrisy of the Aryan Brotherhood and begins to change his racist view of the world with the help of Dr. Sweeny. Reforming his life is not easy though as he still bears the tattooed scars of his neo-Nazi past. While at a frighteningly realistic neo-Nazi concert held at Cameron's house, Derek drags Danny away from the evil underworld he has become caught in, pleading with him to abandon a lifestyle that will only lead to destruction.

By the final moments of the film, both have reformed their views, sincerely wishing to escape the racist bonds of gang violence in Venice Beach. Danny, seeing the truth, rewrites his essay admitting to Dr. Sweeny that "hate is like baggage. Life is too short to be pissed off all the time." Ironically, Danny never manages to hand it in as he is killed moments before class by a member of a rival gang. In this moment, the film concludes by showing that the cycle of violence created by the neo-Nazis and the White Supremacists can be inescapable, often leading to the downfall of all involved.

Key Quotes

Dr Sweeny: *(When talking to Derek in prison referring to his neo-Nazi and gang actions and involvement)* There was a moment... when I used to blame everything and everyone... for all the pain and suffering and vile things that happened to me, that I saw happen to my people. Used to blame everybody. Blamed white people, blamed society, blamed God. I didn't get no answers 'cause I was asking the wrong questions. You have to ask the right questions.....Has anything you've done, made your life any better?

Danny: *(During his final narration after his death)* Hate is baggage. Life is too short to be pissed off all the time.

Seth: *(Singing along to the racist music playing his in truck)* My eyes have seen the glory of the trampling at the zoo/We've washed ourselves in niggers blood and all the mongrels too/We've taken down the zog machine Jew by Jew by Jew/The white man marches on!

Black Hawk Down

2001
Director: Ridley Scott
Starring: Josh Hartnett, Ewan McGregor, Tom Sizemore
144 minutes – Rated R

By Zachary Moilanen

Synopsis:

During 1993, after the starvation of the Somali people by rivaling clan warlords, the United States in conjunction with the United Nations is sent to Somalia to help establish a proper government. *Black Hawk Down* tells the story of the men who were assigned the mission to capture an important Somali clan leader. After locals shoot down two Black Hawk helicopters, the military must discard their original plans and do whatever it takes to secure the helicopters and return safely to base.

Historically Relevant Scenes

00:00:00>00:02:56	- Causes of civil war
00:51:17>00:57:38	- First Black Hawk downed
01:06:58>01:14:05	- Second Black Hawk downed
01:23:38>01:34:25	- Delta Snipers at second crash site
01:55:55>02:09:35	- Extraction
02:11:33>02:16:06	- Casualties and result of the battle

Ratings:

Entertainment - ★ ★ ★ ☆

Historical Accuracy - ★ ★ ★ ☆

Historical Analysis:

In 1991, Somalia was torn apart as the United Somalia Congress overthrew the previous leader Mohammed Siad Barre. After the coup, the Congress divided into two main rivaling forces bent on controlling the government. The civil war between Ali Mahdi Muhammad and Mohammed Farrah Aidid resulted in the massive destruction of the country's agricultural production, which in turn led to serious widespread starvation and malnutrition.

By summer, three more clans, bringing the total to five, were fighting over control of the country while the Somali people suffered.

Then, in June, a ceasefire was signed, but the agreement fell through just as one of the clans, led by Abdel-Rahman Ahmen Ali, seceded from the country of Somalia and formed the Somaliland Republic.

Fighting broke out again in September in the capital of Mogadishu "with over 20,000 people killed or injured by the end of the year." Soon after, international aid began pouring in, but the majority was stolen by the clans, who then exchanged the aid for weapons and munitions. Subsequently, an "estimated 300,000 people died, and another 1.5 million people suffered between 1991 and 1992" as a result of the fighting.

In 1992, the United Nations stepped in, having the clans sign a ceasefire and sending military observers to make sure aid was distributed correctly and efficiently, and by August, Operation Provide Relief began.

The operation was meant to stop starvation and suffering, but when food distribution and safety seemed no closer than prior to U.N. intervention, the United States spearheaded Operation Restore Hope, which would hopefully create a stable government for Somalia. The rest of the year, as well as the first few months into '93 saw a shaky peace as agreements were accepted and then ignored. On July 12, 1993 the crisis turned when the U.S. and U.N. destroyed a complex which was holding fifty of the clans most respected leaders. From this point, the Somalis united against the foreign 'insurgents.'

This is where Ridley Scott's *Black Hawk Down* kicks off.

The film first shows the previous years of starvation and suffering along with some numbers and facts which have just been covered. However, just following that, we see United States Rangers capturing a Somali warlord by the name of General Farah Aidid. As in most Hollywood movies, the antagonist is usually exaggerated, as it were here: Aidid (actually Atto in the movie) is seen as the stereotypical 'bad guy' – adorned with sun glasses and gold chains while smugly offering General Garrison a cigar. After watching the movie, Aidid stated that the movie did him and the other warlords injustice by their portrayals. "I am not smoking cigars. I have no earring on my ears." In addition, Aidid contradicts the entire motor-pool scene where he was captured. He remembered:

"When I (Aidid) was caught on 21 September, I was only traveling with one Fiat 124, not three vehicles as it shows in the film...[a]nd when the helicopter attacked, people were hurt, people were killed...The car we were travelling in, (and) I have got proof, it was hit at least 50 times. And my colleague Ahmed Ali was injured on both legs."

This is completely opposite to what we see in the movie where a Delta member, flying in a Black Hawk helicopter, takes one single shot at Aidid's vehicle, hitting the oil tank in the engine and bringing the car to an immediate stop. Although we love to think our soldiers can take out a warlord and his motor-pool in one shot, it was obviously not accurate.

The movie moves quickly and we soon find ourselves watching the American soldiers depart for their mission to capture and secure one of Aidid's top officials inside the city of Mogadishu.

Once the US Delta Force, being offloaded from small 'Little Bird' helicopters, successfully secures the building with the clan officials inside, the ground convoy moves in to load the prisoners. Up until this point, the only problem in the entire operation was Pvt. Blackburn falling from his helicopter, but in reality, the convoy also ran into trouble and was slow to arrive at the Delta-held building because of barricades in the street. Unlike in the movie where their arrival is quick and painless, in reality, one five-ton truck was hit with a Rocket-Propelled Grenade (RPG) before they were even close to loading prisoners.

Not long afterwards, an American Black Hawk helicopter is hit by an RPG and crashes in the middle of the city. Normally, a crash is secured within minutes, but because of poor communication, "[t]he assault team and the ground convoy waited for twenty minutes out of sight of each other, ready to move, but each under the impression that they were to be first contacted by the other."

During this time, the Black Hawk flown by Chief Warrant Officer Michael Durant is also hit by an RPG and crashes, posing another problem for the ground forces which are already heading to the first site.

Here, we see two snipers, Sergeant First Class Randy Shughart and Master Sergeant Gary Gordon, request permission to help secure the second site as there are currently no forces coming to help the downed crew. After being denied twice, command finally allowed them to protect the crew

Although the movie does a great job at getting the overall gist of what Shughart and Gordon did, there are a few points missing, which make their actions even more commendable.

Firstly, the two were not dropped right next to the crash site as it were shown in the film, but, "armed with only their personal weapons and sidearms, had to fight their way to the location of the downed Blackhawk." Once there, the snipers removed Durant, as well as the other crew members before securing a defensive area around the helicopter. Fighting literally to their last bullet, Gordon was the first to be hit. Soon after, Shughart is also killed as the Somalis overrun the Black Hawk.

While that is happening at the second crash site, the rest of the operation runs into trouble as Somali resistance increases and the convoy is forced to leave the Rangers and Delta members and head back to base. Alone for the night, the soldiers hold up in their buildings as enemy troops swarm the area.

As command sees the events unfold, they eventually decide that assistance from the United Nations would be required to extract the soldiers stuck in Mogadishu. However, the Pakistani-led UN forces are slow to react as they were not informed of the mission, which prolongs the operation even longer.

Finally, the troops are deployed and the American soldiers receive air support. By daybreak, the bodies of the Black Hawk crew are extracted and the United Nations pulls out with the Rangers trailing behind. Although the extraction looks pretty straightforward, the United Nations actually lost a Malaysian soldier to an RPG attack.

The film ends with the cinematically-overused coffin/anti-war scene and is followed by the 19 American soldiers who were killed during the mission. If you were to go back through the movie and recount all the deaths, you would find there to be only 18, but Delta Sergeant First Class Matt Rierson was killed when a mortar exploded two days after the operation.

Although Operation Gothic Serpent was a small mission, the end resulted in the eventual withdrawal of US forces in Somalia. Even with a few errors, *Black Hawk Down* does a pretty good job retelling the story of those men who survived and those who were killed on the botched mission that was meant to end war and bring aid to the people of Somalia.

Key Quotes

Hoot: (*while discussing why he fights*) When I get home people'll ask me, 'Hey Hoot, why do you do it man? Why? You some war junkie?' You know what I'll say? I won't say a goddamn word. Why? They won't understand. They won't understand why we do it. They won't understand that it's about the men next to you, and that's it. That's all it is.

Atto: (*after being captured*) You shouldn't have come here. This is a civil war. This is our war, not yours.
Garrison: 300,000 dead and counting. That's not a war Mr. Atto. That's genocide.

Abdullah 'Firimbi' Hassan: (*while talking with Durant*) Do you think if you get General Aidid, we will simply put down our weapons and adopt American democracy? That the killing will stop? We know this. Without victory, there will be no peace. There will always be killing, see? This is how things are in our world.

Blood Diamond

2006
Director: Edward Zwick
Starring: Leonardo DiCaprio, Djimon Hounsou, Jennifer Connelly
143 minutes – Rated R

By Wanwen Wu

Synopsis:

Set in 1999 during the Sierra Leone Civil War, *Blood Diamond* tells the story of Mende fisherman Solomon Vandy and white "Rhodesian" smuggler Danny Archer who work together to recover a big pink diamond and reunite Vandy with his family. After the attack on Vandy's village by the Revolutionary United Front (RUF), the rebel group taking over Sierra Leone, Vandy's family flees, but his son Dia is taken to be a child soldier, and Solomon is sent to mine diamonds for the RUF, where he finds and hides a big pink diamond. Danny Archer later hears about the diamond and is keen on pursuing it, convincing Vandy to work with him in seeking it out. As Solomon Vandy and Danny Archer make their way to the Kono mining fields to retrieve the precious stone, they encounter countless RUF attacks and learn that Captain Poison of the RUF and Colonel Coetzee a South African mercenary both desire that same diamond as well.

Historically Relevant Scenes	
00:03:15>00:06:35	- Revolutionary United Front (RUF) attacks
00:43:00>00:47:00	- Revolutionary United Front (RUF) attacks
00:06:36>00:08:55	- G8 Conference and diamond mining
00:34:44>00:37:39	- RUF child soldiers' training
02:12:34>02:14:48	- G8 and other nations meeting to discuss conflict diamonds

Ratings:

Entertainment -

Historical Accuracy -

Historical Analysis:

Before the movie *Blood Diamond*, the horrors that occurred during Sierra Leone's eleven year civil war lay unknown to the majority of the world. Nominated for five Academy Awards, the movie opened the eyes of consumers regarding conflict, or "blood," diamonds and as stated in an article from the *Washington Times*, "By showing us the effects of greed on one African family -- and throwing in some exciting chase and fight scenes -- Mr. Zwick [the director] has done what his journalist suspects is impossible: He makes us care." Sorious Samura, who experienced first hand the atrocities in Sierra Leone during the civil war, served as the consultant for the movie. Even though the story revolves around a fictional plot of a man finding a big pink diamond, as Leonardo DiCaprio, who plays the film's White "Rhodesian" smuggler, stated, "segments from this film are *directly* taken from Sorious' accounts of what he's seen first hand."

To fully understand the situation in Sierra Leone, a little bit of history needs to be covered. Presently, Sierra Leone is at peace, but it remains one of the poorest countries in the world. In 1808, Sierra Leone became a British colony, which it remained until its independence in 1961. The country depended heavily on agriculture and fishing, although diamond smuggling provided revenue for many. People lived in slums under a society ruled economically and politically by the white minority. This racial imbalance continued and is reflected in one of the initial exchanges between the white Danny Archer and the black African Mende Solomon Vandy. For example, when Archer tries convincing Vandy to work with him, he states that without him Vandy would be "just another black man in Africa." Archer often attempts to control Vandy, even preventing him from going down and seeing his son.

Sierra Leone had never been a strong nation; however, the situation worsened when problems in neighboring Liberia, resulting from President Charles Taylor gaining control in 1989, spilled over into Sierra Leone. Taylor created the Revolutionary United Front (RUF), the rebel group which terrorized Sierra Leone during the civil war to gain control of Sierra Leone's most prized resource: diamonds.

In March 1991, the RUF made its first move into Sierra Leone and targeted the diamond mines in the capital of Freetown. In 1996, even with a new president in Sierra Leone and a peace agreement supposedly ending the war in November, the RUF continued their attacks. The following year, the Armed Forces Revolutionary Council (AFRC) took over the government and invited the RUF to join them, but in 1998 Nigeria's Economic Community Cease-fire Monitoring Group (ECOMOG) peacekeeping force successfully pushed them out. In 1999, the period depicted in *Blood Diamond*, the opposing forces continuously pushed each other back and forth despite the earlier Lome Peace Agreement, which like the one in 1996 failed in its attempt to end the civil war. But at least the ECOMOG had ousted the AFRC by then. By 1999, an estimated 50,000 or more people were dead and over one million displaced, shifted into refugee camps on the neighboring Guinean border.

Instead of being in a safe haven, the camps' proximity to the border made them vulnerable to continual RUF cross border attacks. People in the camps lived in fear as rumors of RUF infiltration spread and human rights abuses (including children who prostituted themselves for food for their family) increased. Despite those problems within the refugee camps, UN-related programs such as the United Nations Children's Fund (UNICEF) and World Food Programme (WFP) continued to provide food and education and attempted to improve conditions for those displaced from their country.

By 2000, the Lome Peace Agreement finally effectively reduced RUF attacks, and the UN initiated a global embargo on diamonds from Sierra Leone to stem the flow of conflict diamonds, which provided arms to rebel groups. At the same time, members of the RUF received government posts, including the appointment of an RUF leader as vice president. Officially, Sierra Leone's eleven year civil war ended in 2002 when RUF leaders began receiving punishment for their war crimes, but the UN only pulled its troops out of the area at the end of 2005 since the area remained sensitive.

At the center of the civil war stood Foday Sankoh, the RUF leader strongly allied with Liberia's President Charles Taylor. Unlike most rebel groups, the RUF didn't appear to want to overthrow the government, but remained a "bandit organization" that opposed the "corrupt political elite" who "plundered the nation's mineral wealth." The RUF claimed that in taking over the diamond mines, they freed the people and the mines from foreign control. One segment of the movie shows rebels walking through expansive grassland and singing that the RUF "is fighting for Sierra Leone." In reality, this anthem resembles the actual RUF lyrics "RUF is fighting to save Sierra Leone, RUF is fighting to save our people, RUF is fighting to save our country...RUF is the saviour we need right now." And in their "Footpaths to Democracy," the RUF claimed they fought for democracy and political and economic liberation for the people. Illegal diamond trade and aid from Liberia, Burkina Faso, Libya and Ukraine (without the Ukrainian government's knowledge), provided the RUF rebels with AK-47s, light assault rifles easily used by their child soldiers, rocket-propelled grenade launchers, and G3 assault rifles, all of which they used in their spontaneous attacks on villages in the country.

Blood Diamond's director, Edward Zwick, stated that he attempted to make scenes "appear to be as chaotic as it was" to accurately depict what occurred during RUF guerilla attacks, including looting and destruction of houses, and the preponderance of murder, rape, and abduction. In speaking about the scene in which Archer and Vandy are in the town under attack by the RUF, the movie's consultant Samura commented, "Frankly what is happening here is almost like what happened in Freetown being played back in slow motion." While some escaped, such as Solomon Vandy's family did in the movie, those who didn't became diamond miners for the RUF or got to know the RUF specialty of chopping off limbs, especially hands and arms, to symbolically prevent voting by making villagers literally and figuratively have "no hands" to vote. Exactly as the RUF offered Solomon Vandy the choice of "short sleeve or long sleeve" in the movie, one civil war amputee Suleiman Sesay remembers, "They gave us a choice, 'do you want short sleeves or long sleeves?'" with "short sleeves" indicating being amputated at the elbows and "long sleeves" at the wrists. This depraved behavior became normal in a world of violence and drugs. In one of the RUF celebrations depicted in the movie, the rebels start a bonfire, drink, smoke and take drugs; in reality they did the same, burning tires and trees for a bonfire and making little cuts on their faces to rub cocaine powder in, supposedly toughening themselves up.

Several different groups opposed and tried overcoming the menacing RUF forces, including the previously mentioned Nigerian ECOMOG force and the Sierra Leone government's army, although to no avail, since their untrained, disorganized recruits mostly originated from slums. While the government ineffectively tried protecting the people from the rebel group, the Kamajors, a group of local militia shown hiding in the forest in the movie, effectively defended the people. Kamajors, Mende tribal hunters, sided neither with the rebels nor with any of the government troops. Even though the Kamajors were known for their "undisciplined nature and frequent marijuana use," rumored cannibalism, use of "juju" for magical protection and composition mostly of uneducated teenage boys and sometimes child soldiers, they received British aid and respect from civilians since the areas under Kamajor control lay unharmed by the civil war. In the movie, the Kamajors were only briefly shown standing guard in the area around Benjamin Margai's refugee home for children. Their recruitment of child soldiers and specific habits and behavior were ignored. Although, like the RUF, Kamajor forces included child soldiers, food and shelter were provided instead of brainwashing.

Children abducted during RUF attacks became used as brainwashed child soldiers (as depicted in the movie), forced labor, or beings to be sexually exploited. RUF recognized that children, unlike adults, could be controlled and made fearless much more easily. Under penalty of death, the RUF forced the children to shoot their own parents or family members and later coerced the children into becoming child soldiers through indoctrination, even enticing them by assigning them military ranks. In the movie, Solomon Vandy's son Dia's experience accurately illustrates what children abducted by the RUF went through in becoming killing machines. The children trained two to three months, and the RUF killed any who tried to escape or disobey. Dia Vandy's training in the movie involved him blindfolded, unknowingly shooting and killing an innocent civilian, reflecting how in reality, the RUF forced the children to kill people who attempted to escape during RUF attacks.

In the celebration after the attacks, accurately depicted in the movie, the child soldiers, just like all the other older rebels, drank, smoke, fired their AK-47s in triumph, and also voluntarily or were forcibly injected drugs, including marijuana, cocaine, heroine or a strong palm oil wine, which supposedly made them loyal, tough, courageous and invincible. Although Dia Vandy eventually reunites with his father Solomon in the movie, in actuality something like that would most likely not have occurred. Many child soldiers became orphans since their families often died during RUF attacks, sometimes even under the hands of the children themselves. Even if the family of a child soldier survived, the children usually wouldn't return to their village for fear of being hunted by the militia or ostracized by their family and village for their participation in the RUF. Not everyone was as forgiving as the fictional Solomon Vandy who proclaims to his son, "I know they made you do bad things, but you are not a bad boy."

Like the Sierra Leonean children, journalists in Sierra Leone, represented by Jennifer Connelly's character Maddy Bowen in the movie, also lived in fear of the RUF. Although Jennifer Connelly's character fills the role of a "patronizing Westerner" seemingly always present in foreign movies such as this one, she comes off sometimes as a flat character, only placed in the movie as a romantic interest for Danny Archer. During the civil war, Sierra Leone "officially became the most dangerous country in the world in which to be a journalist," since the RUF often purposely targeted them, shown in the movie with the RUF attacks on buses and cars with journalists in them. The movie's consultant Sorious Samura had been the sole journalist remaining in Freetown at the time of the civil war, making his accounts significant. Sometimes government forces accidentally killed journalists, mistaking them for RUF rebels since the journalists were in the wrong place at the wrong time. Many journalists ended up murdered, missing or abducted at the hands of the RUF, while many others darted around the country in hiding, knowing that the RUF would seek them out and kill them. The RUF definitely targeted journalists like Maddy Bowen because their attempts to reveal the illegal diamond trade threatened the RUF's funding for the civil war.

While fighting for control of diamonds likely started the war in the first place, the illegal diamond trade financed the war and provided the rebels with arms during the eleven year civil war. Because of Sierra Leone's rich source of diamonds, 65 to 70% coming from the Kono mining fields discovered in the 1930s where Solomon Vandy discovers the big pink diamond in the movie, diamonds have stayed important both legally and illegally. Now, although only 1% of the world's diamonds probably still originate from conflict areas, that 1% enables rebel groups to afford the arms they need for wars.

Smugglers, as depicted by Danny Archer, played a prominent role in providing the RUF with arms necessary for their attacks through illegal diamond and arms trade during the civil war. In the movie, Danny Archer attempts to smuggle diamonds over the Liberian border by hiding them under the skin of goats, but government troops prevent him from doing so. Over the years, although diamond smuggling has remained prominent, officials now recognize common methods of hiding diamonds and can more effectively prevent smuggling. Those common methods include sewing diamonds into clothes and shoes, stuffing them into bread or hiding the diamonds inside one's mouth.

Those methods applied more to small scale smuggling though. In larger scale smuggling, which Leonardo DiCaprio's Danny Archer takes part in, the diamonds often involved the RUF or even government troops, and most often smugglers transported the diamonds into neighboring Liberia and sold them to Monrovia as Liberian diamonds. From there, the diamonds traveled to Antwerp, Belgium where the lax origin certification regulations increased the chances of blood or conflict diamonds entering the market undetected. As described in the movie, most diamonds then traveled to India to be cut, where clean and blood diamonds mixed to be sold to all other countries that then unknowingly purchased blood diamonds. For instance, the United States, which buys more than half the diamond jewelry available and imports over one million dollars a year of rough diamonds, may easily have unknowingly been involved in purchasing conflict diamonds over the years.

Although companies sometimes knowingly bought conflict diamonds, they usually went through many intermediaries instead of dealing directly with the smugglers in Africa. The form of conflict diamond trade depicted in the movie exaggerates the process and the role of diamond company officials. Critics and the film's general audience say the van de Kaap diamond company in the movie represents De Beers, a prominent South African diamond company founded in 1888. De Beers, who supplies and owns around half the diamonds in the market today, claimed they had unknowingly involved themselves in conflict diamonds until around 1999 or 2000 when they first found out. Critics of the company have said De Beers knew all along that they had conflict diamonds and only pretended not to know when the world became highly aware of the conflict diamond situation. Around 1999 or 2000 when they supposedly first found out about their involvement in conflict diamonds, De Beers stopped buying Angola's civil war diamonds and diamonds in Antwerp, Belgium to reduce the likelihood of involvement in conflict diamonds, although one often can't trace diamonds to their exact origin and "given [De Beers'] dominance in the diamond field, some question whether De Beers has been as untouched by conflict diamonds as it has claimed or whether there aren't blood diamonds in its vast vault of stones."

With the issue of blood or conflict diamonds gaining prominence, many nations came together and signed the Kimberley Process in 2003 to stop the flow of conflict diamonds. The Kimberley Process required rough diamonds to be accompanied by certification of origin, but if Sierra Leonean diamonds are smuggled, like in the movie, over into Liberia and certified as being mined in Liberia, the Kimberley Process has no way of telling. Since the process' initiation, conflict diamonds in the world decreased from up to 15% or more to only around 1% of the world's diamonds. But as Sorious Samura points out in his documentary, most miners in African countries today, including Sierra Leone, have never heard of the Kimberley Process and diamond certification, and even if they did, they prefer selling to smugglers than proper dealers since smugglers often pay more.

Even today in Sierra Leone smugglers have their place. During the RUF's reign of terror, the role of smugglers was even more prominent. They provided the RUF with arms and brought RUF diamonds into the markets, so consumers unknowingly ended up buying conflict diamonds linked to violence against civilians. When Danny Archer and Maddy Bowen first meet, Bowen says, "People back home [in America] wouldn't buy a ring if they knew it cost someone their hand," a point Archer disputes. Archer's point of view may regrettably be true of some diamond dealers and retailers though. With his undercover camera, Samura showed that dealers in big cities such as New York, who definitely have heard of the Kimberley Process and proper diamond certification, ignored the proper documentation and voluntarily purchased conflict diamonds due to the low price. As for diamond retailers, in a 2004 Global Witness report, only five out of the thirty diamond retailers questioned regarding their conflict diamond policies actually responded, prompting Global Witness' Corinna Gilfillan to think that "some of the largest US and international retailers are paying only lip-service," claiming that they avoid conflict diamonds as a marketing strategy to please consumers.

Critics and those familiar with what occurred during the civil war have stated that the movie accurately tells a part of the whole story, potentially harming the reputation of diamond companies, including companies who claim they definitely don't involve themselves in conflict diamonds. But the Global Witness report may suggest otherwise regarding those companies and their conflict diamond policies. Made several years after the end of the civil war and the era of intense illegal diamond trade in Sierra Leone, critics and those in the diamond business have claimed the movie makes it seem as if what occurred in the movie still occurs at the same level right now, harming the economies of countries that depend heavily on diamonds. Another small detail of criticism involves the setting, since although the movie takes place in Sierra Leone, it was filmed in Mozambique 3500 miles South, so the animals shown and the expansive land inaccurately portrays Sierra Leone.

After the release of *Blood Diamond* in late 2006, formerly unaware consumers learned of rebel group's conflict diamonds and the desperation involved in fighting for the diamonds. Although documentaries have been made informing consumers about blood or conflict diamonds, this movie "impressively encapsulates the terror of a nation in free fall in visceral explosions of violence," capturing the attention of many. Although no 100% guarantee exists in ensuring diamonds originated from non-conflicts areas, the movie reminds consumers to keep an eye open and take responsibility in avoiding purchases of conflict or blood diamonds.

Key Quotes

Solomon Vandy: (*sitting in a tent in the rain on the way back to Kono*) I understand White people want our diamonds, yes. But how can my own people do this to each other? I know good people who say there is something wrong with us inside our black skin, that we were better off when the White men ruled.

Danny Archer: (*after seeing children singing in Benjamin Margai's refugee home*) Sometimes I wonder, will God ever forgive us for what we've done to each other? Then I look around and I realize, God left this place a long time ago.

Old man in abandoned village: (*when Archer and Vandy walk through an abandoned village*) And tell the *poomui* not to shoot me. [referring to Archer]
Solomon Vandy: He is crazy for diamonds like everyone else.
Old man: Let's hope they don't discover oil here. Then we'd have real problems.

Danny Archer: (*upon meeting Maddy Bowen*) In America it's bling-bling, but out here it's bling-bang, huh?

Historical Film List

	Movie	Era/Topic
1	Untouchables	1920s
2	American Graffiti	1950s
3	Grease	1950s
4	Pleasantville	1950s
5	JFK	1960s
6	RFK	1960s
7	Saturday Night Fever	1970s
8	Flashdance	1980s
9	Footloose	1980s
10	Urban Cowboy	1980s
11	American History X	1990s
12	Boyz in the Hood	1990s
13	Groundhog Day	1990s
14	Mean Girls	1990s
15	Truman Show	1990s
16	Babel	2000s
17	Brokeback Mountain	2000s
18	Crash	2000s
19	High School Musical	2000s
20	Transamerica	2000s
21	Lions for Lambs	Afghanistan
22	Black Hawk Down	Africa
23	Blood Diamond	Africa
24	Cry Freedom	Africa
25	Cry the Beloved Country	Africa
26	Hotel Rwanda	Africa
27	Interpreter, The	Africa
28	Last King of Scotland	Africa
29	Sarafina	Africa
30	Shaka Zulu	Africa
31	Tears of the Sun	Africa
32	And the Band Played On	AIDS
33	Philadelphia	AIDS
34	Battle of Algiers	Algerian Independence
35	War Letters	American Wars
36	300	Ancient Greece
37	300 Spartans	Ancient Greece
38	Alexander	Ancient Greece
39	Alexander the Great	Ancient Greece
40	Clash of the Titans	Ancient Greece
41	Matrix	Ancient Greece

42	Troy	Ancient Greece
43	Lord of War	Arms Trade
44	Attila	Attila the Hun
45	Life of Brian	Bible
46	Passion of the Christ	Bible
47	Ten Commandments	Bible
48	Behind Enemy Lines	Bosnia
49	Harrison's Flowers	Bosnian War
50	Killing Fields	Cambodia
51	Joy Luck Club	China
52	Last Emperor	China
53	Myth, The	China
54	4 Little Girls	Civil Rights
55	Ghosts of Mississippi	Civil Rights
56	Hairspray	Civil Rights
57	Malcom X	Civil Rights
58	Mississippi Burning	Civil Rights
59	Murder of Emmett Till	Civil Rights
60	Remember the Titans	Civil Rights
61	Rosewood	Civil Rights
62	Separate But Equal	Civil Rights
63	Time to Kill	Civil Rights
64	Town Turns to Dust	Civil Rights
65	Uncle Tom's Cabin	Civil Rights
66	Birth of a Nation	Civil War
67	Civil War	Civil War
68	Cold Mountain	Civil War
69	Gettysburg	Civil War
70	Glory	Civil War
72	Gone with the Wind	Civil War
73	Ride with the Devil	Civil War
74	Santa Fe Trail	Civil War
75	Charlie Wilson's War	Cold War
76	Day After	Cold War
77	Dr. Strangelove	Cold War
78	Forrest Gump	Cold War
79	Good Shepherd	Cold War
80	Hunt for Red October	Cold War
81	K19: The Widowmaker	Cold War
82	Red Dawn	Cold War
83	Thirteen Days	Cold War
84	Truman	Cold War
85	War Games	Cold War
86	1492	Colonization
87	Black Robe	Colonization
88	Colonial Williamsburg	Colonization
89	Crucible	Colonization

90	Mission	Colonization
91	New World	Colonization
92	Pocahontas	Colonization
93	Scarlet Letter	Colonization
94	Civil Action	Corporations
95	Coca Cola	Corporations
96	Constant Gardener	Corporations
97	Corporation	Corporations
98	Erin Brockovich	Corporations
99	Insider	Corporations
100	Roger & Me	Corporations
101	Supersize Me	Corporations
102	Kingdom of Heaven	Crusades
103	Inconvenient Truth	Ecology
104	Outbreak	Ecology
105	Soylent Green	Ecology
106	Hours, The	Feminism
107	Mona Lisa Smile	Feminism
108	Last of the Mohicans	French and Indian War
109	Affair of the Necklace	French Revolution
111	Les Miserables	French Revolution
112	Man in the Iron Mask	French Revolution
113	Master and Commander	French Revolution
114	Napoleon	French Revolution
115	Scarlet Pimpernel	French Revolution
116	Tale of Two Cities	French Revolution
117	Citizen Kane	Gilded Age
118	Gangs of New York	Gilded Age
119	There Will be Blood	Gilded Age
120	Titanic	Gilded Age
121	Eleanor and Franklin	Great Depression
122	Grapes of Wrath	Great Depression
123	King Kong	Great Depression
124	Seabiscuit	Great Depression
125	Gulf War, The	Gulf War
126	Three Kings	Gulf War
127	Miracle Worker	Helen Keller
128	Conspiracy	Holocaust
129	Grey Zone	Holocaust
130	Into the Arms of Strangers	Holocaust
131	Jakob the Liar	Holocaust
132	Life is Beautiful	Holocaust
133	Long Way Home	Holocaust
134	Miracle at Midnight	Holocaust
135	Night and Fog	Holocaust
136	Nuremberg	Holocaust
137	Pianist	Holocaust

138	Schindler's List	Holocaust
139	Sophie's Choice	Holocaust
140	Uprising	Holocaust
141	Messenger: Joan of Arc	Hundred Years War
142	Avalon	Immigration
143	Once Upon a Time in America	Immigration
144	Gandhi	India
145	Year of Living Dangerously	Indonesia Revolution
146	Oliver Twist	Industrial Revolution
147	Great Dictator	Interwar Period
148	Hitler	Interwar Period
149	Sound of Music	Interwar Period
150	Control Room	Iraq War
151	Embedded	Iraq War
152	In the Valley of Elah	Iraq War
153	Over There	Iraq War
154	Message: Story of Islam	Islam
155	Eagles Attack at Dawn	Israel
156	Munich	Israel
157	Last Samurai	Japan
158	Ran	Japan
159	Seven Samurai	Japan
160	Shogun	Japan
161	Shattered Glass	Journalism
162	12 Angry Men	Judicial System
163	People vs. Larry Flynt	Judicial System
164	Brotherhood	Korean War
165	Hunters	Korean War
166	Korea: The Forgotten War	Korean War
167	North Country	Labor
168	On the Waterfront	Labor
169	Hoffa	Labor Unions
170	Evita	Latin America
171	Innocent Voices	Latin America
172	Maria Full of Grace	Latin America
173	Motorcycle Diaries	Latin America
174	Official Story	Latin America
175	Salvador	Latin America
176	Mr. Smith Goes to Washington	Legal System
177	Knight's Tale	Middle Ages
178	Name of the Rose	Middle Ages
179	Princess Bride	Middle Ages
180	Timeline	Middle Ages
181	Syriana	Middle East
182	Century of Warfare	Military
183	Few Good Men	Military
184	GI Jane	Military

185	Whale Rider	New Zealand - Cultural Heritage
186	All the Presidents Men	Nixon
187	Dick	Nixon
188	Nixon	Nixon
189	Courage Under Fire	Persian Gulf War
190	Jarhead	Persian Gulf War
191	Bob Roberts	Politics
192	Bowling for Columbine	Politics
193	Congress	Politics
194	Daily Show	Politics
195	Fahrenheit 451	Politics
196	History of Diplomacy	Politics
197	Indecision 2004: Jon Stewart	Politics
198	Man of the Year	Politics
199	Primary Colors	Politics
200	Star Wars	Politics
201	V for Vendetta	Politics
202	Wag the Dog	Politics
205	West Wing	Politics
206	Wizard of Oz	Populism
207	2001: A Space Odyssey	Prehistoric Man
208	Elizabeth	Queen Elizabeth
209	Elizabeth: The Golden Age	Queen Elizabeth
210	Day Reagan was Shot	Reagan
211	Good Night, Good Luck	Red Scare
212	Majestic	Red Scare
213	Luther	Reformation
214	Man for All Seasons	Reformation
215	Jefferson	Revolutionary Era
216	National Treasure	Revolutionary Era
217	Thomas Jefferson	Revolutionary Era
218	1776	Revolutionary War
219	Patriot	Revolutionary War
220	Great Gatsby, The	Roaring Twenties
221	Ben Hur	Roman Empire
222	Gladiator	Roman Empire
223	Spartacus	Roman Empire
224	The Last Legion	Roman Empire
225	Titus	Roman Empire
226	Animal Farm	Russian Revolution
227	Braveheart	Scotland
228	Flight 93	September 11, 2001
229	Homerun	Singapore
230	Amistad	Slavery
231	Roots	Slavery
232	Apollo 13	Space Race
233	October Sky	Space Race

234	Right Stuff	Space Race
235	Rough Riders	Spanish American War
236	For Whom the Bell Tolls	Spanish Civil War
237	Eight Men Out	Sports
238	Field of Dreams	Sports
239	Glory Road	Sports
240	Hoop Dreams	Sports
241	Hurricane	Sports
242	Invincible	Sports
243	Karate Kid	Sports
244	Million Dollar Baby	Sports
245	Miracle	Sports
246	Natural	Sports
247	Raging Bull	Sports
248	Rocky I	Sports
249	Rocky II	Sports
250	Rocky III	Sports
251	Rocky IV	Sports
252	Rocky V	Sports
253	Rookie	Sports
254	Rudy	Sports
255	We Are Marshall	Sports
256	Executive Decision	Terrorism
257	Fahrenehit 9/11	Terrorism
258	Siege	Terrorism
259	Team America: World Police	Terrorism
260	The Kingdom	Terrorism
261	Capote	Truman Capote
262	10 Days...Changed America	US History
263	Alistair Cooke's America	US History
264	Schoolhouse Rock	US History General
265	Pride and Prejudice	Victorian England
266	Vietnam: A Television History	Vietnam
267	Apocalypse Now	Vietnam War
268	Born on the Fourth of July	Vietnam War
269	Casualties of War	Vietnam War
270	Coming Home	Vietnam War
271	Deer Hunter	Vietnam War
272	Full Metal Jacket	Vietnam War
273	Good Morning Vietnam	Vietnam War
274	Hamburger Hill	Vietnam War
275	Path to War	Vietnam War
276	Platoon	Vietnam War
277	Quiet American	Vietnam War
278	Rescue Dawn	Vietnam War
279	Tigerland	Vietnam War
280	We Were Soldiers	Vietnam War

281	Starship Troopers	War Propaganda Satire
282	3:10 to Yuma	West
283	Alamo	West
284	Dances with Wolves	West
285	Far and Away	West
286	Geronimo	West
287	Heaven's Gate	West
288	Lewis and Clark: Burns	West
289	The Assassination of Jesse James	West
290	Tombstone	West
291	Unforgiven	West
292	West: Burns	West
293	Civilisation	World History
294	Days that Shook the World	World History
296	History of the World	World History
297	Millenium: Volume 1	World History
298	Millenium: Volume 2	World History
299	Millenium: Volume 3	World History
300	Millenium: Volume 4	World History
301	Millenium: Volume 5	World History
302	World at War	World War
304	All Quiet on the Western Front	World War I
305	Blue Max	World War I
306	Flyboys	World War I
307	Grand Illusion	World War I
308	Joyeux Noel - Merry Christmas	World War I
309	Lawrence of Arabia	World War I
310	Legends of the Fall	World War I
311	Lost Battalion	World War I
312	Trench	World War I
313	Very Long Engagement	World War I
314	Anne Frank	World War II
315	Atonement	World War II
316	Aviator	World War II
317	Band of Brothers	World War II
319	Battle of Britain	World War II
320	Battle of the Bulge	World War II
321	Big Red One	World War II
322	Bridge on the River Kwai	World War II
323	Casablanca Express	World War II
324	Catch 22	World War II
325	Cold War Killers	World War II
326	Commandos	World War II
327	Das Boot	World War II
328	D-Day to Berlin	World War II
329	Destination Tokyo	World War II
330	Downfall	World War II

331	Eagle Has Landed	World War II
332	Eagles Attack at Dawn	World War II
333	Empire of the Sun	World War II
334	Enemy at the Gates	World War II
335	Enemy Below	World War II
336	Enigma	World War II
337	Execution of Private Slovak	World War II
338	Fat Man and Little Boy	World War II
339	Fog of War	World War II
340	From Here to Eternity	World War II
342	Go For Broke!	World War II
343	Grave of the Fireflies	World War II
345	Great Escape	World War II
346	Great Raid, The	World War II
348	Guns of Navarone	World War II
349	Hart's War	World War II
350	Hitler SS: Portrait of Evil	World War II
351	Hitler's SS: Portrait of Evil	World War II
352	Ike: Countdown to D-Day	World War II
353	Longest Day	World War II
354	Memoris of a Geisha	World War II
355	Memphis Belle	World War II
356	Midway	World War II
357	Paths of Glory	World War II
358	Patton	World War II
359	Pearl Harbor	World War II
360	Saving Private Ryan	World War II
361	Slaughterhouse Five	World War II
362	Snow Falling on Cedars	World War II
363	Thin Red Line	World War II
365	Tora, Tora, Tora	World War II
366	Tuskegee Airmen	World War II
367	Twelve O'Clock High	World War II
368	U571	World War II
369	Victory	World War II
370	War of the Century	World War II
371	Waterfront	World War II
372	When Trumpets Fade	World War II
373	Windtalkers	World War II
374	Yank in Libya	World War II
375	Yankee Doodle Dandy	World War II

Bibliography

10,000 B.C.
"10,000 BC: Answers in Genesis." Answers in Genesis. 2008. Gospelcom.net.
      25 Mar 2008.
      <http://www.answersingenesis.org/articles/2008/03/10/10000-bc>.
"10,000 BC (film)." *Wikipedia, The Free Encyclopedia*. 24 Mar 2008, 14:17 UTC.
      Wikimedia Foundation, Inc. 25 Mar 2008.
      <http://en.wikipedia.org/w/index.php?title=10%2C000_BC_%28film%29&oldid
      =200541711>.
"Climate Change Rocked Cradle of Civilization." September 10, 2006.
      Science Daily. March 29, 2008.
      <http://www.sciencedaily.com/releases/2006/09/060910143119.htm>.
"Dreadlocks: Encyclopedia II – Dreadlocks – Meaning and Popularity."
      2008. Global Oneness. March 29, 2008.
      <http://www.experiencefestival.com/a/Dreadlocks_-
      _Meaning_and_popularity/id/1289082>.
"History of Domestication of Animals." 2008. History World. March 29,
      2008.
      <http://www.historyworld.net/wrldhis/PlainTextHistories.asp?historyid=ab57>.
"How Realistic is 10,000 B.C.? Not much." Classes and Careers. March 29,
      2008.
      <http://www.classesandcareers.net/education-careers/2008/03/10/10000-bc-
      fact-or-fantasy/>.
"Invention Timeline Illustrating the History of Inventions and Gadgets."
      2008. Invention Reaction. March 29, 2008.
      <http://www.inventionreaction.com/invention-timeline/>.
"Letaba Elephant Hall – Home of the Magnificent Seven." 2008. South
      African National Parks. March 29, 2008.
      <http://www.sanparks.org/parks/kruger/elephants/about/history.php>.
Padrusch, David. "The History Channel Presents Journey to 10,000 B.C.".
      A&E Home Video. March 9, 2008.
"Stone Age Habitats." 2008. Aerobiological Engineering. March 25, 2008.
      <http://www.aerobiologicalengineering.com/wxk116/StoneAge/Habitats/>.

Troy
"Achilles". Wikipedia. The Free Encyclopedia. May 7, 2007. Wikimedia Foundation. May 8,
      2007.
      <http://en.wikipedia.org/wiki/Achilles>.
"Helen of Troy". Wikipedia. The Free Encyclopedia. May 7, 2007. Wikimedia
      Foundation. May 8, 2007.
      <http://en.wikipedia.org/wiki/Helen_of_Troy>.
"Historiocity of the Iliad". Wikipedia. The Free Encyclopedia. May 7, 2007. Wikimedia
      Foundation. May 8, 2007.
      <http://en.wikipedia.org/wiki/Historicity_of_the_Iliad>.
Hunter, James. "Achilles". Encyclopedia Mythica. November 30, 2005. May 7, 2007.
      <http://www.pantheon.org/articles/a/achilles.html>.
Korfmann, Manfred. Was There a Trojan War? May/June 2004. Archaeological Institute of
      America. December 21, 2007.
      <http://www.archaeology.org/0405/etc/troy.html/>.

Reilly, Mary. "A Test on Troy: What's Real vs. What's Reel". University of Cincinnati. April 22, 2004. May 7, 2007.
    <http://www.uc.edu/news/NR.asp?id=1589>.

Rose, Mark. "Trojan Wars: On the Big and Little Screen". Archaeology Magazine. May 14, 2004. May 7, 2007.
    <http://www.archaeology.org/online/reviews/troy/index.html>.

Sailer, Steven. "Troy". The American Conservative. June 7,2004. May 7, 2007.
    <http://www.isteve.com/Film_Troy.htm>.

"Trojan Horse". Wikipedia. The Free Encyclopedia. May 7, 2007. Wikimedia Foundation. May 8, 2007.
    <http://en.wikipedia.org/wiki/Trojan_Horse>.

"Troy (film)". Wikipedia. The Free Encyclopedia. May 7, 2007. Wikimedia Foundation. May 8, 2007.
    <http://en.wikipedia.org/wiki/Troy_(film)>.

Vergano, Dan. "Homeric Feat: Legend vs. Fact". USA Today. McLean, Va.: May 20, 2004. pg. D.10

Walsh, David. "Warrior and Anti-Warrior." June 19, 2004. World Socialist Website. December 21, 2007.
    <http://www.wsws.org/articles/2004/jun2004/troy-j19.shtml>.

300

"300 (film)". Wikipedia. The Free Encyclopedia. December 23, 2007. Wikimedia Foundation. December 24, 2007.
    <http://en.wikipedia.org/wiki/300_(film)>.

Gill, N.S. "Persian Wars – Basics on the Battle at Thermopylae." December 23, 2007. About.com: Ancient/Classical History. December 24, 2007.
    <http://ancienthistory.about.com/cs/weaponswar/p/blpwtherm.htm>.

Griswold, Doug. "300 vs. History". Bay Area Newsgroup. March 4, 2007. San Jose Mercury News. December 24, 2007.
    <http://bayareanewsgroup.com/multimedia/mn/entertainment/300_history_031407.pdf>.

Hanson, Victor Davis. "'300' – Fact or Fiction?" March 22, 2007. Real Clear Politics. December 23, 2007.
    <http://www.realclearpolitics.com/articles/2007/03/300_fact_or_fiction.html>.

Kar, Cyrus. "The Truth Behind '300'" March 25, 2007. Spenta Productions. December 23, 2007.
    <http://www.spentaproductions.com/300themovie_the_truth_behind_300.htm>.

Karnick, S.T. "'300' Movie's Historical Accuracy." March 6, 2007. The American Culture. December 23, 2007.
    <http://stkarnick.com/blog2/2007/03/300_movies_historical_accuracy.html>.

"Leonidas the Spartan." Racial Nationalist Library. December 23, 2007.
    <http://library.flawlesslogic.com/leonidas.htm>.

Lytle, Ephraim. "Sparta? No. This is Madness." March 11, 2007. The Toronto Star. December 23, 2007.
    <http://www.thestar.com/article/190493>.

Miller, Neil. "The *300* Controversy. Fact v. Fiction." March 20, 2007. Film School Rejects. December 23, 2007.
    <http://www.filmschoolrejects.com/opinions/the-300-controversy-fact-or-fiction.php>.

Padrusch, David. "The History Channel Presents Last Stand of the 300 - The Legendary Battle at Thermopylae". A&E Home Video. July 31, 2007.

Papakyriakou, Ellen. "The Training of Youth." July 9, 2006. Ancient Greek Cities. December 23, 2007.

<http://www.sikyon.com/sparta/agogi_eg.html>.
"Spartan Pederasty." Wikipedia. The Free Encyclopedia. December 23,
2007. Wikimedia Foundation. December 24, 2007.
<http://en.wikipedia.org/wiki/Spartan_pederasty>.
"The Anti-'300' Debate." March 7, 2007. The Columbus Movie Guy.
December 23, 2007.
<http://www.columbusmovieguy.com/news/the-anti-300-debate/>.
"The Graeco-Persian Wars: The Ionian Revolt." September 29, 2006. BBC –
H2G2. December 23, 2007.
Twight, Mark. "300: The So-Called Program." Gym Jones. December 23,
2007.
<http://www.gymjones.com/knowledge.php?id=35>.
Vergano, Dan. "This is Sparta. The history behind the movie '300.'" March
5, 2007. USA Today. December 23, 2007.
<http://www.usatoday.com/tech/science/columnist/vergano/2007-03-05-300-
history_N.htm?csp=1>.
Walsh, Bill. "True Thermopylaes." March 16, 2007. The Weekly Standard.
December 23, 2007.
<http://www.weeklystandard.com/Utilities/printer_preview.asp?idArticle=134
03&R=112AC33B>.

Alexander
"Alexander (film)." Wikipedia. 2007. November 16· 2007.
<http://en.wikipedia.org/wiki/Alexander_%28film%29>.
"Alexander in Persia." Williams Students Online. 1996, Jed Taylor. November 24, 2007.
< http://wso.williams.edu/~junterek/persia.htm>.
"Ancient Macedonian Culture" Macedonia. Jovan Pavlovski & Mishel Pavlovski. November
24, 2007.
<http://www.mymacedonia.net/language/aculture.html>.
"Alexander the Boy Wonder." Williams Students Online. 1996, Jed Taylor. November 24,
2007.
<http://wso.williams.edu/~junterek/youth.htm>.
"Alexander the Great" Wikipedia. 2007. November 22, 2007.
<http://en.wikipedia.org/wiki/Alexander_the_Great>.
"Alexander the Macedonian." Macedonia. 2007. November 24, 2007.
<http://www.mymacedonia.net/history/alexander.htm>.
"Armies of the Persian War." Sarissa. November 24, 2007.
<http://www.sarissa.org/war/persian_wars/per_army.php>.
"The Death of Alexander the Great." Livius Articles on Ancient History. November 28, 2007.
<http://www.livius.org/aj-al/alexander/alexander_t28.html>.
Foreman, Laura. *The Epic Story of the Warrior King Alexander.* Da Capo Press. Cambridge,
Massachusetts. 2004.
'Macedonia FAQ: Alexander the Great." Macedonia FAQ. 2000. November 28, 2007.
<http://faq.macedonia.org/history/alexander.the.great.html>.
"Peloponnesian War." Wikipedia. 2007. November 20, 2007.
<http://en.wikipedia.org/wiki/Peloponessian_War>.
"Philip of Macedon Philip II of Macedon Biography."
HistoryofMacedonia.org. December 26, 2007.
<http://www.historyofmacedonia.org/AncientMacedonia/PhilipofMacedon.ht
ml>.
Shultz, Cathy. "Oliver Stone's Costly History Lesson." November 24, 2004.
History in the Movies. December 26, 2007.
< http://www.stfrancis.edu/historyinthemovies/alexander.htm>.

"Sexuality and Alexander." Students Online. 1996, Jed Taylor. November 24, 2007.
< http://wso.williams.edu/~junterek/sex.htm>.
"That Group That Went Hog-Wild in Asia for 11 Years." Williams Students Online. 1996, Jed Taylor. November 24, 2007.
< http://wso.williams.edu/~junterek/army.htm>.

Gladiator
Brown, Craig. "Shock horror socks sandal." The Daily Telegraph. London. May 21, 2005: pg. 23.
"Emperor Commodus." Illustrated History of the Roman Empire. 2007. March 7, 2007.
<http://www.roman-empire.net/highpoint/commodus.html>.
Fulford, Robert. "Marcus Aurelius and Commodus." National Post. May 23, 2000.
"Gladiator (2000 Film)." Wikipedia. 2007. March 7, 2007.
<http://en.wikipedia.org/wiki/Gladiator_(2000_film)>.
Nosotro, Rit. "Emperor Commodus." Hyperhistory.net. 2007. March 7, 2007.
<http://www.hyperhistory.net/apwh/bios/b2commodesch.htm>.
Sanello, Frank. *Reel vs. Real.* First Taylor Trade Publishing. Lanham, Maryland. 2003.
Sethi, Ramit. "Gladiatorial Battles: A Comparison of Ridley Scott's Gladiator and Ancient Literary Sources and Interpretations." Legutko: Ancient Empires. 2001.
"The Roman Gladiator: Female Gladiators." Ablemedia. 2005. March 7, 2007.
<http://ablemedia.com/ctcweb/consortium/gladiator6.html>.
Winner, David. "A blow to the temples." Financial Times. London. January 29, 2005: pg. 34.

Kingdom of Heaven
Ahmez, Parved. "Film Review: Kingdom of Heaven". May 2, 2005.
About.com: Islam. December 24, 2007.
<http://islam.about.com/od/activism/a/kingdom_heaven.htm>.
Arlandson, James M. "Islamic Crusaders vs. Christian Crusaders."
Answering Islam. December 24, 2007.
<http://www.answering-islam.org/Authors/Arlandson/crusades.htm>.
"Balian of Ibelin". Wikipedia. The Free Encyclopedia. December 23, 2007.
Wikimedia Foundation. December 24, 2007.
<http://en.wikipedia.org/wiki/Balian_of_Ibelin>.
Chattaway, Peter. "Reviews: Kingdom of Heaven". May 5, 2005. Christianity Today Movies. December 24, 2007.
<http://www.christianitytoday.com/movies/reviews/kingdomofheaven.html>.
Dafoe, Stephen. "The Battle of Hattin: July 4, 1187". 1998. A History and Mythos of the Knights Templar. December 24, 2007.
<http://www.templarhistory.com/hattin.html>.
Dajani-Shakeel, Hadia. "Some Medieval Accounts of Salah al-Din's Recovery of Jerusalem (Al-Quds)." 1988. Institute for Palestine Studies. December 24, 2007.
<http://www.fordham.edu/halsall/med/salahdin.html>.
Furnish, Timothy R. "Kingdom of Heaven: What Parts are Real?" May 16, 2005. History News Network. December 24, 2007.
<http://hnn.us/articles/11933.html>.
"Guy of Lusignan". Wikipedia. The Free Encyclopedia. December 23, 2007.
Wikimedia Foundation. December 24, 2007.
<http://en.wikipedia.org/wiki/Guy_of_Lusignan>.
Hirsen, James L. "'Kingdom of Heaven' Truth in Limbo". May 9, 2005.
FirstLiberties.com. December 24, 2007.
<http://www.firstliberties.com/truth_in_limbo.html>.

"Kingdom of Heaven". December 23, 2007. Wikiquote. December 24, 2007.
        <http://en.wikiquote.org/wiki/Kingdom_of_Heaven>.
"Kingdom of Heaven (film)". Wikipedia. The Free Encyclopedia. December
        23, 2007. Wikimedia Foundation. December 24, 2007.
        <http://en.wikipedia.org/wiki/Kingdom_of_Heaven_(film)>.
"Kingdom of Jerusalem". Wikipedia. The Free Encyclopedia. December 23,
        2007. Wikimedia Foundation. December 24, 2007.
        <http://en.wikipedia.org/wiki/Kingdom_of_Jerusalem>.
MacDonald, G. Jeffrey. "Medieval Historians give 'Kingdom' Mixed
        Reviews". May 15, 2005. USA Today. December 24, 2007.
Mariani, Joe. "Kingdom of Heaven: Hollywood vs. History." May 12, 2005.
        MensNewsDaily.com. December 24, 2007.
        <http://mensnewsdaily.com/archive/m-n/mariani/2005/mariani051205.htm>.
Niccum, Jon. "Kingdom of Heaven Launches Successful Crusade." May 6,
        2005. Lawrence Journal World and News. December 24, 2007.
        <http://www2.ljworld.com/news/2005/may/06/kingdom_of_heaven/>.
"Raynald of Chatillon". Wikipedia. The Free Encyclopedia. December 23,
        2007. Wikimedia Foundation. December 24, 2007.
        <http://en.wikipedia.org/wiki/Raynald_of_Chatillon>.
Schultz, Cathy. "Making the Crusades Relevant in Kingdom of Heaven."
        May 6, 2005. History in the Movies. December 24, 2007.
        <http://www.stfrancis.edu/historyinthemovies/kingdomofheaven.htm>.
"Sibylla of Jerusalem". Wikipedia. The Free Encyclopedia. December 23,
        2007. Wikimedia Foundation. December 24, 2007.
        <http://en.wikipedia.org/wiki/Sibylla_of_Jerusalem>.
Svesnik, Shlomo. "Oy Vez, Jerusalem." May 10, 2005. World War 4 Report.
        December 24, 2007.
        <http://www.ww4report.com/node/451>.
"The Crusaders Capture Jerusalem, 1099." 2000. EyeWitness to History.
        December 24, 2007.
        <http://www.eyewitnesstohistory.com/crusades.htm>.
"The First Crusade: Conquering of Jerusalem." The Latter Rain Page.
        December 24, 2007.
        <http://latter-rain.com/crusade/curone.htm>.

Braveheart
"King Edward II". Soylent Communications. December 28, 2007.
        < http://www.nndb.com/people/710/000093431/>.
"Official Police Reports Include Gibson's Remarks". July 31, 2006. AP.
        December 28, 2007.
        < http://www.msnbc.msn.com/id/14123734/>.
Sanello, Frank. *Reel vs. Real*. First Taylor Trade Publishing. Lanham,
        Maryland. 2003.
Stiles, Paula. "Braveheart: How Mel Gibson won the Battle of Scottish
        Independence and Lost the War of Historical Accuracy." July 9,
        2006. Suite 101.com. December 28, 2007.
        <http://medievalhistory.suite101.com/article.cfm/film_review__braveheart>.
"Wars of Independence – William Wallace". BBC.Co.UK. December 28,
        2007.
        <http://www.bbc.co.uk/history/scottishhistory/independence/features_indepe
        ndence_wallace.shtml>.

Pocahontas

Auld, Kiros. "Pocahontas: Patron Saint of Colonial Miscegenation?" 2002.
    Powhatan Museum of Indigenous Arts and Culture. December 31,
    2007.
    <http://www.powhatanmuseum.com/Pocahontas.html>.
"Captain John Smith." The Association for the Preservation of Virginia Antiquities. 2000.
    November 24, 2007.
    <http://www.apva.org/history/jsmith.html>.
Chagollan, Steve. "Pocahontas Takes New Trip To Hollywood." The International Harold
    Tribune. November 28, 2005.
Chief Roy Crazy Horse. "The Pocahontas Myth." Powhatan Renape Nation.
    December 31, 2007.
    < http://www.powhatan.org/pocc.html>.
"Exploring Florida." University of South Florida. 2002. November 24, 2007.
    < http://fcit.usf.edu/Florida/lessons/menendz/menendz1.htm>.
"History of Jamestown." The Association for the Preservation of Virginia Antiquities. 2000.
    November 24, 2007.
    <http://www.apva.org/history/index.html>.
"London Company." Wikipedia. The Free Encyclopedia. January 3, 2008.
    Wikimedia Foundation. January 4, 2008.
    <http://en.wikipedia.org/wiki/London_Company>.
Montgomery, Dennis. "Such a Dish as Powdered Wife I Never Heard Of." Colonial
    Williamsburg. December 28, 2007.
    <http://www.history.org/Foundation/journal/Winter07/jamestownSide.cfm>.
"Pocahontas." 2007. The Association for the Preservation of Virginia
    Antiquities. December 31, 2007.
    <http://www.apva.org/history/pocahont.html>.
"Powhatan Indian Tribe History." Access Genealogy. 2007. November 24, 2007.
    <http://www.accessgenealogy.com/native/tribes/powhatan/powhatanhist.htm
    >.
Lee, Cotton. "Powhatan Indian Lifeways." July 1999. Historic Jamestown. National Park
    Service. December 31, 2007.
    <http://www.nps.gov/jame/historyculture/powhatan-indian-lifeways.htm>.
Stone, Edward T. "Columbus and Genocide." American Heritage Magazine. 2007.
    November 24, 2007.
    <http://www.americanheritage.com/articles/magazine/ah/1975/6/1975_6_4.sh
    tml>.

National Treasure: Book of Secrets

"Abraham Lincoln assassination." *Wikipedia, The Free Encyclopedia.* March 25,
        2008, 16:05 UTC. Wikimedia Foundation, Inc. March 26, 2008
        <http://en.wikipedia.org/w/index.php?title=Abraham_Lincoln_assassination&o
        ldid=200821577>.
"City of Gold Info." 1997 Microsoft Encarta Encyclopedia. March 24, 2008.
        < http://www.mysteriouscitiesofgold.org/
        r_city_of_gold_info.htm>.
"HMS Resolute." 2005. Athropolis Productions Limited. March 24, 2008.
        <http://www.athropolis.com/arctic-facts/fact-resolute.htm>.
"The Jesuit Connection to the Assassination of Abraham Lincoln." 1999.
        Truth on the Web Ministries. March 26, 2008.
        < http://members.aol.com/KHoeck777/Abe.htm>.
"Mount Rushmore." Wikipedia. March 24, 2008.
        < http://en.wikipedia.org/wiki/Mount_Rushmore>.

"National Treasure Book of Secrets, Mistakes, Goofs and Blunders." March
        24, 2008
        < http://www.moviemistakes.com/film7128>.
"Presidential HMS Resolute Desk." Citymax.com. American Presidential
        Museum. March 24, 2008.
        <http://www.americanpresidentialmuseum.com/catalog/item/1700409/113268
        4.htm>.
"Collectible Japanese Secret Trick Puzzle Box Himitsu Bako." 2004 Northern
        Options. March 24, 2008.
        < http://www.puzzleboxworld.com>.
"Statue of Liberty National Park: History." 2008 APN Media, LLC. American
        Park Network. March 24, 2008.
        <http://www.americanparknetwork.com/parkinfo/content.asp?cat
        id=85&contenttypeid=35>.

Gangs of New York
"Analysis of Gangs of New York." Backintime.com. February 2, 2008.
        <http://www.backintime.com/moviereviews/gangsofny/>.
Anbinder, Tyler. Interview. "Is Gangs of New York Historically Accurate?"
        Gotham Gazette.
        December 23, 2002. February 2, 2008.
        <http://www.gothamgazette.com/article/feature
        -commentary/20021223/202/162>.
"Bowery Boys." Wikipedia.com. 2008. Wikipedia. March 2, 2008.
        <http://en.wikipedia.org/wiki/Bowery_Boys>.
Brown, Joshua. "The Gang's Not All Here." Common-place.org. April 2003.
        February 2, 2008. <http://www.common-place.org/vox-pop/200304.shtml>.
Burnett, Eric. *The Best American History Book in the World*. Lincoln, NE:
        iUniverse, 2003.
Carle, Frances. "Bill the Butcher." Herbertasbury.com. 1999. February 2,
        2008.
        <http://herbertasbury.com/billthebutcher/billp.asp>.
Carle, Frances. "Gangs of New York." Herbertasbury.com. 1999. February 2,
        2008.
        <http://herbertasbury.com/gangsofnewyork/>.
Chamberlain, Ted. "'Gangs of New York': Fact vs. Fiction."
        News.nationalgeographic.com.
        March 24, 2003. National Geographic. February 2, 2008.
        <http://news.nationalgeographic.com/news/2003/03/0320_030320_oscars_gangs.ht
        ml>.
"Draft Riots." Infoplease.com. 2007. February 2, 2008.
        <http://www.infoplease.com/ce6/history/A0816049.html>.
        "Early Irish Gangs of NY, The." Network54.com. February 21, 2006.
        February 2, 2008.
        <http://www.network54.com/Forum/402609/thread/1140521414/last-
        1140521414/The+Early+Irish+Gangs+of+NY>.
"Five Points Study Guide." Excerpt from *Gangs of New York: Making the
        Movie*.
        Miramax Books, 2003. DVD. *Gangs of New York*.
Gangs of New York. Dir. Martin Scorsese. Perf. Leonardo DiCaprio, Daniel
        Day-Lewis, and
        Cameron Diaz. Miramax, 2002.
"Gangs of New York." *All Things Considered*. National Public Radio.

December 23, 2002.
February 2, 2008. <http://hnn.us/comments/6212.html>.
"Gangs of New York." Wikipedia.com. 2008. Wikipedia. February 2, 2008.
　　　<http://en.wikipedia.org/wiki/Gangs_of_New_York>.
Grinspan, Jon. "America's Worst Immigration War." Americanheritage.com.
　　　November 4, 2006. American Heritage Inc.. February 2, 2008.
　　　<http://www.americanheritage.com/events/articles/web/20061104-know-nothing-
　　　nativism-american-party-immigration-catholicism.shtml>.
"History of the Five Points." DVD. *Gangs of New York*. Miramax, 2002.
London, Herbert. "Real Gangs." Nationalreview.com. January 16, 2003.
　　　National Review Online. February 2, 2008.
　　　<http://www.nationalreview.com/comment
　　　/comment-london011603.asp>.
Mandelbaum, Carola. "Requiem for Bill 'The Butcher' Poole."
　　　Thebrooklynrail.org. April, 2003. The Brooklyn Rail. February 2, 2008.
　　　<http://www.thebrooklynrail.org/film/april03/requiem.html>.
"New York Draft Riots, The." Civilwarhome.com. March 3, 2002. February 2,
　　　2008.
　　　<http://www.civilwarhome.com/draftriots.htm>.
"P.T. Barnum." Ringling.com. February 2, 2008.
　　　<http://www.ringling.com/explore/history/ptbarnum_1.aspx>.
"Tweed Ring, The." U-s-history.com. 2002. February 2, 2008.
　　　<http://www.u-s-history.com/pages/h703.html>.
"Tweed, William Marcy." History1900s.about.com. 2007. February 2, 2008.
　　　<http://history1900s.about.com/gi/dynamic/offsite.htm?site=http%3A%2F%2Fww
　　　w.infoplease.com%2Fce6%2Fpeople%2FA0849803.html>.
"Uncovering the Real *Gangs of New York*." Discovery Channel.
　　　Prod., writ., dir. Harry Hanbury. Prod. Susan Aasen. Narr. Bob Brown.
　　　Parrhesia Pictures, Inc., ABC Inc., 2002.
"US Immigration History." Visa2003.com. 2003. February 2, 2008.
　　　<http://www.visa2003.com/world-immigration/us-history.htm>.

From Hell
Barbee, Larry S. "Casebook: Jack the Ripper - From Hell: Fact
　　　or Fiction?" Casebook. 19 Mar 2007.
　　　<http://www.casebook.org/dissertations/dst-fromhellfact.html>.
"From Hell (2001)." IMDb. 19 Mar 2007.
　　　<http://imdb.com/title/tt0120681/maindetails>.
"Jack the Ripper." Wikipedia. The Free Encyclopedia. 2007. Wikimedia Foundation. March
　　　19, 2007.
　　　<http://en.wikipedia.org/wiki/Jack_the_Ripper>.
Sanello, Frank. *Reel vs. Real*. First Taylor Trade Publishing. Lanham,
　　　Maryland. 2003.
Scheib, Richard. "From Hell (2001)." Moria. 19 Mar 2007.
　　　<http://www.moria.co.nz/horror/fromhell.htm>.

Flyboys
"Death of a Zeppelin, 1916." 2005. Eyewitness to History. January 4, 2008.
　　　<http://www.eyewitnesstohistory.com/pfzeppelin.htm>.
"Eugene Bullard." Wikipedia. The Free Encyclopedia. January 3, 2008.
　　　Wikimedia Foundation. January 4, 2008.
　　　<http://en.wikipedia.org/wiki/Eugene_Bullard>.

"Flyboys." <u>Wikipedia. The Free Encyclopedia.</u> January 3, 2008. Wikimedia Foundation. January 4, 2008.
<http://en.wikipedia.org/wiki/Flyboys>.

"Flyboys – I'm Not Hopeful." August 15, 2006. <u>The Miniatures Page.</u> January 4, 2008.
<http://theminiaturespage.com/boards/msg.mv?id=83482>.

King, Tim. "Movie Review:*The Flyboys* Shoots Myths About WW1 Pilots Down in Flames." July 4, 2006. <u>Salem-News.com.</u> January 4, 2008.
<http://www.salem-news.com/articles/july042006/the_flyboys_7406.php>.

"Lafayette Escadrille." <u>Wikipedia. The Free Encyclopedia.</u> January 3, 2008. Wikimedia Foundation. January 4, 2008.
<http://en.wikipedia.org/wiki/Lafayette_Escadrille>.

Lemire, Christy. "'Flyboys' an Earnest War Picture." 2006. Associated Press. January 4, 2008.
<http://movies.msn.com/movies/movie.aspx?m=585397&mp=r>.

Stone, Jay. "Review: Flyboys." September 22, 2006. <u>CanWest News Service.</u> January 4, 2008.
< http://movies.msn.com/movies/movie.aspx?m=585397&mp=r>.

"The Red Baron Scores Two Victories, 1917." 2005. <u>Eyewitness to History.</u> January 4, 2008.
<<u>http://www.eyewitnesstohistory.com/pfzeppelin.htm</u>>.

"Zeppelin." <u>Wikipedia. The Free Encyclopedia.</u> January 3, 2008. Wikimedia Foundation. January 4, 2008.
<http://en.wikipedia.org/wiki/Zeppelin>.

Lawrence of Arabia

Belt, Don. "Lawrence of Arabia: A hero's journey" <u>National Geographic</u>. Washington: Jan 1999. Vol. 195, Iss. 1; p. 38 (24 pages).

Crowther, Bosley. "A Desert Warfare Spectacle" New York Times. 16 May 2007.
<http://www.nytimes.com/packages/html/movies/bestpictures/lawrence-re.html>.

Hughes, Matthew. "T. E. Lawrence" <u>The Journal of Military History.</u> Lexington: Oct 2005. Vol.69, Iss. 4; pg. 1232, 2 pgs.

Hodson, Joel. "Lowell Thomas, T.E. Lawrence and the creation of a legend" <u>American History</u>. Harrisburg: Oct 2000. Vol.35, Iss. 4; pg. 46, 7 pgs.

Leach, Hugh. "Lawrence in Arabia." <u>History Today</u>. London: Oct 2005. Vol.55, Iss. 10; pg. 4, 3 pgs.

Shuster, Mike. "The Middle East and the West: WWI and Beyond." <u>All Things Considered</u>; NPR. August 20, 2004. 7 May 2007.
<http://www.npr.org/temp lates/story/story.php?storyId=3860950>.

Shuster, Mike. "The Mideast: A Century of Conflict." NPR. September 2002. 16 May 2007.
<http://www.npr.org/news/specials/mideast/history/>.

"T. E. LAWRENCE ON GUERILLA WARFARE" 16 May 2007.
<http://pegasus.cc.ucf.edu/~eshaw/lawrence.htm>.

Williams, Hywel. "Comment & Analysis: Lies in the sand" <u>The Guardian</u>. Manchester (UK): Jun 3, 2002. pg. 16.

Woodward, David R. "The Middle East during World War One" BBC. 16 May 2007.
<http://www.bbc.co.uk/history/worldwars/wwone/middle_east_01.shtml>.

The Untouchables

"Al Capone- the Man." <u>Al Capone Museum</u>. 15 Mar. 2008. 22 Mar. 2008
    <http://www.alcaponemuseum.com/>.
Bardsley, Marilyn. "Crooked Cops." <u>Crime Library</u>. 2007. 22 Mar. 2008
    <http://www.crimelibrary.com/gangsters_outlaws/cops_others/n
      ess/15.html>.
Bardsley, Marilyn. "Eliot Ness: the Man Behind the Myth." <u>Crime Library</u>.
    2007. 22 Mar. 2008
    <http://www.crimelibrary.com/gangsters_outlaws/cops_others/ness/3.html>.
Bergreen, Laurence. Capone: The Man and the Era. New York: Touchstone,
    1994.
High, Stanley. "Cleveland versus the Crooks." Reader's Digest 32(February
    1939): 48-51.
Kobler, John. <u>The Life and World of Al Capone</u>. New York: G.P. Putnam'S
    Sons, 1971.
"Labor & Crime V. Wilkerson." <u>TIME Magazine</u>. 11 Apr. 1932. 17 Mar. 2008
    <http://www.time.com/time/magazine/article/0,9171,743497,00.ht
    ml>.
"Temperance Movement." <u>American Law Encyclopedia Vol.9</u>. 2008. 18 Mar.
    2008.
    <http://law.jrank.org/pages/10714/TemperanceMovement.html>.
"Temperance Movement." <u>Wikipedia</u>. 15 Mar. 2008. 15 Mar. 2008
    <http://en.wikipedia.org/wiki/Temperance_movement>.
"The Untouchables." <u>Wikipedia</u>. 17 Mar. 2008. 21 Mar. 2008
    <http://www.crimelibrary.com/gangsters_outlaws/cops_others/n
      ess/15.html>.

The Aviator

Brand, Paul. "Nice Town. I'll Take It." <u>Bright Lights Film Journal.</u> 2005.
    February 2005.
    <http://www.brightlightsfilm.com/47/hughes.htm>.
"Howard Hughes: A Chronology." <u>Channel 4</u>. 2007. December 2004.
    <http://www.channel4.com/history/microsites/H/history/e-h/hughes.html>.
"Howard Hughes." <u>PBS.com</u>. 2007.
    <http://www.pbs.org/kcet/chasingthesun/innovators/hhughes.html>.
"Howard Hughes." <u>Wikipedia.</u> 2007. December 19, 2007.
    <http://en.wikipedia.org/wiki/Howard_hughes>.
Hunter, Stephen. "Howard Hughes, Spreading His Wings."
    <u>Washingtonpost.com.</u> 2005.
    December 19, 2004.
    <http://www.washingtonpost.com/wp-dyn/articles/A7811-2004Dec17.html>.
Hyde, Douglas. "The Hughes-Hepburn affair." <u>CNN.com.</u> 2007. February
    23, 2005.
    <http://edition.cnn.com/2005/SHOWBIZ/Movies/02/23/hughes.hepburn/ind
    ex.html?iref=newssearch>.
Rosenberg, Jennifer. "Howard Hughes." <u>About.com</u>. 2007.
    <http://history1900s.about.com/od/people/p/hughes.htm>.
Schultz, Cathy. "The Aviator." <u>History in the Movies.</u> 2007. December 23'
    2004
    <http://www.stfrancis.edu/historyinthemovies/aviator.htm>.
"The Crash of the XF-11." <u>Check-six.com.</u> 2007. November 10, 2007.
    <http://www.check-six.com/Crash_Sites/XF-11_crash_site.htm>.

Enemy at the Gates
"Battle of Stalingrad." Wikipedia. 2007. November 10, 2007.
    < http://en.wikipedia.org/wiki/Battle_of_Stalingrad>.
May, Tom. "Historical Background." Geocities.com. 2007. November 10,
    2007.   <
    http://www.geocities.com/tommay_e17/enemybackground.html>.
Meek, James. "Under Fire." Guardian Unlimited. 2001. November 10, 2007.
    <http://film.guardian.co.uk/features/featurepages/0,,452300,00.
    html>.
Smith, Scott L. "A for History, D for Entertainment." The Journal for
    Historical Review. 2001. November 10, 2007.
    < http://www.ihr.org/jhr/v20/v20n2p45_Annaud.html>.
"Soviet War Crimes" Wikipedia. The Free Encyclopedia. January 3, 2008.
    Wikimedia Foundation. January 4, 2008.
    <http://en.wikipedia.org/wiki/Soviet_war_crimes>.
"Soviet Women Soldiers in WWII: Three Biographical Sketches – Excerpt."
    BNET Research Center. 2000. November 10, 2007.
    <http://findarticles.com/p/articles/mi_m0EXI/is_2000_Fall
    -Winter/ai_73063465>.
"The Battle of Stalingrad." Stalingrad Military-Historical Club. 2007.
    November 10, 2007.
    < http://stalingrad.ic.ru/main.html>.
"Vasily Zaitsev's Sniper Count" 2003. The Voice of Russia. January 4, 2008.
    <http://www.vor.ru/Russia/Stalingraders/Defenders_8_eng.html
Yoder, Mike. "Rattenkrieg." 2003. Military History Online – Battle of
    Stalingrad. January 8, 2008.
    <http://www.militaryhistoryonline.com/wwii/stalingrad/rattenkrieg.aspx>.

Patton
"Battle of El Guettar." Wikipedia. 2007. April 4, 2007.
    <http://en.wikipedia.org/wiki/Battle_of_El_Guettar>.
"Death & the General." Time.com. 1945. March 11, 2007.
    <http://www.time.com/time/magazine/article/0,9171,886708,00.ht
    ml>.
"George S. Patton." Wikipedia. 2007. March 1, 2007.
    <http://en.wikipedia.org/wiki/George_S._Patton>.
"Hammelburg Raid, The." Taskforcebaum.de. 2006. March 1, 2007.
    <http://www.taskforcebaum.de/main1.html>.
"HyperWar: U.S. Army Campaigns of WWII – Tunisia" Ibiblio.org. March
    19, 2007.
    <http://www.ibiblio.org/hyperwar/USA/USA-C-
    Tunisia/index.html>.
Lord, Walter. "The Finish Line Was Messina." November 27, 1988. The New
    York Times. January 10, 2008.
    <http://query.nytimes.com/gst/fullpage.html?res=940DE4D91531F
    934A15752C1A96E948260&sec=&spon=&pagewanted=all>.
Parkes, J.A.. "Solid biopic of controversial figure." Amazon.com. 2002. March
    1, 2007.
    <http://www.amazon.co.uk/Patton-two-disc-set-George-
    Scott/dp/rentals/B00005AA0N>.
"Patton (film)." Wikipedia. 2007. March 4, 2007.
    <http://en.wikipedia.org/wiki/Patton_%28film%29>.
"People & Events: George S. Patton Jr. (1885-1945)." Pbs.org. 2001. March 1,

2007.
<http://www.pbs.org/wgbh/amex/bulge/peopleevents/p_patton. html>.

Sanello, Frank. *Reel vs. Real*. First Taylor Trade Publishing. Lanham, Maryland. 2003

Stroupe, Frank. "George Patton Biography." Freeinfosociety.com. March 1, 2007.
<http://www.freeinfosociety.com/site.php?postnum=517>.

The Motorcycle Diaries

"About the Production." The Motorcycle Diaries. Focus Features. 28 Nov 2007.
<http://www.motorcyclediariesmovie.com/home.html>.

"Alberto Granado." Wikipedia.org. November 2007. Wikipedia. 17 Nov 2007.
<http://enwikipedia.org/wiki/Alberto_Granado>.

Castaneda, Jorge G. Companero: The Life and Death of Che Guevara. Vintage, 1998.

Dorfman, Ariel. "Che Guevara." TIME 100: Che Guevara. June 14, 1999. November 2007.
<http://www.time.com/time/time100/heroes/profile/guevara01.html>.

Guevara, Ernesto. The Motorcycle Diaries: Notes on a Latin American Journey. Havana, Cuba: Centro de Estudios Che Guevara, 2004.

"My Ride with Che." My Ride with Che | Interview. February 13, 2004. The Guardian. 28 Nov 2007.
<http://film.guardian.co.uk/interview/interviewpages/0,6737,1146746,00.html>.

Russell, Lawrence. "The Motorcycle Diaries." The Motorcycle Diaries (Diarios de motocicleta). 2004. Culture Court. 28 Nov 2007.
<http://www.culturecourt.com/F/Latin/MotorCycleDiaries.htm>.

Short, Glen David. "Salles', Guevara's and Granado's Motorcycle Diaries: A Comparative Review." Glen David Short at ScribeCentral.com. 2004. 28 Nov 2007.
<http://www.scribecentral.com/GLENDAVIDSHOT/archives/000357.html>.

Stodden, William. "Chronology of the Economic Ministry of Comrade Guevara after the Revolution in Cuba." Chronology While in the Economic Ministry. May 17, 2000. Marxists. 28 Nov 2007.
<http://www.marxists.org/archive/guevara/biography/econ-ministry.htm>.

""The Motorcycle Diaries" ("Diarios de motocicleta")." Maoist review of "The Motorcycle Diaries". 2004. Etext. 28 Nov 2007.
<http://www.etext.org/Politics/MIM/movies/long/diaries.html>.

"The Motorcycle Diaries." Channel 4 – The Motorcycle Diaries. Channel 4. 28 Nov 2007.
<http://www.channel4.com/film/cinemadvd/microsites/M/motorcycle_diaries/tyretracks_t.html>.

Quiz Show

""A Sop to the Public at Large": Contestant Herbert Stempel Exposes Contrivances in a 1950s Televsion Quiz Show" History Matters, March 1, 2007.
<http://historymatters.gmu.edu/d/65565>.

Alleva, Richard. "A pop quiz -- Quiz Show" Commonweal. New York: Oct 21, 1994. Vol. 121, Iss. 18; pg 17, 2 pgs.

"Barbarians at the gate – Quiz Show" Time. New York: Sept 19, 1994. Vol. 144, Iss. 12; pg. 77, 1 pgs.

Bernstein, Richard. "For $64,000, What is 'Fiction'?" New York Times. New York, N.Y.: Sept 4, 1994. pg. A. 1.

Blake, Richard A. America. "Rerun -- Quiz Show" New York: Mar 11, 1995. Vol. 172, Iss. 8; pg. 32, 2 pgs.

"Charles Van Doren" PBS, March 1, 2007.
    <http://www.pbs.org/wgbh/amex/quizshow/peopleevents/pande02.html>.
Cornwall, Rupert. "Out of America: Questioning an age of innocence lost." The
    Independent. London, UK: Oct 12, 1994. pg. NOPGCIT
Epstein, Joseph. Commentary. "Redford's Van Doren & mine" New York: Dec 1994. Vol. 98,
    Iss. 6; pg 40, 7 pgs.
""Every Effort Was Made to Control the Shows": A Televsion Producer Details and Defends
    Deceptive Quiz Show Practices" History Matters, March 1, 2007.
    <http://historymatters.gmu.edu/d/6557>.
Frankel, Max. "WORD & IMAGE; This is Your Life" New York Times. New York, N.Y.: Oct
    9, 199. pg. A. 32.
"Questionable questions – Quiz Show" National Review. New York: Oct 10, 1994. Vol. 46,
    Iss.19; pg. 76, 3 pgs.
"QUIZ SHOW SCANDALS" Museum of Broadcast Communications, March 1, 2007:
    <http://www.museum.tv/archives/etv/Q/htmlQ/quizshowsca/quizshowsca.h
    tm>.
"QUIZ SHOW; Entertainment Versus History" New York Times. New York, N.Y.: Sep 25,
    1994. pg. A. 4.
"QUIZ SHOW; Acceptable Dramatic License?" New York Times. New York, N.Y.: Sep 25,
    1994. pg. A.4.
Sumner, Gregory D. "America -- Quiz Show" The American Historical Review. Washington;
    Oct 1995. Vol. 100, Iss. 4; pg. 1206.
""The Truth is the Only Thing with Which a Man Can Live": Quiz Show Contestant Charles
    Van Doren Publicly Confesses to Deceiving His Television Audience" History
    Matters, March 1, 2007: <http://historymatters.gmu.edu/d/6566>.
"Truth or consequences – Quiz Show" directed by Robert Redford" The New Republic.
    Washington: Oct 10, 1994. Vol. 211, Iss, 15; pg 32, 2 pgs.
"Twenty-One" BBC, March 1, 2007: <http://www.bbc.co.uk/dna/h2g2/A2586530>.
"Twenty-One (game show)" Wikipedia, March 1, 2007:
    <http://en.wikipedea.org/wiki/Twenty_One_%28game_show%29
Venanzi, Katie "An Examination of Television Quiz Show Scandals of the
    1950s University Honor Program," 1997, March 1, 2007:
    <http://honors.umd.edu/HONR269J/projects/venanzi.htm>.

Capote

Capote, Truman. *In Cold Blood*. Vintage International Publishing. New York. 1965.
Geringer, Joseph. "The Clutter Family Killings: Cold Blood." Crime Library. 2007.
    November 11, 2007.
    <http://www.crimelibrary.com/notorious_murders/family/clutter/4.html>.
Gibbons, Phil. "Capote vs. Capote." Fair. March 2006. November 11, 2007.
    <http://www.fair.org/index.php?page=2880>.
La Ferla, Ruth. "Unearthing The Notebook That Unnerved Society." The New York Times.
    November 25, 2001. November 11, 2007.
    <http://www.nytimes.com/ads/capote/capote_2.html>.
Maloney, J.J. "In Cold Blood: A Dishonest Book." Crime Magazine. May 7, 1991. December
    2, 2007.
    <http://crimemagazine.com/CrimeBooks/incold.htm>.
Moe, Doug. "Capote's Last Book Still A Mystery." The Capital Times. November 21, 2005.
    November 11, 2007.
    <http://www.madison.com/archives/read.php?ref=/tct/2005/11/21/051121011
    3.php>.
O'Connor, John J. "How Capote Blurred Border Between Fact and Fiction." The New York
    Times. November 22, 1996. November 11, 2007.

<http://query.nytimes.com/gst/fullpage.html?res=9905E0DB163DF931A15752C
1A960958260>.

Rocha, Guy Louis. "Truman Capote's In Cold Blood: The Nevada
Connection." Nevada State Library and Archives. March 14, 2006.
November 11, 2007.
<http://dmla.clan.lib.nv.us/docs/nsla/archives/spec-feat.htm>.

Schneider, Dan. "Capote Directed by Bennett Miller." International Writers Magazine.
November 2005. November 11, 2007.
<http://www.hackwriters.com/capote.htm>.

"Truman Capote." Wikipedia. 2007. November 11, 2007.
<http://en.wikipedia.org/wiki/Truman_capote>.

Full Metal Jacket

"Blanket Party." Wikipedia. 2007. November 24, 2007.
< http://en.wikipedia.org/wiki/Blanket_party>.

"Full Metal Jacket." Full Metal Jacket: The Movie. November 24, 2007.
< http://full_metal_jacket_25.tripod.com/ha2.htm>.

"Full Metal Jacket essays." Full Metal Jacket. 2007. November 24, 2007.
< http://www.megaessays.com/viewpaper/38719.html>.

Goldburg, Robert and Johnson, Brandon. "Boot Camp Violence: Abuse in
Vietnam." Journal of Undergraduate Research. 1995. November 24, 2007.
<http://www.lib.utah.edu/epubs/undergrad/vol6/johnson.html>.

"Mai Lai Massacre." Wikipedia. 2007. November 24, 2007.
< http://en.wikipedia.org/wiki/My_Lai>.

"National Front for the Liberation of South Vietnam." Wikipedia. 2007.
November 24, 2007.
< http://en.wikipedia.org/wiki/Viet_Cong>.

"Tet Offensive." Wikipedia. 2004. December 10, 2007.
<http://en.wikipedia.org/wiki/Tet_Offensive#South_Vietnam>.

"Vietnam." Wikipedia. 2007. November 24, 2007.
< http://en.wikipedia.org/wiki/Vietnam>.

"Vietnam People's Army." Wikipedia. 2007. November 24, 2007.
<http://en.wikipedia.org/wiki/People%27s_Army_of_Vietnam>.

Apollo 13

Apollo 13. Dir. Ron Howard. Perf. Tom Hanks, Kevin Bacon, Bill Paxton, Gary Sinise, and
Ed Harris. Universal, 1995.

"Apollo 13." Wikipedia. 2007. November 25, 2007.
<http://en.wikipedia.org/wiki/Apollo_13>.

Arnold, Martin. "Plight of 3 Apollo 13 Crewmen Stirs World Interest." The New York
Times. April 15, 1970. November 25, 2007.
<http://partners.nytimes.com/library/national/science/nasa/041570sci-nasa-
arnold.html>.

Banke, Jim. "What Caused the Apollo 13 Disaster?" Space.com. April 13, 2000. November
25, 2007.
<http://www.space.com/news/spacehistory/apollo13_focus_failure_000413.ht
ml>.

Chaikin, Andrew. "Apollo 13 Astronauts Remember." Space and Science. April 19, 2000.
November 25, 2007.
<http://www.space.com/peopleinterviews/apollo13_lovell_sidebar_000419.html
>.

Compton, David W. "The Flight of Apollo 13." NASA. May 22, 2000. November 25, 2007.
<http://liftoff.msfc.nasa.gov/Academy/History/APOLLO-13/compton.html>.

"Goofs for Apollo 13." The Internet Movie Database. 2007. November 25, 2007.
        <http://www.imdb.com/title/tt0112384/goofs>.
King, Susan. "Author cites the best and worst films for historical accuracy." Los Angeles
        Times. November 25, 2007. <http://archive.southcoasttoday.com/daily/02-
        00/02-12-00/b03li072.htm>.
Lovell, James A. "Houston We Have a Problem." Ch 13.1. November 25, 2007.
        <http://history.nasa.gov/SP-350/ch-13-1.html>.
"NASA." Wikipedia. December 9, 2007. December 10, 2007.
        <http://en.wikipedia.org/wiki/NASA#History>.
Redmond, Charles. "Apollo 13- Chronology of Events Surrounding Accident." NASA.
        January 26, 2004. November 25, 2007.
        <http://www.hq.nasa.gov/pao/History/apollo/problem.html>.

The Day After

Corry, John. "TV View; 'The Day After': TV as a Rallying Cry." The New York
        Times. New York, N.Y. 20 Nov. 1983: pg. A.1
The Day After. Dir. Nicholas Meyer. Perf. Jason Robards, Steve Guttenberg,
        John Lithgow. DVD. American Broadcasting Company, 1983.
"The Day After." Wikipedia, The Free Encyclopedia. 21 Mar 2008. Wikimedia
        Foundation, Inc. 23 Mar 2008.
        <http://en.wikipedia.org/w/index.php?title=The_Day_After&oldid=199797190
        >.
Fischer, Benjamin B. "A Cold War Conundrum: the 1983 Soviet War Scare."
        Central   Intelligence Agency. 21 Nov. 2007. Central Intelligence Agency. 26 Feb.
        2008.
        <https://www.cia.gov/library/center-for-the-study-of-intelligence/csi-
                publications/books-and-monographs/a-cold-war-
        conundrum/source.htm>.
George, Alice L. Awaiting Armageddon: How Americans Faced the Cuban
        Missile Crisis. Chapel Hill: The University of North Carolina Press, 2003.
Hanes, Sharon M., and Richard C. Hanes. Cold War Almanac. Ed. Lawrence
        W. Baker. Detroit: U-X-L, 2004.
"Introduction: A New Nuclear Threat." The Challenge of Nuclear Weapons.
        Watson Institute for International Studies, Brown University, 1989.
Niccum, Jon. "Fallout from 'The Day After'" Lawrence.com. 19 Nov. 2003. 26
        Feb. 2008. <http://www.lawrence.com/news/2003/nov/19/fallout_from/>.
"Peace Memorial City, Hiroshima." The City of Hiroshima. 2002. Hiroshima
        Peace Culture Foundation. 4 Mar. 2008.
        <http://www.city.hiroshima.jp/kikaku/joho/toukei/History-E/c05.html>.
Rennell, Tony. "September 26th, 1983: The Day the World Almost Died." The
        Daily Mail 29 Dec. 2007. 4 Mar. 2008.
        <http://www.dailymail.co.uk/pages/live/articles/news/news.
        html?in_article_id=505009&in_page_id=1770>.

Lord of War

"Charles Taylor (Liberia)." Wikipedia. 2007. November 04, 2007.
        <http://en.wikipedia.org/wiki/Charles_G._Taylor>.
Doyle, Mark. "Charles Taylor - preacher, warlord and president." BBC
        NEWS. June 4. November 04, 2007.
        <http://news.bbc.co.uk/2/hi/africa/2963086.stm>.
Bennett, Brian. "How the Lord of War Was Nabbed." Time Magazine. March
        7, 2008. March 9, 2008.
        <http://www.time.com/time/world/article/0,8599,1720555,00.html?imw=Y>.

"Monrovia." Wikipedia. 2007. November 04, 2007.
  <http://en.wikipedia.org/wiki/Monrovia>.
Smith, Dan. The Penguin Atlas of War and Peace. Penguin Books.
  Harmondsworth, Middlesex, England. 2003.
"Viktor Bout." Wikipedia. 2007. November 04, 2007.
  <http://en.wikipedia.org/wiki/Victor_Bout>.

American History X
Berlet, Chip. "Overview of U.S White Supremacist Groups." Journal
  of Political and Military Sociology 34(2006):
Brown, Timothy. "Subcultures, Pop Music and Politics: Skinheads
  and "Nazi Rock" in England and Germany." Journal
  of Social History 38(2004):
Charney, Marc. "Word for Word / The Skinhead International; Some
  Music, It Turns Out, Inflames the Savage Beast." The
  New York Times 02 Jul 1995:
Dees, Morris. "You have right to hate, but not right to hurt."
  USA TODAY 03 Jun 1991:
"Hitler Youth." Wikipedia. 2008. February 29, 2008.
  <http://en.wikipedia.org/wiki/Hitler_Youth>.
Salamon, Julie. "On the Fringe of Rock 'n' Roll, Music with a Heart Full of
  Hatred."
  The New York Times 18 Feb 2002:
Tagliabue, John. "The New Hitler Youth Are Troubling Germany."
  The New York Times 15 May 1991:

Black Hawk Down
"Battle of Mogadishu (1993)." Wikipedia. 9 May 2007. 30 Apr. 2007
  <http://en.wikipedia.org/wiki/Battle_of_Mogadishu_%281993%29
"BBC News | AFRIC | Warlord Thumbs Down for Somalia Film." BBC. 29
  Jan. 2002. 14 May 2007
  <http://news.bbc.co.uk/2/hi/africa/1789170.stm>.
"Black Hawk Down (2001)." IMDb. 12 Jan. 2002. 14 May 2007
  <http://www.imdb.com/title/tt0265086/>.
"Black Hawk Down (Film)." Wikipedia. 12 May 2007. 14 May 2007
  <http://en.wikipedia.org/wiki/Black_Hawk_Down_%28film%29>.
"Gary Gordon." Wikipedia. 7 May 2007. 30 Apr. 2007
  <http://en.wikipedia.org/wiki/Gary_Gordon>.
"Randy Shughart." Wikipedia. 7 May 2007. 30 Apr. 2007
  <http://en.wikipedia.org/wiki/Randy_Shughart>.
Snyder, R. "Operation Restore Hope, Battle of Mogadishu, 1993." NVCC. 10
  Sept. 2002. 14 May 2007
  <http://novaonline.nvcc.edu/eli/evans/his135/Events/Somalia93
  /Somalia93.html>.

Blood Diamond
"'Blood Diamonds' Still Sold By U.S. Retailers." Commondreams.org. April
  1, 2004.
  OneWorld.net. November 10, 2007.
  <http://www.commondreams.org/headlines04/0401-12.htm>.

"Blood Diamonds: Timeline of Conflict." Cnn.com. January 18, 2001. Cable
  News Network. November 10, 2007.

<http://archives.cnn.com/2001/WORLD/africa/01/18/diamonds.timeline/index.h tml>.

"Blood Diamond- Under Siege." Ifilm.com. March 16, 2007. November 10, 2007.
<http://www.ifilm.com/video/2833106>.

Blood on the Stone. Dir. C. Von. DVD. Insight News TV, 2007.

"Brutal Child Army Grows Up." Bbc.co.uk. May 10, 2000. BBC News. November 10, 2007.
<http://news.bbc.co.uk/2/hi/africa/743684.stm>.

Campbell, Greg. "The Sordid History Behind Africa's Conflict Diamonds." Csmonitor.com.
December 11, 2006. The Christian Science Monitor. November 10, 2007.
<http://www.csmonitor.com/2006/1211/p09s01-coop.html>.

"Child Soldiers: Children of Conflict." Bbc.co.uk. BBC World Service Trust. November 10, 2007.
<http://www.bbc.co.uk/worldservice/people/features/childrensrights/childrenofc onflict/soldier.shtml>.

Chimhete, Caiphas. "ZimConservation Archives." Zimconservation.com. February 11, 2007. November 10, 2007.
<http://www.zimconservation.com/archives7-31.htm>.

"Culture of Sierra Leone." Everyculture.com. November 10, 2007.
<http://www.everyculture.com/Sa-Th/Sierra-Leone.html>.

"De Beers." Wikipedia.com. 2007. Wikipedia. November 10, 2007.
<http://en.wikipedia.org/wiki/De_Beers>.

Duke, Lynne. "Blood Diamonds: A River or a Droplet?" Washingtonpost.com.
December 27, 2006. The Washington Post. November 10, 2007.
<http://www.washingtonpost.com/wp-dyn/content/ article/2006/12/26/AR2006122601013.html>.

Durham, Dick. "Diamond Trade Fuels Bloody Wars." Cnn.com. January 18, 2001. Cable News Network. November 10, 2007.
<http://archives.cnn.com/2001/WORLD/africa/01/18/diamonds.overview/index.ht ml>.

"Footpaths to Democracy- Revolutionary United Front of Sierra Leone." Fas.org. November 10, 2007.
<http://www.fas.org/irp/world/para/docs/footpaths.htm>.

"Guinea: Living on the Edge." Irinnews.com. IRIN. November 10, 2007.
<http://www.irinnews.org/InDepthMain.aspx?InDepthId=17&Report Id=62733>.

"IFEX: Sierra Leone: More journalists murdered and reported missing." Ifex.org. IFEX. November 10, 2007.
<http://www.ifex.org/es/content/view/full/24080/>.

Koinange, Jeff. "Sierra Leone Amputees in a League of Their Own." Cnn.com. April 3, 2006. Cable News Network. November 10, 2007.
<http://edition.cnn.com/2006/WORLD/africa/04/03/btsc.koinange/index.htm l>.

"Kono JV." Manoriver.com. Mano River Resources Inc. November 10, 2007.
<http://www.manoriver.com/s/Diamond_SL_Kono_JV.asp>.

Lennox, Emma J.. "Montage: Blood Diamond." Montagefilmjournalism.blogspot.com.
January 27, 2007. University of Glasgow. November 10, 2007.
<http://montagefilmjournalism.blogspot.com/2007/01/blood-diamond-review-by- emma-j-lennox.html>.

McElroy, Claudia. "Special Report: Sierra Leone." Cpj.org. November 10, 2007.
    <http://www.cpj.org/attacks99/africa99/africaSP.html>.

McKenzie, Glenn. "Cannibalistic, Unruly Militia Defends Sierra Leone Against Its Rebels."Freerepublic.com. July 4, 2007. Free Republic. November 10, 2007.
    <http://www.freerepublic.com/forum/a3962c1ef7afa.htm>.

Pearsey, Rebecca. "InkTank: Movies." Wjcblog.typepad.com. April 2, 2007. The Washington Journalism Center Blog. November 10, 2007.
    <http://wjcblog.typepad.com/ink_tank/the_news/index.html>.

"Revolutionary United Front (RUF)." Globalsecurity.org. November 10, 2007.
    <http://www.globalsecurity.org/military/world/para/ruf.htm>.

"Sierra Leone Rebels Forcefully Recruit Child Soldiers." Hrw.com. May 31, 2000. Human Rights Watch. November 10, 2007.
    <http://www.hrw.org/press/2000/05/sl0531.htm>.

"Sierra Leonean Refugee Children Neglected." Hrw.com. July 29, 1999. Human Rights Watch.November 10, 2007.
    <http://www.hrw.org/press/1999/jul/guinea729.htm>.

"Sierra Leone Timeline." Globalintegrity.org. Global Integrity. November 10, 2007.
    <http://www.globalintegrity.org/reports/2006/SIERRA%20LEONE/timeline.cfm>.

Soggot, Mungo. "Making a Killing- Conflict Diamonds are Forever." Publicintegrity.org. November 8, 2002. The Center for Public Integrity. November 10, 2007.
    <http://www.publicintegrity.org/bow/report.aspx?aid=152>.

235

Notes

Made in the USA
San Bernardino, CA
25 June 2013